A LIFE IN THE SADDLE

Memoirs of a Pioneer, Circuit Rider and Missionary

A Life in the Saddle
Memoirs of a Pioneer, Circuit Rider and Missionary

Brian Hogan

©2021
Fayetteville, Arkansas

Copyright Page

Copyright ©2021 Asteroidea Books.
All rights reserved. No part of this book shall be reproduced, stored in a retrieval system, or transmitted by any means, electronic, mechanical, photocopying, recording, or otherwise, without prior written permission.
All Bible verses from the King James Version.

Illustrations: engravings, photos, maps are either the property of the author, Creative Commons, Public Domain, or used with permission.

Cover: Methodist circuit rider in stained glass, Methodist Sky Chapel, Chicago, Illinois. Licensed under the Creative Commons Attribution-Share Alike 4.0 International.

Cover Design by Kimberly K. Williams, www.KimberlyKWilliams.com

Library of Congress Control Number: 2021905457
ISBN: 978-0-9986111-6-7
Printed by INGRAM SPARK

The author thanks:
Andrew Johnson National Historic Site N.P.S., Greeneville, TN
Bell County Historical Society, Middlesboro, KY
Betty L. Fletcher, Director, Greenville - Greene Co. History Museum
Bushwhacker Museum, Nevada, Missouri
Cumberland Gap National Historical Park N.P.S., KY, TN,
Greenville - Greene County History Museum, Greeneville, TN
Historical Foundation of the Cumberland Presbyterian Church and their list of CPC Ministers: www.cumberland.org/hfcpc/minister
Huntsville-Madison County Public Library, AL
KATY Trail State Park, Missouri State Parks
Lexington Historical Museum, MO
Maryville College Archives, Maryville, TN
President Andrew Johnson Museum, Tusculum University
Susan Knight Gore, Historian and Archivist, HFCPC
Welcoming landowners and knowledgeable locals along the way
And, above all others, my long-suffering wife, Louise, for putting up with and even encouraging a decade-long obsession to reintroduce Uncle Davie to the world. I don't deserve you.

Any errors or omissions are unintentional and wholly the fault of the author.

PREFACE

A Full Life

Judging from his 1899 memoirs, the Reverend David M. Hogan lived a memorable and amazing life. It's even more astonishing to step back further and see in just how much of his nation's story he played participant and observer. David M. Hogan was born during the term of James Madison, fourth President of the United States, and died during the term of the twenty-sixth, Teddy Roosevelt. Twenty-three Presidents led the USA during the span of his long life. And, of the three former Presidents and Founding Fathers who served before he was born; Adams and Jefferson were alive well into David's teen years!

At this writing, the United States is on its 46th President — his single life spanned twenty-five (more than half) of our Nation's leaders!

Remarkable observations:

Both his patriot grandfathers, Capt. William James Hogan and Moses Dorton, fought in the American Revolution.

His father, General David Hogan — "the second white baby born in Kentucky"— fought in The War of 1812.

He grew up on the Kentucky frontier — that "dark and bloody ground" at the famed Cumberland Gap, the first great gateway to the west, where the Wilderness Road pierced the mountains.

His middle name was either 'Madison' or 'Moses'.

His great grandfather was frontiersman Daniel Boone. Grandmother Sarah Grant was Boone's niece and adopted daughter.

His parents lacked formal education but, out of ten surviving offspring, they produced: a minister, six college grads, four medical doctors (one a surgeon), four Postmasters, a Federal Government civil servant, and successful farmers.

His family of origin pioneered the Missouri and Texas Territories, and he served the spiritual needs of newly settled communities as an itinerant "Circuit Rider" minister.

He was eyewitness to the Cherokee Trail of Tears, and five decades later, a missionary to the Cherokee Nation.

He was a California *Forty Niner* — preaching and mining in the Gold Rush.

He lived in eight states, and yet, barring the California gold camps, his homes were all within an 833-mile diameter circle whose geographic center is Brandywine Island on the Mississippi just north of Memphis — a place he never laid eyes on — but a 417-mile radius from there takes in all his homes.

His wife, Elizabeth Blackburn Hoss, was a renowned pioneer of female education west of the Mississippi River.

His family experienced almost every aspect of the plague of slavery, America's "peculiar institution": ownership, abolition, reconstruction, raids by radicals on both sides and sharp divisions brought on by culture and conscience.

His ranch in Vernon County, Missouri was ground zero for the Battle of Big Dry Wood early in the Civil War. During that war, his son, brothers — even a sister! — were combatants on both Union and Confederate sides.

He lived through the War of 1812, Kansas-Missouri Border War, Civil War, Missouri Mormon War, Mexican American War, Utah Mormon War, and the Spanish-American War.

Though no known photograph exists, he left a mark on his world. His name was bestowed upon river fords, schools, towns, cemeteries, and countless children born in the years surrounding the turn of the 20th Century. His first name went to descendants and nephews, and his last became a popular forename among the Cherokee.

He almost never received a salary for his ministerial labor (preacher, pastor, circuit rider, apostolic church planter, trainer, Presbytery clerk, administrator, officiant at over a thousand weddings, funerals, Sunday School organizer, and missionary), so he worked in varied secular employments: tanner, teacher, Postmaster, Justice of the Peace, entrepreneur, man of business, farmer, rancher, prospector, and builder.

The sheer historical panoply David Hogan strode though in ninety-two years makes most lifetimes seem short and mundane by comparison.

About this Book

This book is an expansion on the account Rev. Davie Hogan left of his own life, which he entitled: *Autobiography of David Hogan (1811-1899)*[1]. The author will quote directly from this work in the following format, as in the following opening passage:

> *I propose on this the 16th day of February A.D. 1899, in the 88th year of my life, to continue the work of writing a biographic sketch of my life, from a very imperfect, or partially kept diary. I will here state, this work is only intended as a manuscript for the information of my children, grandchildren, and those who in the future may be interested in the history this writing may afford. I have tried to keep as far from self-laudation as possible. I therefore pray that whosoever may consult or read it, if they think they see a spirit of exultation, they will account for it, on other grounds than intention of the writer.*

The rest of the text is comprised of quotes from other sources and background information researched and compiled by the author. Davie wrote for an audience with a base of shared experience and knowledge mostly lost to contemporary readers. The author has attempted to fill out Hogan's often terse or detail lacking account with the wealth of information on history, family members, and local color his ancestor neglected to include. By the way, the author, Brian Hogan, is Rev. Hogan's third great grandnephew.

---

1 "Autobiography of David Hogan 1811-1899" Typescript. Typed by David Hogan, 1899, at Cambridge City, Indiana. Resides in the archives of the Cumberland Presbyterian Church, Cordova, TN. Source of original not recorded — Julia Hogan Fraunberg or her heirs assumed.

TABLE OF CONTENTS

MY OLD KENTUCKY HOME (1811-1828) 11

CHILDHOOD'S END (1829-1832) 27

CAPTURED BY CHRIST (1833-1835) 35

STARTING A FAMILY (1836-1837) 55

MISSOURI MINISTER (1838-1839) 73

FINANCIAL RUIN (1840-1848) 85

GOLD RUSH (1849-1857) 99

PROSPERITY AND TRIBULATION (1858-1860) 107

WAR! (1861-1865) 115

RECONSTRUCTION (1866-1881) 131

BEREFT (1882-1883) 151

THE END OF HIS TRAIL OF TEARS (1884-1893) 157

KEEPER OF FAMILY LORE (1894) 181

RETIREMENT (1895-1899) 185

FINISH LINE (1900-1904) 193

'RECAPITULATIONS' 201

    Index of Illustrations 219

    Index of People 224

    Index of Places 229

MY OLD KENTUCKY HOME (1811-1828)

My father and mother, Gen. David Hogan and Elizabeth Palmer (Dorton), his wife, were of Scotch-Irish descent, which determines my extraction.

David M. Hogan, lovingly called 'Uncle Davie' by those who loved and revered him, preacher, missionary, and pioneer, was born of a long and illustrious family line stretching back to the earliest kings of Ireland.

First let us consider his maternal family tree. His mother, Betsy Dorton, came from great-grandparents who had all been born in North America, including one who was Native to this continent. Her grandfather, William F. Dorton, was killed by Indians at Dorton's Fort near Nicklesville, Virginia seven years before Betsy's birth. Betsy's Lewis, Waller and Robertson progenitors all came from England and Wales (Lewis), as did the Dorton's most probably. All her lines had come early to the settling of the New World, arriving beginning in the 1630s.

On his paternal grandmother's side, he traced his decent from William Grant (b. 1696, Scotland), and Margery Venner (b. 1704 in Ireland), who were the parents of his great-grandfather, Gen. William Henry Grant[2] and Eliza Jane Boone's[3] father, Squire Boone, and mother, Sarah Jarman Morgan[4].

David's paternal grandfather's ancestry includes the Lane and Fuller families, English Catholics who sought religious freedom in

---

[2] Gen. William Henry Grant (1726-1804, PA > NC > KY).

[3] Eliza Boone was Davie's great-grandmother.

[4] Squire Boone, born 1696 in Devon, England. Sarah Jarman Morgan was of Welsh descent.

Catholic Maryland (with a notable exception: Capt. Nicholas Martiau[5], a French Huguenot fleeing Catholic persecutors).

Nicolas Martiau came to Virginia as a refugee in 1620 and was the first known forebearer of George Washington in America. He was said to be a Moor (black). Martiau, an engineer and personal representative of Henry, 5th Earl of Huntington, was naturalized in England before coming to Virginia. He was a member of the Virginia Company. He designed the fortifications at Yorktown, Fort Story, Old Point Comfort, and Fort Monroe; British America's first forts. He served in the Virginia House of Burgesses, and as a judge. Martiau's Plantation comprised 1300 acres including the site of Yorktown. His daughter Sarah married Capt. William Fuller, Puritan Governor of Catholic Maryland. In Martiau's will, he provides for, and frees his two Negro servants. This gesture antedated similar actions by Nicholas' descendant George Washington more than a century. Washington was one of the first USA slave owners to do so – if not the first.

The Hogan family[6] derives its name from Davie Hogan's 17th great grandfather — a certain Ógán son of Aitheir. Aitheir was first cousin to Brian Boru, the High King of Ireland. Aitheir and Ógán lived at the turn of the first millennium (1000 C.E.) but the line continues back, through kings and queens of Ireland and Thomond and back more than a thousand years to Crimthann Niadh Nar of Ireland (b.131 B.C.) and from there disappears into the mists of myth (Crimthann Niadh is the purported offspring of Irish deities).

The Hogans continued to live in and near Tipperary County in Ireland until somewhere between 1640 and 1659 when Patrick

---

[5] Davie's sixth great-grandfather through the Fuller line.

[6] Silence Lane married James Shadrack Hogan in 1748. Their first child, Capt. William James Hogan was grandfather to our subject. The 4th child, John Hogan, was the 4th great-grandfather of Norma Jean Baker aka "Marilyn Monroe" (whose grandmother was Della Hogan). This makes actress Marilyn Monroe second cousin four times removed to David Hogan.

My Old Kentucky Home (1811-1828)

Hogan[7] emigrated to Virginia Colony in British America, specifically Brunswick. David's first ancestor born on American soil was William W. Hogan, Patrick's second son, born 1660 in New Brunswick, Brunswick, Virginia. William's grandson, William Griffin Hogan (1705-1783) moved the family into North Carolina where they founded plantations.

William Griffin Hogan's grandson, a Captain William James Hogan II, fought for American Independence and left his home in the Yadkin Valley of North Carolina for the "dark and bloody land" of Kentucky. Hogan was a companion of Daniel Boone on the famed explorer's third trip on the Wilderness Road through the Cumberland Gap. He traversed Boone's Trace (later the Wilderness Road) including The Narrows north of the Gap. The Road cut through a 'water gap' just south of the only place to cross the steep banked Cumberland River. The crossing was Cumberland Ford (later Pineville, KY). William would remember this land and later settle at the Fords of the Cumberland. In 1780, William married Daniel Boone's niece and adopted daughter, Sarah Elizabeth Grant. The young couple started their family at a frontier fort the hardy settlers called Bryans Station. Their firstborn, David[8], was born June 17th, 1781 and bore the double honor of being both the first Hogan born a citizen of the new United States (although the validity of that nation would be contested for another four months until Cornwallis' surrender to General Washington) and the second baby of European ancestry born in Kentucky. The Hogan family were Presbyterian in religious affiliation, preferring, like most Scots-Irish, the tradition and highly educated leadership that church offered.

---

[7] Patrick's father, Conogher Giallbarbh Hogan was born 1585 at County Tipperary's Cranagh Castle, there is nothing to suggest that the family owned or lived within a castle. It is most likely that they'd moved to the castle as construction labor (work began around 1580) and occupied worker's huts at the site. Whether they were still there or had moved back to another Hogan inhabited village in Tipperary County by the time Patrick was born remains unclear.

[8] Gen. David Hogan (1781-1867) father of David M. Hogan and 13 other children.

My Old Kentucky Home (1811-1828)

> *"Heaven must be a Kentucky kind of place."*
>
> Daniel Boone

William and Sarah Hogan were licensed[9] to run a tavern at Cumberland Ford in 1800. Six years later, their eldest, David married Betsy Dorton and settled in with his in-laws, Moses and Dicy Dorton. Moses, licensed to run the tavern (Wm. Hogan sold him Hogan's Tavern, provided the security for Moses' license and began running a ferry across the Cumberland when the water ran too high to ford), rechristened it 'Dorton's Mansion'. David and Betsy planted crops and harvested children: Wilkinson (1807), Sarah Ann (1808) and John D. (1810). His parents, Capt. Wm. James and Sarah Hogan, moved on around 1812 to pioneer what became Huntsville, Alabama. They stayed in Kentucky long enough to witness the birth of their fourth Hogan grandchild[10] (son David's fourth child), David Madison Hogan (who would go by 'Davie') . Grandma Sarah died when Davie was only five, but Grandpa William lived on in Alabama until the lad was 15 years old.

A word about the business pursuits of the Hogan and Dorton families: Both Capt. Hogan and Moses Dorton were making their living off the emigrant flow coming on the Wilderness Road. The main way to prosper in this area of poor farming land was to get the license to operate a tavern, a river ferry, and supplement by providing postal service. Travelers needed a safe fortified place to stay, resupply, pen their animals, and rest from the journey. The answer was Hogan's Cumberland Ford Tavern (1800-1809)[11], which

---

[9] among the six First Licensed Tavern Keepers in Knox County, KY.

[10] Two of their daughters, Nancy Hogan Herndon and Betsy Hogan Beaty had already given them five Herndon and two Beaty grandkids, respectively.

[11] Elijah Hogan, son of Capt. Hogan, b. 1794, grew up working in his dad's tavern and started his own tavern in Starkville, Mississippi in 1834.

became Dorton's Mansion (1810-1837 Moses Dorton; 1837-? James B Dorton), Nancy Hogan Herndon's Tavern in Barbourville (1801-1812) and Dorton's Tavern in Barbourville (1812). They also needed to get their wagons, animals, and belongings across the rivers. Cumberland Ford worked fine when the water level was low, but a ferry was required at all other times. Both Capt. Wm. Hogan and the Dortons (Moses & his son Wm. Dorton) provided licensed ferry service for a price. Hogan's two brothers, James and John were doing the same thing in Nicholasville, KY. And since mail was of vital importance on the frontier — folks paid to collect it, letters were free to post; The Hogans and the Dortons were always quick to snap up the coveted Postmaster appointments. Taverns were ideal places for people to collect their mail. Farmers would call at the tavern or general store on Saturday to get any mail, sit by the stove, talk with neighbors, and have a drink and a chew. The Postmaster was paid out of the revenue from delivered mail. Some Postmasters, like Moses Dorton, established delivery routes over a limited area and would ride these in all weather ("Neither snow nor rain nor heat nor gloom of night stays these couriers from the swift completion of their appointed rounds" was forged in these early days. After Moses, came other Postmasters in the family: Elijah Hogan (MS), Col. Wm. Hogan (Georgetown, MO), Gen. David Hogan (Arator, MO), George M. Hogan (TX), and Rev. Davie Hogan (Deerfield, MO).

The subject of this account announced his entry into the story (and into the World):

"I was born in Harlan County[12], twelve miles from Cumberland Gap, on the second day of December 1811."

---

[12] at the time of David's birth, it was still Knox County, Harlan County's creation being 1819. Uncle Davie is giving the up-to-date county name.

My Old Kentucky Home (1811-1828)

The new infant was sprouting his first teeth and loudly demanding solid food when the infant nation, into which he'd been born a citizen, plunged into war.

The United States declared war on Britain in a conflict known as 'The War of 1812', in June 1812. The war would drag on until Christmas Eve, 1814.

Davie's dad, David Hogan Sr., fought in the Kentucky Militia, 18th Brigade, who found themselves in bloody backwoods battles against Great Britain's Indian allies. Due to the nature of militia service — where the men had crops to tend and families at risk — young David's father was in and out of the Kentucky homestead during his two and a half years of wartime service, as proved by the birth of a fifth child, William M.[13] on 17 November 1813. At war's end, the State of Kentucky granted David Hogan Sr. the State rank of Brigadier General for his service; hence the honorific title "General" he bore for the rest of his days.

On a more personal note, during the 'War of 1812' the Hogan family lost a matriarch. Eliza Jane Boone, Davie's great-grandmother on this father's side, died January 25, 1814 at Bryans Station, the Kentucky log fort where her daughter had given birth to Gen. David Hogan, the second child of European descent born in

---

[13] Gen. David Hogan is a political supporter of James Madison (1809 – 1817) and honors his idol by giving four sons in a row (between 1811-1818) middle names beginning with M. David M., James M., William M. (b. 17 Nov 1813) and George Madison Hogan. In three cases there is no surviving record of the full middle name (the three born during Madison's term), but it is a strong surmise that all four bore the name Madison, with James being a full namesake. The General's habit of naming sons after military and political figures was thrown into confusion by accusations of treason (that became public the year he chose to name Wilkinson) and later, the two court martials of Gen. James Wilkinson by the Madison Administration. Wilkinson was exposed as a troop-killer and an incompetent and went on to involve himself in the treasons of Aaron Burr. Gen. David changed his first son's name to Wilkerson to erase the shame. A good plan considering that Theodore Roosevelt said of James Wilkinson "In all our history, there is no more despicable character."

Kentucky. Eliza was a niece of Daniel Boone and Davie's last surviving great-grandparent.

Davie Hogan later wrote that he and his growing band of siblings were raised on farms. For the first five years of his life, the Hogan farm lay close to the "mansion" of his Dorton grandparents, who tended an inn near the ford of the Cumberland River. A sixth sibling, James M. was born there in 1816. This was the infamous "year without a summer" caused by a volcanic eruption in Indonesia that lowered temperatures dramatically for years. In October of the same year, word came from Davie's grandfather Capt. William James Hogan II in north Alabama, that Grandma Sarah Elizabeth Grant Hogan had passed on, leaving the sixty-six-year-old Captain lonely and probably regretting moving so far away from family.[14]

Eventually, in 1817, soon after hearing James Monroe had been inaugurated the fifth President, General David moved his family eleven miles to another farm just outside the eastern mouth of the Cumberland Gap on the famed Wilderness Road.

> *"When I was about five years of age my father moved to the west foot of Cumberland Mountain, in one mile of the Gap; here I was raised up to my twenty-first year. Near the Gap stands the Corner Tree and stone[15] set by it, of*

---

[14] William James and Sarah Hogan, parents of General David, had moved from Knox County Kentucky to pioneer land in what is now Huntsville, AL in 1812, just as David and Betsy were starting their family.

[15] this reference to a "*Corner Tree" and stone set by it*" at the Tri-State Boundary was greatly exciting to the Cumberland Gap National Park historian I emailed about it. She'd never come across any mention of this before and was eager to see if traces remained. The tree was almost certainly a victim of Civil War fortification building resulting in deforestation of the area, but she hoped to find the stone David mentioned remaining — perhaps tumbled down the hill. She searched as much as she could through the leaf litter of fall and found nothing — but hoped to search again in better conditions. She failed to find the stone

My Old Kentucky Home (1811-1828)

Virginia, Tennessee, and Kentucky. In the days of my boyhood, I have often run round this tree and stone to prove how quickly I could be in three different states. Being raised up here, among the hardy mountaineers, may be somewhat the predicate for my generally great physical strength and even to my present age."

The Hogan's new neighbors had been participating in a religious revival, the Second Great Awakening. Cultural differences between settlers during the First Great Awakening opened a rift among Presbyterians in North America, split between the Old Side (mainly congregations of Scottish and Scots-Irish extraction like the Hogan family) who favored a doctrinally oriented traditional church with a highly educated clergy and a New Side (mainly of English extraction - the majority living around the Cumberland Gap) who put greater emphasis on the experiential revivalist techniques championed by the Great Awakening. The rift had been healed for a time but, during the Second Great Awakening, large numbers of converts had created new congregations in every place of any populace resulting in chronic leadership deficit. The "Old" Presbyterian Church of the USA refused pleas to ordain local ministers to serve these new flocks; insisting that only Princeton University could professionally train ordained leaders. By 1810, the churches of the Cumberland Gap region became so frustrated at this bottleneck that they ordained their own leaders, and the Cumberland Presbytery was expelled by the parent church. Three defrocked ministers formed the Cumberland Presbyterian Church (CPC). This church stressed evangelism, an individual salvation experience, free will (rather than 'fatalistic predestination'), and decentralized authority in church government. One of the three founders was Finis Ewing, a farmer from the Gap area who now pastored the Lebanon CPC in Tennessee but maintained close ties with the Gap CPC congregation that comprised of many of the Hogans' neighbors. Gen. David and his family were staunch "Old Presbyterians", but

---

which quite probably ended up in fortifications itself. The spot is well marked today. (photo pg. 22)

they nevertheless found community among the surrounding Cumberland Presbyterians, whom they quite liked even though finding them over enthusiastic in religion. Davie Hogan will state later that he memorized Scripture in Sunday School when he was "a lad" so it seems that the churches of the area had a non-denominational cooperative Sunday School that the Hogan kids attended. These were an important part of children's education in towns lacking regular weekday school. Their Bible-only curriculum made them palatable across the lines of sectarian strife. Davie would one day organize Union Sunday Schools in Missouri's frontier hamlets.

Two hundred seventy miles away, southwest along the mountains in what would be Huntsville, Alabama[16], Capt. William James Hogan II wrote his Last Will and Testament (alas, not his last) on October 23rd, 1817, dispersing various tracts of land and twenty-four enslaved human beings among his heirs. His behest to Gen. David was to split a ¼ section[17] with his brother William James Hogan III in addition to inheriting "Simon and Nancy". Capt. William would soon remarry and change this Will, causing consternation and grief among his children.

Several months later (1818), Davie welcomed yet another sibling when George Madison was born. There were now seven Hogan children on the farm.

> *In my raising, I worked on the farm in summer, and went to school in fall and winter - to the mud-daubed log schoolhouse, a window being made by cutting a log out full length of the house to give light. I attended school after this sort up to my eighteenth year.*

---

[16] "Madison County Probate Records at Huntsville, AL," Ancestry.com

[17] Designated Huntsville 0004S-0001W, NE¼ of Section 13, This land is on the south side of Huntsville and centers on the intersection of today's Airport Road S and S Memorial Parkway. The graveyard containing the bodies of William and Sarah in somewhere in this parcel, exact location lost to time, but would have been visible from their kitchen window.

My Old Kentucky Home (1811-1828)

Davie may not say as much about his school days as we might like, but he must have enjoyed learning. His first response to pursuing his life's calling would be to seek further education. He was an avid lifelong learner and he hung on the stories passed down to him by parents and grandparents as much as the practical reading, writing and 'rithmatick dispensed by the teachers at the log schoolhouse.

Davie's maternal Grandfather, Moses Dorton, was the first Postmaster of Cumberland Ford, eleven miles away where wagons following the Wilderness Road forded the Cumberland River[18]. Grandpa Dorton would take young David on horseback trips while he delivered mail. For several years after his family moved south to the Cumberland Gap, Davie would ride to Dorton's Mansion with his parents for visits, but by the time he was ten years old he was confidently taking the journey back and forth on his own. No fears of getting lost on Boone's Trace — he was a descendant of Dan'l Boone. His great grandfather famously declared: "I have never been lost but I was bewildered once for three days." The boy reveled in his Grandpa Moses' Revolutionary War tales of the Battle of Kings Mountain, coming through the Gap with Daniel Boone and Davie's Grandpa Hogan, guarding the settlers as an "Emigrant Spy", and serving the famed men of the frontier in his inn. One story captured young Davie's imagination as surely as the twenty-one-year-old Moses pursued and captured a Cherokee chieftain in the story. Davie would carry the details of this account with him throughout his life leading to an extraordinary connection with another Cherokee when both were old men.

General David and Betsy (as Elizabeth Dorton was always called) Hogan already had produced seven children on their farm near the

---

[18] 31 March 1818 Moses Dorton was appointed Postmaster of Cumberland Ford, later Pineville, Bell, Kentucky: He had been running the ferry across the ford with his son, William since at least 1816 when licensed by Knox Co), but probably since 1812 when William James Hogan gave it up to move to Alabama. The site was settled early (ca. 1781) since it was where the Wilderness Road crossed the Cumberland River. Thus, the community was first called Cumberland Ford and the post office of this name was established with Moses Dorton, Postmaster (1818-1826).

My Old Kentucky Home (1811-1828)

Cumberland Ford, and they were only half done! The Hogan family had just moved into their new farm just one mile below the Cumberland Gap and Tri-State Border in a new county: Harlan. Davie was thrilled to cuddle his new brother Moses Dorton, but his entire family was jostling to hold the new babe. Little Moses had come into a crowded log cabin on a bitterly cold January day in 1820. His namesake, Grandpa Moses Dorton, lived within a mile, and he and Grandma Dicy braved frostbite to see their newest grandson.

The joy of new life was often quenched by the passing of older lives in those pioneer days. Nine months later, in September 1820, word came from uncle Nathan Boone of Femme Osage Creek in Missouri Territory that Great-Grandpa Daniel Boone had let go of life at 85 years of age. Missouri was to become a state within a year and, had he lived, Old Dan'l would have "skinned out" for unfamiliar territory. He always chafed at lack of "elbow room".

More siblings followed at regular two-year intervals at the increasingly packed Hogan home. Another brother, Joseph Warren Turley was born in 1822, followed by a second sister, Elizabeth Grant Clay[19] in 1824 and brother Robert Henderson[20] on March 9th, 1826. Just three days later, death knocked again and Grandpa Dorton, the old Indian Fighter, died eleven miles away at Dorton's

---

[19] Henry Clay was the popular and powerful Speaker of the House that year. Grant was her Grandmother Hogan's maiden name. She'd died in 1816 and Elizabeth was the first girl born since though which Gen. David could honor his mother.

[20] The Hogan's liked to name their kids after favorite politicians and Kentucky luminaries. Richard Henderson (1734–1785) was an American pioneer and merchant who attempted to create a colony called Transylvania just as the American Revolutionary War was starting. The Transylvania Colony was in what is now central and western parts of Kentucky, and a chunk of north central Tennessee. Daniel Boone was hired by Henderson to establish the Wilderness Road going through the Cumberland Gap and into southeastern Kentucky to facilitate settlement.

My Old Kentucky Home (1811-1828)

Mansion Tavern[21] at Cumberland Ford. Davie was especially close to Grandpa Dorton and rode the post routes with him every chance he got. He would miss sitting behind Moses' saddle and hearing his thrilling tales of escapes and rescues on the Kentucky frontier.

The following year another patriarch passed. Capt. William James Hogan, Gen. David's father, died at his pioneer cabin near the spring in what was to become Huntsville, Alabama. Davie and his siblings never felt like they really got to know this grandfather. By 1809 he had already grown disenchanted with the territory he'd helped open. Capt. William bought up land in Alabama and became one of the first settlers in Madison County. Much like his father-in-law Daniel Boone, William had no head for capitalizing on his advantages and sold much of Huntsville to a guy named Hunt who platted it out and made a mint. None of the Hogan children had any memory of Grandpa and Grandma Hogan in Kentucky as Wilkinson and Sarah were infants when they'd moved on. Grandmother Sarah had passed when Davie was five and William had remarried in 1819. A new Last Will and Testament to provide for his bride became a cause of disagreement among those he left behind[22].

Sadness doesn't last forever. Another son, Samuel Grant was born to the Hogan's in summer 1829. He was named after his uncle, General David Hogan's youngest brother, Samuel Grant Hogan (1801-1890). Interestingly, his middle name honored Grandmother

---

[21] Today's Pineville, KY. A later historian remarked "By the year 1826, when Moses Dorton died, the Indians had been dispersed, his children were grown, and he had become a rich man for his day. It is believed that he is buried in the Wallsend Cemetery. His wife 'Dicy' went to live with her youngest daughter, Emily, and her husband, Wylie Hibbard, on [Hibbard Branch] Clay County, KY about 1832. She died there in the 1840's."

[22] A year later, in 1827, the widow, Hannah Hill Dupree Hogan, was defendant for his 1826 Will, with William Hogan's disinherited children and grandchildren contesting. The case settled when Hannah gave in and agreed to abide by William Hogan's earlier 1817 Will.

Sarah Elizabeth Grant Hogan, William's first wife, who was adopted and raised by Daniel and Rebecca Ann (Bryan) Boone (and was also their niece, her birth mother being Elizabeth Boone[23]). The last two Hogan children to be born came along quickly after Samuel — and left just as quickly. A stillborn boy and Mary, who only lived a year.

Davie's oldest brother, Wilkinson was 22 years old and ready to begin his own life. The first to leave the nest, he married 20-year-old Polly Lane on New Year's Eve, 1829. The friends and family gathered at the wedding in the Hogan home could talk of little else but the great migration of so many neighbors to new lands opened by Missouri statehood. Wilkinson boldly declared that he and his new bride would be joining the wagon trains as soon as he could put together the funds for the move. The close-knit Hogan clan realized that separations were coming beyond just the expected ones of marrying and moving to a nearby farm. Davie, now just-turned 18 years old and a man, remembered the stories he'd heard as a boy of opening Kentucky and longed for new frontiers himself.

---

[23] Eliza Jane Boone and Gen. William Henry Grant had eleven children including Sarah Elizabeth Grant.

My Old Kentucky Home (1811-1828)

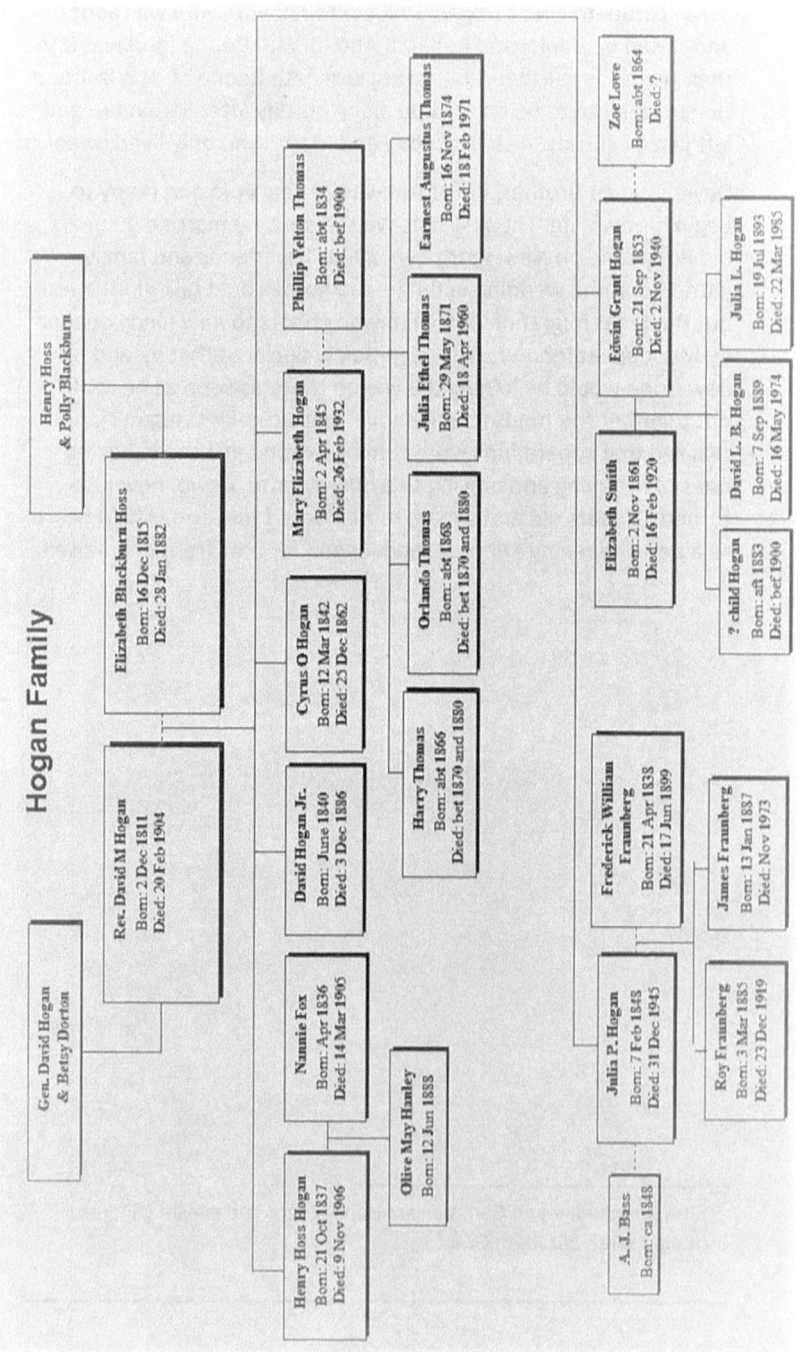

My Old Kentucky Home (1811-1828)

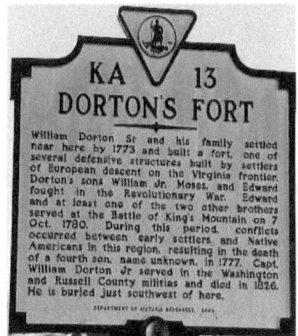

Photo: Dorton's Fort, Nickelsville VA.   *Historic Marker*

Marker Inscription:

DORTON'S FORT William Dorton Sr. and his family, settled here by 1773 and built a fort, one of several defensive structures built by settlers of European descent on the Virginia frontier. Dorton's sons William Jr., Moses and Edward fought in the Revolutionary War. Edward and Moses served at the Battle of King's Mountain on 7 Oct. 1780. During this period conflicts occurred between early settlers and Native Americans in this region, resulting in the death of a fourth son, (Jacob) in 1777. Capt. William Dorton Jr. served in the Washington and Russell County militias and died in 1826. He is buried just southwest of here.

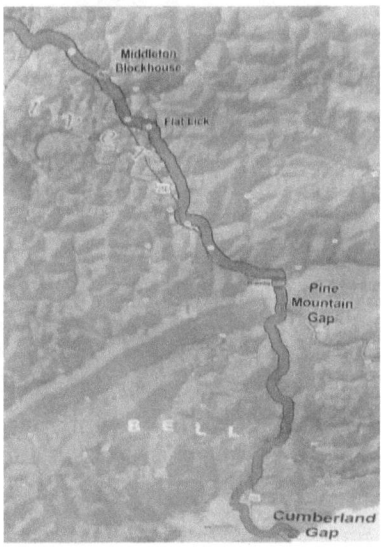

Left: Daniel Boone (1734-1820) American frontiersman, who in 1775 blazed the Wilderness Road through the Cumberland Gap and into Kentucky.

Right: The Wilderness Road (formerly Boone's Trace) from the Cumberland Gap through The Narrows (Pine Mountain Gap) and Cumberland Ford (today's Pineville, where the river crossing west to east continued the trail northward.

My Old Kentucky Home (1811-1828)

Bryans Station under siege.

Cumberland Ford & Narrows

Hogan's Cumberland Ford Tavern (1800). John and David Hogan (seated). From 'Boy Centurions' by B. Hogan. Painting by Helen

Cumberland River Ford at Pineville, KY

Left:
Probable location of Robertson's Station / Hogan's Tavern /Dorton's Mansion on Breastwork Hill and Old Dorton Branch Rd. looming above Cumberland Ford.

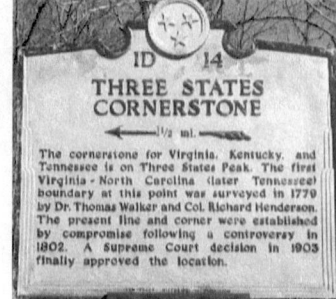

THREE STATES CORNERSTONE: Marker Inscription: The cornerstone for Virginia, Kentucky, and Tennessee is on Three States Peak. The first Virginia - North Carolina (later Tennessee) boundary at this point was surveyed in 1779 by Dr. Thomas Walker and Col. Richard Henderson. The present line and corner were established by compromise following a controversy in 1802. A Supreme Court decision in 1903 finally approved the location.

CHILDHOOD'S END (1829-1832)

At eighteen, Davie was finished with schooling (or so everyone thought) and his thoughts turned to learning a trade. He followed Wilkinson into tanning hides, as becoming an apprentice tanner was easy with his older brother as his sponsor. He writes that he followed "... *after at the tanner's trade to my twenty-first year.*" Sixteen-year-old younger brother, William, had surprised the family by announcing that he was leaving home too. His destination was the shocking thing. William had never seemed to enjoy school or engage the spiritual side of life, but he was off for the Ohio River port of Allegany City[24] to study at the brand-new Western Theological Seminary. His parents were baffled by this sudden change in interests but could only feel relief that it was a good solid school of the "Old Presbyterians" rather than one of the Cumberland variety that captivated their neighbors. It was a four-year course of study and the journey arduous, so even though he'd promised to return home for summer break in 1830, they knew they'd not see much of him from now on.

Even though the neighborhood brand of religion was disconcerting, the Hogans felt like they really fit into the community around the Cumberland Gap. With dismay they realized the sheer number of goodbye parties had been on the rise. It seemed like they were in the road waving to the back end of a neighbor family's team and wagon every week. Almost all who left were setting out for Missouri. The small group that had led the move with Rev. Finis Ewing's congregants had been followed by what was becoming a steady stream. There were always folks from further east ready to buy their lands, but the new neighbors weren't like the friends they were waving off. Letters from Missouri were read publicly at the inn and Gen. David began to wonder at the opportunities presented by the wondrous lands opened up around the new

---

[24]Allegany City was annexed by Pittsburgh as North Pittsburgh.

Childhood's End (1829-1832)

Cumberland Presbyterian paradise of Ewingsville, in Cooper County.

Davie was at the tannery when the Census Taker came to the door of the Hogan's log home. The government was counting the populace of the young growing nation for the fifth time. He was sorry to have missed the excitement of a visit from someone who literally had seen most everyone and had all the news. By the time he came home and washed at the rain barrel (his work being a trial to sensitive noses) Davie had to content himself with his family's (especially smug little brother William, home for summer recess) recounting of all that John Dixon, the Enumerator, had divulged. The busy man was lured into sitting on the porch for a spell when the General offered a cup of bourbon sent down all the way from Barboursville by Davie's Aunt Nancy, wife to Rev. Capt. Richardson Herndon. The Herndons owned the first tavern in Barbourville, Kentucky, and had used the profits to buy up prime downtown lots. Late in life, Richardson turned to pastoring the Cumberland River Baptist Church. Rev. Herndon might not hold with strong drink these days, but Nancy loved her brother and considered the 25-year-old bottles of Kentucky whisky still stored in her basement to be both fine and frugal gifts. This treat so liberally shared with John Dixon ensured the Hogan family got every scrap of news and gossip that could be wrung from his loosened lips.

The most exciting news from abroad was the new treaty between the Federal Government and the Sac and Fox, Mdewakanton, Wahpekute, Wahpeton, Sisiton Sioux, Omaha, Ioway, Otoe and Missouria Nations. The Chiefs had signed the Fourth Treaty of Prairie du Chien, which, when the document was fully signed (the Sioux were holding out) and ratified, would cede to the United States the majority of Minnesota, Iowa and (this got David's attention) Missouri. In return the government was promising the tribe allocations in reservations in "Indian Territory" established by three prior treaties. This agreement went a long way in making the settling of Missouri lands far safer than the same feat in Kentucky had been when Moses Dorton and Capt. Hogan had pushed through the Gap.

Childhood's End (1829-1832)

The process of news was give-and-take. The man had an important and Constitutionally mandated job to do. General David gave a careful accounting of the family and its property. As Mr. Dixon carefully put marks in each column, grouped by gender and age, the General was proud to see that of twenty families already on the page, his was by far the largest. Besides himself, the Hogans recorded nine males ranging from up to 30 yrs., and Betsy and two daughters. Betsy was expecting again though just beginning to show. Unborn individuals were no concern of the census taker who merely needed to mark down all living human beings in the household. Dixon's eyes bugged out a bit when David listed his eleven enslaved workers. This was an increase of seven over the 1820 count. The General noted with pride that there was only one on the page that didn't belong to him. Neighbor John Baughman's family of seven had a single servant. With Wilkinson married and out starting his own household, David noticed something that had hitherto escaped him: there was an equal number of children and servants in his household.

The excitement of the 1830 Census lasted for weeks as the neighborhood traded tidbits back and forth. However, harvest was soon upon them and with David off to work, William back at school in Pennsylvania and Wilkinson getting his first crop in, there was lots of work for all the kids and servants. Betsy, large with child, worked hard in the kitchen to feed all the working bellies. In fact, the granny midwife had stopped by chance and found her grunting through contractions and still standing and stirring greens. That earned Betsy a sharp rebuke and just an hour later baby Mary and a stillborn unnamed male twin were born. Sadly, little Mary didn't last the year. These two little graves marked the end of childbearing (after 14) for Betsy Hogan and a final punctuation on Kentucky for the Hogan family.

In August of 1831, frightening news came over the Gap with travelers fleeing Virginia. An enslaved African named Nat Turner had incited seventy-five of his fellows to rise in armed revolt against their owners. There had been about sixty whites killed and fugitives were still at large. These tidings were uniformly whispered

Childhood's End (1829-1832)

to the General by folks who made sure none of his servants were in earshot. The stated intention of the revolt was to mobilize all the African slaves in the country to rise and throw off the yoke. This possibility spelled more than just financial ruin to General David — it was an existential threat hanging over his family. Immediately, half-hearted conversations about following their friends to Missouri became quickly formed solid plans to pack up and liquidate real estate for a move west as soon as humanly possible. Even with this surge of motivation to flee the increasingly troubled East, pulling out of one of SW Kentucky's more prosperous plantations was no easy undertaking. General David and Betsy knew that Wilkinson and Polly, expecting their first child in January, were less tied to the land and urged the young couple to go on ahead and "spy things out" in Missouri. To sweeten the pot, the General provided a team of oxen and a new Conestoga wagon for their journey and offered John D., his second son as added help, protection, and provision. At 21, John was a fine shot with his grandfather's Kentucky Long Rifle and the family's best hunter. This three-person advance party left almost immediately — seeking to beat freezing temperatures to Missouri.

They made it in record time. In late October, a letter arrived postmarked September 12th, 1831, from Tebo Grove, Missouri. John wrote that he and Wilkinson, with help from neighbors, had erected a log home and a tannery nearby (but downwind) and were settling in nicely in Henry County, Missouri. They'd gone quite a bit further west than the General had directed, but they'd gone through Ewingsville and stayed two nights with former Gap neighbors from Kentucky. In fact, the Cumberland Presbyterian town's name had just been changed to New Lebanon and seemed to be one of Cooper County's tidiest and most wholesome communities. They had exchanged news with other emigrants and become convinced land in Henry County was just as fine and much cheaper, so they'd pressed onward. Still, John's letter encouraged the folks back home greatly. After signing the letter John had appended a postscript to his brother inviting Davie to come out and work in their tannery.

Davie told his dad that he'd much rather stay and help with the big move. The truth was that he loathed tanning hides. It was hot, filthy, smelly work and even his mother's strong lye soap failed to make him feel clean. He had been planning to quit the tannery when it shut for Christmas 1831. After his December 2nd twentieth birthday, Davie could claim to have worked "at the tanner's trade to my twenty-first year" and make the excuse for quitting the noxious job that his family's relocation needs were more pressing. Additional time in the tannery didn't feature in any of Davie's dreams.

> *In November 1832, my father and entire family, except two older brothers who had preceded, moved to Missouri, and for the first year, lived at New Lebanon, renting the farm and dwelling house of Rev. Finis Ewing, who had vacated and moved near Lexington a short time before.*

Davie fails to mention that the party briefly took up residence in Howard County, just north of Cooper County, upon arrival in Missouri. They almost certainly sojourned in the newly minted town of New Franklin[25], since this was the crossroads of trails and the end of their westward route since crossing into Missouri at St. Charles, following the Boonslick Road, a path first explored and blazed by their uncles, the Boone boys[26]. The family's short stay in Howard County turns up in a single record without reason or duration. They almost certainly traveled as part of a larger and

---

[25] The City of New Franklin, founded in 1828 after the town of Franklin washed away in 1826 & 1828 floods, was chartered in 1835. Known as the town where four trails meet — marking the end of the Boonslick Trail, the beginning of the Santa Fe Trail, including the Lewis & Clark Trail and the KATY Trail — history awaits in every direction! (from the town's website)

[26] The Boone's Lick Road or Boonslick Trail was an early 19th Century route from eastern to central Missouri. Running east-west on the North side and roughly parallel to the Missouri River the trail began in the river port of St. Charles. The trail played a major role in the westward expansion of the United States and the development of Missouri's statehood. The trail's eventual terminus at New Franklin was the start of the better-known Santa Fe Trail. First traced by the sons of Daniel Boone, the path originally ended at a salt lick in Howard County used by the pair to manufacture salt. Today the lick is maintained as Boone's Lick State Historic Site.

better protected wagon train. The size and wealth of what they were moving would have made this the only prudent course. It is a good guess that the wagon train was bound for Howard County. Perhaps the trek's rigors and the connections made with their traveling partners made the Hogan family briefly consider settling there. In his 1899 memoirs Davie conveys their ultimate destination was always New Lebanon. Apparently by 1899, the New Franklin stop was forgotten or unworthy of mention.

Regardless, they had close friends that were settled and expecting to welcome them in New Lebanon, so they repacked the wagons and went the final 25 miles to their new Missouri home. Upon arrival, amid many happy reunions for both the parents and the children, they found that the CPC founder, Rev. Finis Ewing and his wife 'Aunt Peggy', had recently vacated their fine New Lebanon house and farm to occupy a city house in Lexington. As Davie was to learn for himself, one didn't make a living from the ministry on the frontier. Rev. Ewing had friends in high places and, in 1831, it paid off. President Andrew Jackson, his childhood friend, appointed Finis to a federal post in Lexington, Missouri. The arrival of the Hogan family was timely and fortuitous as a large two-story house in the center of the little town on the prairie was for rent and move-in ready.

The next year (1820) Finis Ewing moved to Missouri and settled in Cooper County among his old neighbors from Kentucky who had preceded him. He soon had an organized congregation, a meetinghouse, and, of course, a campground. This church, New Lebanon, has had a remarkable history, and has shared largely in the work for the Master in that State.

In 1821 R.D. Morrow and Finis Ewing opened a school of the prophets. Morrow taught science and Ewing theology. No charge was made for the young preachers' tuition or boarding. McGee Presbytery had already enrolled many candidates for the ministry, and these eagerly availed themselves of the advantages here offered. There was a long summer vacation which was spent in preaching toters [lugging supplies for ministers] and camp meetings, Morrow and Ewing accompanying the young preachers. [27]

---

[27] *History of the Cumberland Presbyterian Church,* Benjamin McDonnold 1899.

Childhood's End (1829-1832)

Davie's happiness and vacation were both short lived. Within the month John rode over for a visit and Wilkinson, Polly and their infant son, Samuel Lane Hogan soon followed. During hugs and exchanges of news, his brothers "worked" their dad to send Davie home with them to help in the tannery. He caught the General's eye and shook his head to kill the idea in the budding, but when they mentioned his wages would really help the family to settle in and partially recoup moving expenses, their father was all in with the notion. With his arms full of new nephew and surrounded by persuasive and determined older brothers and a very insistent father, Davie, now 21 and an adult, he supposed, really didn't have a chance. By March first he was back up to his elbows in the odiferous hell of tannery work!

When recounting this years later, Davie has the perspective of time and a learned ability to trust the Lord's leading even in unpleasant circumstances. He voices no complaints:

> *So soon as the family were comfortably located in this home, my eldest brother, who had the year before built a tannery in Tebo Grove, and in want of help, I left the home and went to his relief the 1st of March 1833, and in June following returned to New Lebanon.*

It is worth noting that Davie only lasted little more than three months at this hated labor.

CAPTURED BY CHRIST (1833-1835)

A few days after my return [from Tebo Grove], *the annual Camp-meeting came on at that place* [New Lebanon], *at which, on Monday the 15th day of June 1833, I professed religion; also, my eldest sister[28] professed. Now to give a fair statement of my character up to the day I professed religion, it sufficeth to say, no man was more foolishly proud or wicked, and intentionally profane - which habits were intended to assist me in opposing Christianity and to cultivate a spirit of infidelity. I will now disclose the accompanying facts of my conversion.*

The sister above spoken of, had been a penitent and seeker of religion for more than a year, and on the first day of the meeting she went forward, to what was in those days called the 'mourner's seat.' My pride greatly revolted at her course; I resolved to try to talk and reason with her, and possibly get her out of that way of doing. I said to her, "Father and Mother are Old Presbyterians - they know of no such fanaticism," but she would have none of my admonitions. She wept, she prayed aloud, often in tones indicative of desperate despair. This was her condition from Thursday night till Monday about twelve o'clock, when she professed, she triumphantly rejoiced, often exclaiming, "Glory to God!" with many other expressions of a happy soul. She was filled with laughter and tears of joy. This caused many of her religious friends to offer her their happy

---

[28] Sarah Ann Hogan, age 21, single.

greetings and there was a general shouting in the crowd about or around her.

Now, this was too much for my pride and opposition longer to bear. I resolved to take her out of that crowd. I stood at the upper end of the large shed which covered most the congregation: she was sitting in a chair at the lower end of the shed shouting aloud. I started from where I stood, with a full determination to take her out and also, to desperately hurt anyone who might by force attempt to prevent my purpose.

I was comparatively a stranger among that people, as I had only been a few days among them, and made a partial or limited acquaintance.

When I started for her (she being 20 steps distant) the following thoughts came to my mind: "You are a stranger among this people, and the best and most intelligent are around her, and heartily rejoicing with her, and today's action may bring a reproach on you, of which you can never get clear." I then determined to get nearer her seat, to observe her actions, and by such observation, in my mind decide whether there existed such thing as heartfelt religion, or experimental knowledge of God's pardoning mercy.

One clear look at her made the evidence overwhelming, and I at once determined to seek for that which gave her such joy. I turned to leave the throng and put in execution my purpose of seeking; I found myself trembling and so weak in my lower limbs, I feared I might fall if I should start to walk out of the crowd. I rebuked myself for being so affected and determined to stand a few minutes till my knees would recover strength, and I would get it ['religion'] *in secret. By the time this thought was fully formed, I found I could not stand longer on my feet, and to hold myself up, I* put my arm around a post which supported a girder of the shed; it, however, availed me nothing; the arm weakened with the whole physical system.

Just at this moment an old lady vacated a chair that stood touching the post I was hugging; I fell into that chair, and as I fell my pride was so subdued, I cried aloud, and prayed aloud for God to save me, the vilest sinner on earth. Many persons talked to and advised me to trust - to believe - but it appeared to me, I could not do as they directed. When I had despaired, my sister came to me, placing her hands on my head with these words, "Oh, my brother! Believe on the Lord Jesus; claim him, take him as yours for life, for death and eternity." This determined me; I will trust and claim him! If he damns me, it will be just; if he saves me, it will be his infinite mercy.

From the moment of that trust, I have never been able to show or express, the fullness I, at that moment, saw in Christ Jesus for the salvation of all the world: even the chief of sinners, as he had saved me.

I stood amid the throng, and called aloud for my two younger brothers, William, and James[29], and a number of young men whose acquaintance I had made, saying to them, if they wanted religion, and would come and occupy the bench I stood on, I would tell them in five minutes, so plainly, that they would certainly succeed. At least a score came to the bench, my brothers in the number, for whom I was particularly interested. I kneeled between them, as they were side by side; I urged them to claim Christ - not to hesitate a minute, for he came into the world to save sinners; and when I claimed him by faith, he saved me, and you

---

[29] William is 20, James 18, and the two follow Davie in birth order.

know, I was the worst sinner in the world. My words only appeared to increase their convictions, and distress of mind. Directly, I concluded they were surely dull of apprehension - the true theory I had in my experience, but they had neither. "No man knoweth the Son but the Father, and no man knoweth the Father save the Son, and he to whom the Son will reveal him."(Matt. 11: 27)

For I have always dated my call to the ministry to the day of my conversion, as from that day, I felt I must persuade men in Christ's stead to be reconciled to God. Though, I often after strove to throw off the impression. I employed two months reading and comparing the Westminster, Cumberland and Methodist Episcopal Confessions of faith[30], in order to determine the church I should join, and on the last Sunday in August, 1833, my sister and I joined the Cumberland Presbyterian Church[31], at New Lebanon, Missouri, Rev. Archibald McCorkle, Pastor, and September 15, 1833, I was received under the care of New Lebanon Presbytery; a candidate for the ministry.

Once sure of a direction, Davie resolutely "set his face like flint" to follow it. He was elected as Candidate for Cumberland Presbyterian ministry just three weeks after becoming a church member.

"I had a fair common school education, but desired a more thorough, and on the 1st day of March 1834, I left

---

[30] The camp-meeting was a cooperative affair, and Davie is trying to choose between the sponsors: Methodist and CPC, and his parents' Presbyterian Church. He employs each group's *Confessions of Faith* to make his decision.

[31] Also recalled in *The Cumberland Presbyterian*, June 16, 1904, page 764 (cumberland.org/hfcpc/minister/HoganDavid.htm).

home, traveling on horseback, to the Southern and Western Theological Seminary at Maryville, East Tennessee.[32]

The overland journey from central Missouri to eastern Tennessee was a grueling one. Davie spent an entire month on horseback.

The seminary was not a chartered institution, but taught the full college curriculum, or classic course. Isaac Anderson, D.D. was President, Darius Hoyt, D.D. Professor of Languages, and Fielding Pope, D.D. Professor of Mathematics and English Science. All were New School, properly, followers of Samuel Hopkins, D.D.

"New School" or Hopkinsianism was a theological scheme and a form of Calvinism which later adherents called "consistent Calvinism." The view evolved into a distinct theology which dominated theological thinking in New England. The whole theological movement was important in the Second Great Awakening. It was opposed generally by the "Old Presbyterian" theologians of Princeton. This may be the first time Davie's cultural views of slavery were challenged as Samuel Hopkins was fiercely abolitionist.

I pursued the educational course at Maryville from the 1st of April 1834 to the 1st of August 1836.

There is something remarkable leading to, and attendant upon, my work among the Cherokee Indians, of which I will make a brief statement. While I was a student in the Southern and Western Seminary at Maryville, East Tennessee, Mr. John B. Jones[33] *was my fellow student; he*

---

[32] Rev. Isaac Anderson opened the Southern and Western Theological Seminary in 1819 to educate more church leaders for the territory. In 1842, the name changed to "Maryville College" and continues to operate to this day in Maryville, Blount County, Tennessee.

[33] ***Champions of the Cherokees: Evan and John B. Jones;*** by William G. McLoughlin, 1990, Princeton University Press

was born and raised among the Cherokees and learned their language just as the Indian children learned it. His father was a Baptist missionary. Young Jones was being educated by his father for Mission work, when he should occupy his father's place. He and I boarded in the same family and slept in the same bed. Now, his talks about the Indians caused me to think much about their moral and spiritual wants, and awakened in me a great desire, if I were prepared by the understanding of their language, to preach the gospel to them, which ever abided to my seventy-second year, when I was commissioned.

God caused the paths of John Buttrick Jones and Davie Hogan to cross when both men were incredibly young. David was twenty-three and "Young Jones" was only eleven! Issac Anderson operated both a Preparatory School and a Seminary (Sam Houston was an earlier student who tested the headmaster's patience). John B. Jones was the son of a famous Welsh Baptist missionary to the Cherokee, Evan Jones, who would lead a group of Cherokee on the Trail of Tears in just two years; Both Jones' would serve among them in Indian Territory (Oklahoma) and both were already ardent abolitionists. As they boarded together and shared a bed there must have been heated discussions about slavery between the missionary kid and the newly saved seminarian raised on a plantation. Davie's worldview was being hammered repeatedly. His young roommate would go on to be an amazing missionary to the Cherokee in his own right and the two would certainly cross paths on the Nation when Davie finally arrived. It would be fully fifty years before David Hogan was able to answer the call he received during his long talks with John B. Jones.

October 1835 was a vacation month of the Seminary with me. I attended the regular session of the Knoxville Presbytery of the Cumberland Presbyterian Church at Madisonville, Monroe County, Tennessee. From a sedentary life, and close study, I was in a weak state of health, and for the benefit of my health, the Knoxville Presbytery thought it proper to license me, and that I should rest for two months from Seminary studies, and ride horseback. Whereupon, on the 15th day of October, the Knoxville Presbytery passed the following order: "Ordered, That David Hogan ride two rounds on the Sequachee Valley district in the next two months and report his ministerial work in the next regular session of Presbytery." I immediately bought a pony and started for the circuit; fifty miles distant from the Seminary.[34]

In these days mission work was the circuit or district work, to which the Presbytery would send a man to preach. If an ordained man, he was authorized by his Presbytery to organize churches and do all the work of an ordained minister. If only a licensed man, he was required at the different preaching points to give opportunity to all who wish to join the Cumberland Presbyterian Church to come and give him their hand and he would enroll their names and report to the Presbytery. These missionaries had no Board to give them a salary or support. The mission had to give the support, or the missionary did without.

---

[34] *Circuit riders were the first step towards evangelizing the area encompassed by a presbytery. Some parts of the Cumberland Presbyterian Church disliked the term "circuit rider" (a usage popularized by the Methodists) and preferentially utilized the phrase "itinerant missionary." But by whatever name, the early preachers rode circuits. The bounds of the circuits were established by the Presbytery and assignments for preaching in each were made at each of the semi-annual meetings. In the earlier days the circuit riders were often young men not yet ordained. Their mission was to spread the gospel in the circuit assigned to them and, when possible, to collect enough persons to form a church; later an ordained minister would come and formally organize the congregation.* History of New Lebanon Cooper County Missouri, Chapter IV

Who supported those sent out by our church? They went at God's call and commission and God moved the people to take care of them: true, often the missionary would have to do as Paul did, resort for a period to "tent making", which in my own case, was to teach a school for one to five months.

Only a few days before (being commissioned to ride circuit) I had loaned James W. Ramsey all the money I had, he being a Cumberland Candidate for the ministry; also, a classmate. The borrowed money was to be paid to me by his father, Col. Ramsey, who lived on the way to my circuit, about thirty miles from the Seminary. I only had one dime in my purse. Yet I was not uneasy, as I would be able to get to Col. Ramsey's that day, only thirty mile's ride, and my dime would pay my ferry across the Clinch River. But I had the misfortune to lose my way after I got into Roane County, Tennessee, which caused me to fall short of my destination that night, ten miles.

Now comes my first trouble as a preacher and circuit rider. I, however, got to Kingston, the County seat of Roane County; the moon shone brightly, and at or near the edge of the town stood a cottage house with the sign hoisted, 'Private Entertainment.' When I came in front of it, I sat on my jaded pony some minutes, deciding what was best to do.[35]

---

[35] Young Minister Hogan is understandably reluctant to enter a "public house" as a newly minted preacher. These establishments had a reputation for immoral and unsavory activities and questionable clientele and also likely spots for inexperienced travelers to be robbed, or worse.

I concluded to call the landlord[36] to the front gate and make known to him my misfortune. I stated to him, I had that day lost my way in travel and as "You see, Sir, it is now in the night and the country is strange to me, and if this is Kingston, I am about ten miles from where I expected to lodge tonight, at Col. Ramsey's. I have no money, except a dime, with which I expected to pay my ferry; if you will let me stay with you, I will send you my bill from Col. Ramsey's." He apprehended my situation at once, struck the hostler[37] bell, and asked me to light [dismount] *and come in. When we got in the room, I said, "Sir, this is the first time I have ever had to beg such favor."*

He saw my humiliation, and replied, "Don't let it trouble you, sir, it is all right." He had at once commenced interrogating "Are you acquainted with Col. Ramsey?"

"Not personally."

"Where did you start from this morning?"

"From Maryville."

"Is Col. Ramsey's the end of your journey?"

"No sir; I am going to Sequachee Valley."

"What part of the valley are you going too?"

"No particular part."

"Do you live in or near Maryville? Is it your home?"

---

[36] This landlord was Col. Joseph Byrd (39 yrs. old), whose father Jesse was the first ferryman at what was Byrd's Ferry, now Sevier's Ferry. In youth he served in the Indian war under Gen. Jackson, (hence the Col. honorific Davie later mentions) and at his majority married Ann Pride. He was a farmer who occasionally boated from Kingston to Huntsville, AL. He served eight years as sheriff of Roane County, and a justice. They were Methodists.

[37] Hostler: a man employed to look after the horses of people staying at an inn.

"No sir; my home is in Missouri." At the last answer he expressed astonishment.

"Missouri! Oh! You are a great way from home." The next minute he added: "Excuse me sir, I am questioning to find out all about you. What is your name?"

"My name is Hogan." Then he said, again, "Excuse me, I'm questioning not to harm you, but for good. I see you are young. Have you any relatives in this State of your name?"

"I have an uncle in Athens, McMinn County, if he has not lately moved."

"Ah, Colonel William James Hogan III.[38]"

"Yes, Sir?"

"I know him well. He has moved to Talladega, Alabama. I can talk to you now, not as a stranger. May I ask what your purpose is in going to Sequachee Valley?"

"Yes, Sir. I have been confined three sessions in the Seminary at Maryville and the confinement has, and is, breaking down my health and strength. I came from Missouri to that institution to educate myself for the ministry, and my failing strength required a rest. One week since, the Knoxville Presbytery of the Cumberland Presbyterian Church thought it best to license me to preach and placed me on the Sequachee Valley circuit for two months, hoping thereby to restore my lost strength." Mr. Byrd, the landlord, appeared pleased and satisfied with his examination, and so expressed himself. After supper, on lighting me to bed, I said to him, "I want an early start in the morning to get to Col. Ramsey's for breakfast."

---

[38] 1788-1855. Brother of Gen. David Hogan. Settled on Muskogee (Creek) Tribal lands near Talladega in 1834.

He replied, "No sir, you will breakfast with me - but I will give you an early start."

The breakfast was eaten just at day light. He asked me to hold prayers with the family. Whilst we were eating breakfast, he informed me the ferry belonged to him. On bidding farewell, he handed me an unsealed note, telling me to please hand it to the ferry man. I did so. The ferry man opened and read "Set this man over free, and hand him this five-dollar bill. The very man handed me the five dollars, and asked, did you stay at Col. Byrd's last night?"

I answered, "I did."

Before we shook hands Col. Byrd requested that on my return to Maryville I should hold a two days meeting for them and Kingston, saying, he would secure the use of the Methodist Church. Also stating, that his wife and daughter had professed religion two months since at a Cumberland Camp-meeting near Athens and wished to join the church. I promised him, if my health and strength improved, as I hoped, I would comply with his request, which I did.

Now the truth and blessing to be drawn from the above related incident is this: When the true child of God is overtaken by misfortune or disappointment, if he be faithful to trust God, such misfortune or tribulations have the promise of the Father. "All things shall work together for good to them that love God, to them who are called according to his purpose." (Rom. 8:28) This is how we know, by experience.

Incidental to my work in Sequachee Valley is the following: It required one month to make one round; hence, I could only make two rounds according to the order of the Presbytery, which would give me two services at each preaching place on the circuit, from the upper end to the *lower end of the valley, where the Sequachee River empties into the Tennessee. From the head of the valley, I traveled down the west side of the beautiful river, and in return, on the east side; preaching in every schoolhouse, but oftener, in the dwelling houses (according to order of places on circuit and names given by my predecessors).*

My first appointment was Pinhook, in the upper end of the Valley, and the appointment for service was at candle lighting. There was no coal oil, gas, or electric lights in those days. The Presbytery had enjoined me on the duty of taking collections for the support of myself and those who should be next sent or were already in the Mission Field.

I said to them that night, "I was ordered by the Presbytery to make two rounds on this circuit and my appointment one month hence will close my work with you. Now at my next and last appointment, I want everyone who desires to have preaching by me or any other preacher, to be ready with a dime to put in the collection. Should you have much more money, I am glad, but keep it. Be sure and put in a dime, whether you are a member of the church or not. (The dime at that time was a newly adopted coin by the U. S. Government and constituted a large part of the fractional currency.) I also said, "I hope no one will put in the hat a larger piece of money, or more than one dime." At every place of preaching round the circuit, the hat collection was appointed for the next appointment, and the same cautions were given relating to the dime. The happy results will be given farther on.

At this first appointment they had had a house raising that day, and the larger portion of the house raisers remained for supper, and to be at preaching that night. The preaching was in the old log dwelling which was soon to be abandoned for the new one, which they had that day raised. The old house was not large, but every nook and corner was crowded with people either sitting or standing. As was the custom in the house raisings of those days, they had used "Tennessee White Face" (whiskey) and some of them felt its effects; but they kept good order and apparently listened well to what I said. My pulpit consisted of a small table and chair placed rather to the side of the middle door between the two rooms of the cabin. So soon as it was a little dark, a candle was lighted and placed on the little table, also several lights in each room. When all was ready, I arose, announced the page, number, and meter of my hymn; after reading it, I gave the two first lines again, stating the meter, and saying, "I will thank some friend to set the tune." No one responded. I tried and failed and was about to lay my hymn book on the table, when over in an opposite corner an elderly looking man arose and seemed to be a little under the influence of "white face". He asked me to read the first two lines again, saying, he thought he could set the tune. I read the lines and he set the tune, and all went on well to the close of the service.

My next appointment was ten miles distant, at Pikeville[39], I reached the town next morning by 11:00. Here I was honored to hold services in the town Academy. After service I rode home with a brother six miles, who had come that distance to hear me preach. He lived on the way to my

---

[39] The city is situated in the northern half of the Sequatchie Valley, a deep, narrow, and fertile valley that presents as a large rupture in the southern Cumberland Plateau. The walls of the plateau, namely Walden Ridge and Little Mountain, rise prominently to the east and west, respectively. The Sequatchie River passes through the eastern section of Pikeville.

next day's appointment. I tarried the night with him. My appointment for the next day (on Thursday at 11:00 AM) was at Spring's. Brother Spring, in that day, was called a wealthy farmer, and had built his house for church service, as well as for a dwelling, having folding partitions for the entire lower part of his roomy building.

On my travel to Spring's, about one mile before I came to his house, there was quite a hill, covered with young pines. From the top of this hill, his house was in plain view in the valley below. I saw a considerable number of horses hitched along the front yard fence. This indicated to me there was already a congregation in waiting; I felt in want of a better preparation; I turned my horse and rode a few steps among the pine bushes, hitched my horse, got out my Bible and prayed; then I read the third chapter of the Epistle to the Romans, but got no new light therefrom. I then looked at my watch for the time - it was near 11:00. I mounted my horse, as I rode down to the house, I determined to preach from Isaiah 3:10-11. The Lord led me out into a large place; that is, he gave me light and liberty, while treating of the righteous character and the reward. Many appeared to be happy in the audience. In delineation of the wicked character and the reward of his hands, there was a general breakdown; the effect was such the congregation was not dismissed till the sun rose next morning. They made count of twenty professions. This wonderful display of the power of God stood in my way for some time after. Satan tempted me to be proud, as though I had accomplished much.

In making the first round on this circuit, I formed a good general acquaintance with the people. When I got back to the upper end of the valley, the family at Pinhook had gotten into the larger new house, and although they had much more room than in the old, the new house was not sufficient to hold all the people that came out that night. Before I commenced services that night, I privately planned with two young men, whose acquaintance I had made (neither of them religious), that when I should call for them, they would use their hats in collecting the dimes, charging them to give everyone in the audience an opportunity. I afterward counted the pieces and was led to believe each one in the audience must have put in a dime, which I think was probably the case in each place of preaching on the second and last round. At least, I will say, my common size purse became full and I had to make a purse of one of my socks.

At the next regular session of Presbytery, my report was one hundred professions, ninety of whom have given me their hands and names, joining the CPC. When I emptied my sock of dimes on the Clerk and Treasurer's table, he was, or appeared to be, astonished, and called on the Moderator for help to count them (Clerk and Treasurer was the lamented Rev. Robert Tate[40]). There were two hundred and twenty dollars in dimes. Now, many may have exceeded the order I gave for no one to put in more than one dime. However, Bro. Tate said, no preacher of that circuit had ever before that taken up more than ten dollars, for six- or twelve-months' work.

He requested me, to state to the Presbytery the course I had pursued in taking collections, saying, "There must be something peculiar causing such success." I stated that I thought the limitation to one dime, and for everyone who

---

[40] Robert Tate (ca 1793-1837) was pioneering Texas for the CPC and home in Tennessee for this meeting and some personal monetary interests. He died on the return journey to Texas, Sept. 17, 1837.

wanted to hear the gospel from me or any other preacher to put a dime in the hat at my next appointment; however, more especially, they appear to be moved by the Holy Spirit.

When I was a lad in Sunday School, much of the work was memorizing the scriptures. On one occasion, I committed to memory the parable of the "Ten Virgins." I did it so well that I have ever since been able to repeat it. From the memory of the parable, the following occurred in my ministry. On my return from Sequachee Valley to Maryville, East Tennessee, I made an appointment to preach near the County Seat of Rhea County, Tennessee. The day was inclement, was snowing. Ten young ladies composed the entire audience. This peculiar fact presented to my mind the memorized parable for a text. I was familiarly acquainted with these ladies, three of them devout Christians.

As soon as I announced my text their minds took hold, at least, of its applicability. The Lord helped me to preach and they gave a hearing ear. At the close of the discourse, I invited those who felt that they were not prepared to meet the Bridegroom to kneel in prayer and seek the readiness at once. The unconverted seven quickly bowed, and four of them confessed the Savior joyfully, before the benediction was pronounced. I learned the remaining three professed a short time after. Now, when a boy in Sunday School, I did not think of the good that might come to myself and others from memorizing scripture.

While Davie was cutting his teeth in pioneering church planting ministry, his family back in Missouri made a move. General David had been looking for enough land to farm like the plantation he'd had in Kentucky. He found it on the border of Cooper and Pettis Counties in a newly minted small town called Arator. He moved his wife and remaining children onto the land from the rented Ewing

Home in New Lebanon and went through the legal process of homesteading the land from the Federal Government. In 1834 and 1835 he added to this acreage by purchase until he had a farm large enough for his fifty slaves and large family. Davie received letters about the move and understood the cliché "you can never go home." He loved New Lebanon for being a heart for the Cumberland Presbyterians and for providing the holy ground where he had surrendered to Jesus Christ. But it would never be his home again.

Finis Ewing home in New Lebanon, MO which the Hogan family occupied in 1833. Photographed in later years with the upper story removed.

Interior of New Lebanon Cumberland Presbyterian Church

Modern Headquarters of Rev. Davie Hogan's beloved church, in Cordova, TN

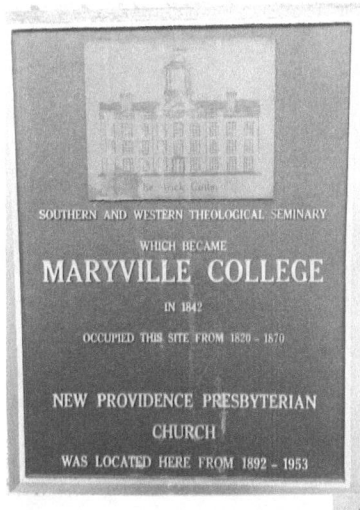

Clockwise from top left:
Plaque at historic site of Southern and Western Seminary – Maryville College,
.Isaac Anderson, founder and David Hogan's seminary professor.
The campus in 1834, the Brick Seminary and the Frame College.
A Circuit Rider much like Davie looked as he rode the Sequatchee Valley Circuit.
Prof. Fielding Pope, D.D. Davie Hogan's Professor of Mathematics and English Science.

STARTING A FAMILY (1836-1837)

David Hogan was ready to take the next step in his education and he'd chosen Greeneville College, then located 3 miles south of Greeneville, Tennessee on the farm of its late founder Hezekiah Balch, a New Lights Presbyterian. In August of 1836, the lovely and intelligent Elizabeth Blackburn Hoss, eldest child of Henry Hoss, President of Greeneville College, was finishing up a degree in Education at that place of higher learning. This rare pursuit for a young woman of that day no doubt caught the interest of Davie Hogan as he interviewed with President Hoss to finish his education at Greeneville. David must have made a fine first impression on Mr. Hoss. He was not only accepted into the College; he was accepted as a son-in-law by Henry and Polly Hoss[41], even though he'd clearly stated his intent to move back to Missouri! He was no sooner officially engaged to the beautiful Elizabeth when the campus was thrown into unexpected sorrow. President Henry Hoss dropped dead on August 29th. Davie and Elizabeth comforted each other in their shared grief; Elizabeth mourning her father and David having just learned of the death of his 14-year-old brother, Joseph. The young boy had died in early July at the family home in Arator, but the mail from the Missouri frontier was slow — the sad news didn't reach David in Tennessee until late August, even though posted by his brother William M. Hogan, Postmaster of Georgetown. Davie was far away when the family gathered in the small churchyard near their farm to bury the lad.[42]

---

[41] Davie and Elizabeth were third cousins once removed through the Boone family. Whether they connected the dots or maybe this facilitated the rapid incorporation of young Hogan into the Hoss family is unknown.

[42] Providence Cemetery is 6 miles east of Smithton on Hwy 50, north on 135 for 3 miles to the church at the corner of 135 & Providence Rd.

In September 1836, I entered Greeneville College[43], near Greeneville, East Tennessee. In August I had made my arrangements with the President of the College, Henry Hoss, to there finish my college course. It was vacation month, and he was suddenly removed by death before the commencement day of the college year. The curators elected Alfred[44], his oldest son, to the chair vacated by the death of his father: he had graduated in his nineteenth year, one month before his father's death.

With the whirlwind of college studies, engagement and living with grieving soon-to-be in-laws, Davie was still drawn powerfully to church planting. He rode a circuit for the Cumberland Presbyterians while still a ministerial student. He demonstrated gifts of prophetic preaching and effective evangelism.

The following occurrences took place while I was at Greeneville College. While there I preached every Sabbath at some point reachable and return in the day. On one occasion, I had made an appointment across the Nolichucky River, four miles from the College. There was quite a rise in the river, I had to ferry. My text that day was Amos 4:12. "Therefore thus will I do unto thee, O Israel: and because I will do this unto thee, prepare to meet thy God, O Israel." In concluding my discourse, I felt for and pleaded with the

---

[43] Tusculum College is a private four-year college affiliated with the Presbyterian Church located in Tusculum, Tennessee, a suburb of Greeneville, Tennessee. The college was founded as Greeneville College in 1794, making it the oldest college in Tennessee and the 28th oldest college in the United States.

[44] Alfred Hoss (1817-1892) President of Greenville College 15 Sep 1836 to his resignation 14 Aug 1838. President Lincoln appointed him to a position in the War Department. Buried in the Congressional Cemetery in D.C.

youth of the audience to prepare to meet God. They might be called to meet God that evening.

There was in the audience that day, a young man and two young ladies, who crossed the river in a canoe. After service when the young man and two young ladies started for their canoe, one of his young friends addressed him, "Jim, take care in crossing the river, that you don't get your call this evening." He replied, "No danger, I have heard such warnings ever since I was a little tad." That evening he and the two young ladies somehow turned the canoe and were drowned.

On another occasion, I went a short distance from the College to hear Charles Coffin, D. D. , Ex-President of the College. He insisted that I should preach for him, as he had a severe cold. I yielded. My text was Romans 10:8-9[45]. About the middle of my discourse a young man, who at that time was a student attending the college, professed religion. He quickly rose to his feet, rejoicing and telling how blessed is he whose trust is in the Lord. Suffice to say, I did not finish my sermon.[46]

October the 27th, 1836, I was married to Miss Elizabeth Blackburn Hoss, eldest daughter of the late

---

[45] "But what saith it? The word is nigh thee, even in thy mouth, and in thy heart: that is, the word of faith, which we preach; That if thou shalt confess with thy mouth the Lord Jesus, and shalt believe in thine heart that God hath raised him from the dead, thou shalt be saved."

[46] These three paragraphs are included here for chronological order but were originally typed by D. Hogan in the 'Recapitulations' at the end of his Memoirs. The author has so rearranged where it improves narrative flow.

deceased president.⁴⁷ Our engagement was before his death and had his approval.

---

⁴⁷ #3906 Tennessee Marriage Records, Greene County. Witnessed by George W. Foute, Greene County Clerk* and Valentine Sevier, District Court Clerk. Legally executed Oct 27, 1836 by Robert Frazier, Minister of the Gospel.
* Foute went on to attest to future President Andrew Johnson's 1839 sale of the home he'd bought in 1831. His tailor shop was on the same property.

Starting a Family (1836-1837)

Encounter On The Walk
Julius Pratt

Around 1800, the Presbyterian Church suffered a division in theology, in large part, over ordination of ministers and revivals. This painting represents a chance encounter by Reverends Samuel Doak (old school) and Hezekiah Balch (new school) on a boardwalk after a tremendous rain. Doak told Balch, "Sir I do not give way to the devil" to which Balch replied, "Sir I always give way to the devil, you may pass." Upon which Balch stepped off the walk into mud over his ankles.

Encounter on the Walk depicts Hezekiah Balch, founder of Greeneville College engaged in a doctrinal dispute with Samuel Doak (Old Presb.).

Emancipation Movement: Rev. Coffin on left, Doak with cane.

Emancipation Movement
Joe Kilday

Under the influence of the Reverends Samuel Doak and Charles Coffin, Greeneville became a center for emancipation. Pictured are Samuel Doak, Charles Coffin and Benjamin Lundy, editor of The Genius of Universal Emancipation, published in Greeneville from 1822 to 1824.

Starting a Family (1836-1837)

Henry Hoss' gravestone Washington College Station Cemetery. Davie certainly attended the burial.

Charles Coffin, the abolitionist minister who put Davie Hogan in his pulpit. (Greeneville Greene County History

Mordecai Lincoln, Greenville College Board Member, and town shoemaker. Close friend of Andy Johnson and relative of Abe Lincoln.

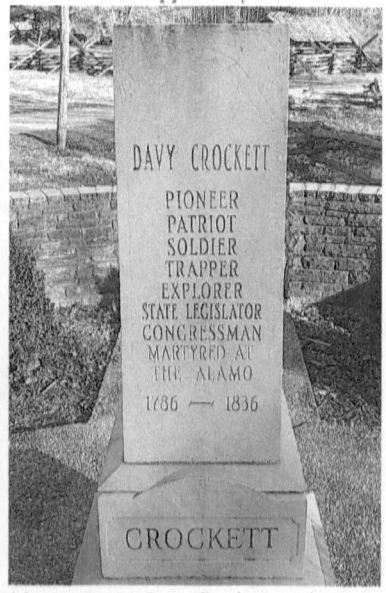

Monument to Davy Crockett, at his birthplace near Greenville on the Nolichucky River. Killed at the Alamo in Texas in 1836 the year Davie Hogan arrived

It's intriguing that future President Andrew Johnson was the tailor (already active in local politics) in Greeneville, the county seat where Davie registered their marriage. Andy was auditing oratory classes out at Greeneville College where he surely met Davie. Since Andy's home shop was only three miles from campus, he likely was tailor for both the Henry Hoss funeral and Hogan-Hoss wedding. He was locally famous for his wedding frock coats. His thorough workmanship inspired the local song *Long Tailed Blue*.

Andrew Johnson, Greeneville tailor. 17th President of the United

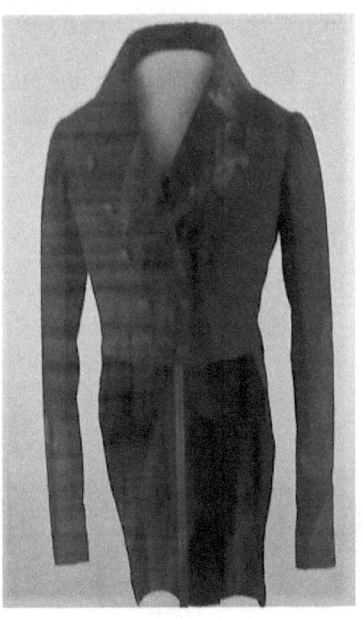

Blue wedding frock made by Andrew Johnson, circa 1836.

If you want the girls to love you

To love you good and true,

Go down to Andy's tailor shop

And get a long-tailed blue.

Andy's close friend and neighbor was Mordecai Lincoln,[48] first cousin once removed of Abraham Lincoln. Mordecai was a tanner and shoemaker, a Board Member and Trustee of Greeneville College (1835-1837) and another probable vendor for both funeral and wedding. Robert Frazier, the Cumberland Presbyterian Minister who officiated their wedding was two years David's senior, a fellow student at Greeneville and newly minted "Minister of the Gospel". Frazier would later create, publish, and edit the *Cumberland Presbyterian Messenger*.

> *My marriage in the family, and their knowledge of my intention to locate in Missouri, determined the whole family*

Andy's wife, Eliza, reads to him while he works. Perhaps a book on public speaking borrowed from Davie's college where he was auditing oratory classes. (NPS.gov)

Johnson Tailor Shop and early home in Greeneville, TN.

> *to move to Missouri at the close of the college year, and at once, all preparations were made for removal the next September 1837.*
>
> *For various advantages in the settlement of the family, I determined to come to Missouri in advance and make some*

---

[48] As justice of the peace, Mordecai Lincoln officiated at the wedding of Andrew Johnson and Eliza McCardle on May 17, 1827.

preparations for their location. Hence, I only spent from October till March at Greeneville College. Had I continued to the close of the collegiate year, I should have graduated, at least, with respectable honors.

The practical issues of re-homing a large and bereaved family were daunting. The responsibility placed upon young Davie with his mother-in-law's determination to join her daughter in Missouri forced him to abruptly abandon the studies he'd come to Greeneville College to complete. Henry Hoss had left a 45-year-old widow, Polly Blackburn Hoss, and seven children — and all of them except Alfred, the new College President, were Missouri-bound. Names and ages of the Hoss children at the time of the family's immigration to Pettis County, Missouri: Elizabeth Hoss Hogan (21), Alfred (20), Sam (19), Julia (15), Edwin (11), Archie (10) and Emma (5).

Davie wisely concluded that such a dangerous and complicated journey should be scouted out, so he and Elizabeth prepared to be the advance party on the move from Tennessee to his parents' home in Missouri.

In March 1837, when I left Greeneville College for Missouri, I was in my twenty-sixth year and my wife in her twenty-second. Elizabeth and I placed ourselves and some little effects on a flatboat, with a family who had built the same to float to the mouth of the Tennessee River, on their move to Missouri.

A Word about River Travel: Traveling by river was the longest way to get to your destination because you had to follow the path and flow of the river, which isn't exactly straight. Sometimes the river would flow the opposite direction from your destination. By choosing this route, Davie and his new bride had to load and board a flatboat at the Nolichucky River boat launch close to their home on the Greeneville College campus. Then float down the Nolichucky to the French Broad River, onto the Tennessee River at Knoxville, down to Huntsville, Alabama, and back north on the Tennessee river to Paducah, Kentucky. At that point the couple with whom they were traveling would sell their flatboat as scrap lumber (about $16) or perhaps intact to someone taking goods down the Mississippi to New Orleans. Both couples probably sold barrels of Tennessee whiskey to get their fare money for the next stage of travel, whisky being the main commodity that left Greene County by flatboat. They certainly didn't travel with cash as the rivers were beyond the law's reach. The party paid for economy passage on a steamboat and, their pace now increased up to 12 mph, took the Ohio River to Cairo, Illinois, then north up the Mississippi to St. Louis, Missouri, then east on the Missouri River to Boonville, Missouri - the mother of westward migration trails. Not exactly a direct route.

The primary advantage to taking this longer route was the Flatboat. As you can see in the illustration, flatboats were not exactly a sleek,

modern mode of transportation. They were awkward one-way craft. You were basically in a big wooden box that was drifting along with the current. The advantage of this box was that it was made of heavy timber, so it shielded its passengers from outside attack. It also afforded a small cabin and a place for any livestock. For moves like this one, typical mid-range flatboats were about 55 ft long by 16 ft wide and were called Broadhorns, Kentucky Boats, or Natchez Boats. The party would have purchased guidebooks, which would plot a suggested course downriver, provided you could get your boat to cooperate! They probably hired a guide at Huntsville to help steer the craft through the most dangerous stretch of river — the treacherous Muscle Shoals rapids in northwest Alabama. Of course. there were other places along the route where the wise (and inexperienced) would employ the services of river guides. The river portion of this trip could take four months or more, depending on the time of year and any stops along the way.

David doesn't specify their departure date, but March 15th is a good guess, as there was surely an ardent desire by the Hoss family to celebrate Easter together. Easter Sunday fell on March 14th that year. Progress on a flatboat was slow, and it took the party over a month to transit from Balch Farm Greeneville College campus to Havana in Decatur County, Tennessee. They launched their crowded flatboat from a boat launch[49] just a couple miles from campus into the Nolichucky River. It was all-hands-on-deck since a flatboat required at least three people to navigate. Boarding their shared floating home, they navigated the winding stream for about fifty miles to its confluence with the French Broad River. This took them another 72 miles into Knoxville, where they floated onto the broader flow of the Tennessee River south for 175 miles to Chattanooga. Floating down the Tennessee River was challenging

---

[49] The author was able to locate where they began by finding the 1837 site of Greeneville College (Balch farm 3 miles from Greenville) and then the nearest possible place to launch a flatboat. The Nolichucky is all bluffs in that area, and their only option was and is the present day Kinser Park boat launch.

for heavily loaded flatboats. Some ten miles below Chattanooga there was a narrow gorge called *The Suck*, a.k.a. *The Valley of the Whirlpool Rapids*, and there were the *Muscle Shoals* in North Alabama. From Chattanooga, probably with a hired river guide aboard, they floated 291 miles westward and north to Havana (town now a memory), arriving May 22nd.[50]

> *While we were floating down the Tennessee River, an upriver wind stopped us at a little town, Havana, for a day or two. I was impatient under the detention. On the second day a steamboat, the Black Hawk, came down the river loaded with Cherokees, five hundred male and female, big and little. They were the least civilized of the tribe and the United States Government had to catch and force them to their present home. They were landed on a small river island close to our flatboat and allowed to recreate on the little island for several hours.*[51]
>
> *I at once proposed to my dear wife, that we would take our few goods and provisions off the flatboat on to the steamer and go with these Indians and be their missionaries the rest of our lives. We stood on the roof of our flatboat where we could look over most of the island. She looked at their wild, denuded state, and said she could not consent to go and spend her life with them.*

The chance meeting of the Hogan party's flatboat and a group of Native Americans on the Trail of Tears via the steamboat, Black Hawk, is pegged in history for the evening of May 23rd, 1837. Lieutenant Edward Deas left a journal that recounted the setting

---

[50] A 38-day journey. Flatboats could make at best 5.5 miles on a good day with spring flow. Greeneville to Havana would have taken a minimum of twelve 9-hour days with no stops and perfect conditions. For the two non-nautical couples, 38 days seems reasonable (about ⅓ maximum speed).

[51] *"On the second day"* May 23rd, 1837. The island was Eagle Nest Island: Latitude: 35° 24' 45.10" N; Longitude: 88° 4' 51.50" W. See photo pg. 62

from an official perspective. Davie can be forgiven misidentifying the bedraggled Native Americans as "Cherokees". They were Muscogee, also known as Creek, who'd fled the removal of their own people in 1832 and hid among the Cherokee. This only bought them another five years in Alabama. The soldiers undoubtedly regaled Davie with the difficulty of capturing the "Indians" and weren't too particular about the tribal divisions. There'd been escapes in the beginning of the voyage, so the 472 remaining captives were put on the island to prevent desertions.

This event is David Hogan's second call to missionary work with Native Americans. The first occurred through a roommate who grew up among the Cherokee as an M.K.[52], and now this strong urge standing on the roof of a flatboat. He thought they were Cherokees, and ironically, he would be a missionary to the Cherokee just a little over 50 miles from the Muscogee Nation in Oklahoma. David, 25 years old, sadly poles the flatboat away from the people God has bound his heart to. It will be another 45 years before he can answer the call.

He must have thought of the admonition of Paul the Apostle in First Corinthians 7:1,7-8 "Now for the matters you wrote about: It is good for a man not to marry. . ... I wish that all men were as I am. But each man has his own gift from God; one has this gift, another has that. Now to the unmarried and the widows I say: It is good for them to stay unmarried, as I am."

> *I have often thought since, we were young and capable of learning their language and teaching them ours, and we might have accomplished more than we have. Perhaps God controlled in her decision, and I reckon He did.*

On May 24th, a relieved Elizabeth, her resigned husband, and their friends continue their river journey north toward the Ohio River in Paducah, another 159 miles (they made better time on this last flatboat leg, only 4 days). David knows that he could have made no other choice and still honor the vows he had made less than four months before. What he didn't know was Elizabeth was pregnant.

---

[52] MK: Missionary Kid

Starting a Family (1836-1837)

She may have been more game for adventure if her body wasn't flooded with maternal hormones.

The two young couples were able to book passage on a steamboat headed to their destination and made much better time on this portion of the journey. After 47 miles the stern-wheeler stopped in Cairo at the southern tip of Illinois and then turned upriver for 194 miles on the mighty Mississippi. They didn't stop at Kaskaskia, Illinois but what a thrill to see it slide by! The Captain provided commentary about this former first capital of Illinois that had been the capital of the Northwest Territory before that. Davie could hardly imagine the town he saw as the capital of French Upper Louisiana over a hundred years before. He could see the old stone church the French and Indians had built. But when the Captain declared that Kaskaskia had been an Indian capital for a thousand years before the French arrived David plopped down on a huge grain sack. This was unimaginable!

St. Louis, Missouri was the next large port-of-call and above that frontier city their steamer left the Mississippi and went west on the Missouri River, following the 1804 trail of explorers Lewis and Clark for 191 miles. It had only been 33 years and yet there were towns and settlements everywhere. Places along the way had been settled by Davie's great grandfather Daniel Boone and his sons. Their destination, Boonville, had been first called Boone's Lick and was a saltworks pioneered by Nathan and Daniel Morgan Boone, brothers of Davie's Grandma Sarah Hogan. Both the Boone brothers were still alive, but they'd moved on from Boonville by 1837. Boonville was the westward end of the Boone's Lick Trail that overland settlers followed into Central Missouri and the jumping-off-place for the Santa Fe Trail they took further west to Mexico. It must have been extremely exciting to unload their things at the dock and move among pioneers from all over heading into parts unknown. Going down the gangplank at Boonville Landing just four days out of Paducah felt wonderful. The end of their long move was just a day's wagon ride away.

It needs no explanation, to say we were greatly relieved when our floating craft landed at Paducah, Kentucky. We

> *immediately took a steamer and got to Boonville, Cooper County, the 1st day of June 1837, and to Arator, thirty miles distant, the Hogan home, the 2nd day of June.*
>
> *Here we were comfortably homed and after a good rest, I joined myself in constant daily, or nearly so, preaching, in the entire bounds of the New Lebanon Presbytery, in company with the Rev. Barnett Miller, D. D., of precious memory. There were many precious revivals, many souls were saved and added to the church.*

Davie fails to mention that Elizabeth was the one most needing rest after the arduous three-month move from Tennessee. She was into her second trimester with their first child when they arrived at his parents' home. General David, his dad, was a popular fellow in the community, having been appointed Postmaster of Arator the year before. He'd been shown the ropes by his son, William, who'd been Georgetown Postmaster since 1835. The new Minister was living in the perfect home to meet all the folk of the surrounding area and share the Good News with them as they received their earthly news in the post. He immediately threw himself into the work of riding circuit and holding revival meetings.

At the same time, he was constantly working out arrangements to enable the Widow Hoss and her children, to make the move west and join the newlyweds. The schedule hastened by the coming baby and Elizabeth's desire for her mom's help.

> *During my first year of work there was a Camp-meeting on Haw Creek, and the first ever held at that place; there I preached a funeral sermon of a Mrs. Read, the mother of Rev. Robert Read, of precious memory. Robert was hardly grown to manhood. At that meeting he professed, also, Rev. Mitch Miller[53], who at that time was perhaps a boy of twelve*

---

[53] Fleming Mitchell Miller, C.P.C. Minister, 1824 – 1890.

years; each prominently useful and died in the midst of their manhood days.

Fifty years after this camp-meeting, Rev. N. J. Crawford and myself were in the Indian Territory - were traveling by train from Muscogee to Chouteau. Mr. Crawford made the acquaintance of an old gentleman on the car, whom he found to be a Cumberland Presbyterian. He brought him to my seat and introduced us. When my name was spoken, the old gentleman appeared to be astonished "Hogan! Hogan! Did you hold a camp-meeting once in 1837 on Haw Creek, Morgan County, Missouri?" I replied, "I did." Giving me his hand again with tears in his eyes, he said; "Brother Hogan, there I gave myself to the Lord, when you called me to the mourner's bench, nearly fifty-one years ago. I am happy in that heavenly light today."

Brother Miller[54] was very anxious for my ordination and arranged for a called session of the presbytery for that purpose, and on the 21st day of October 1837, I was ordained by the New Lebanon Presbytery at Elkton, Cooper County, Missouri.

Davie fails to mention another significant event that very Licensure Day. Elizabeth bore him their first child, Henry Hoss Hogan - named for her late father, Henry Hoss. We don't know if Mrs. Hoss and the children had completed their move to join the couple by the time the baby came. They began in September and could have made it if they had spent a bit more and made the entire trip by stern-wheeler.

---

[54] John Miller (1788-1886) Missouri State Senator and Representative. In the incident above he was on a one-year break between Senate and House. Miller was the original landholder in New Lebanon and sold Finis Ewing his property there.

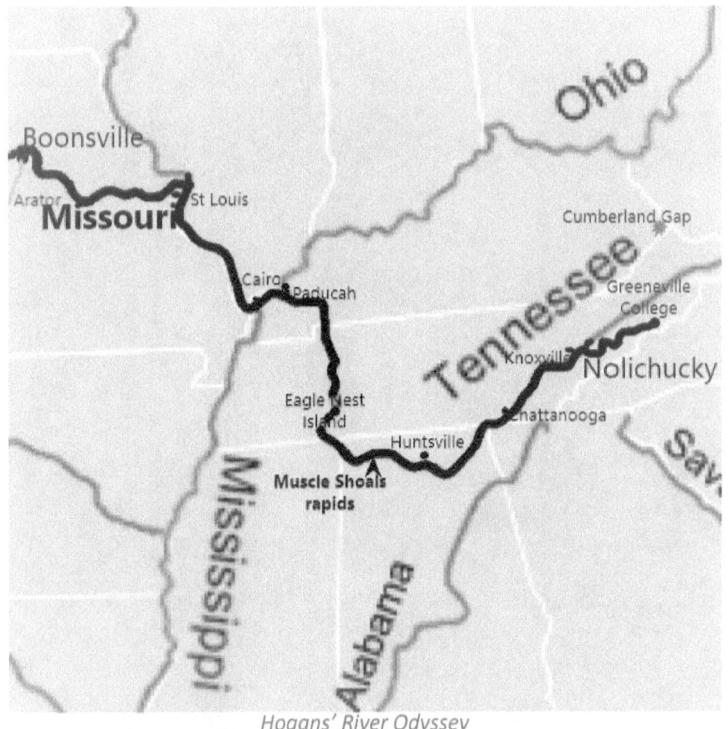
Hogans' River Odyssey

Their launching point on the Nolichucky River near Greeneville College

Starting a Family (1836-1837)

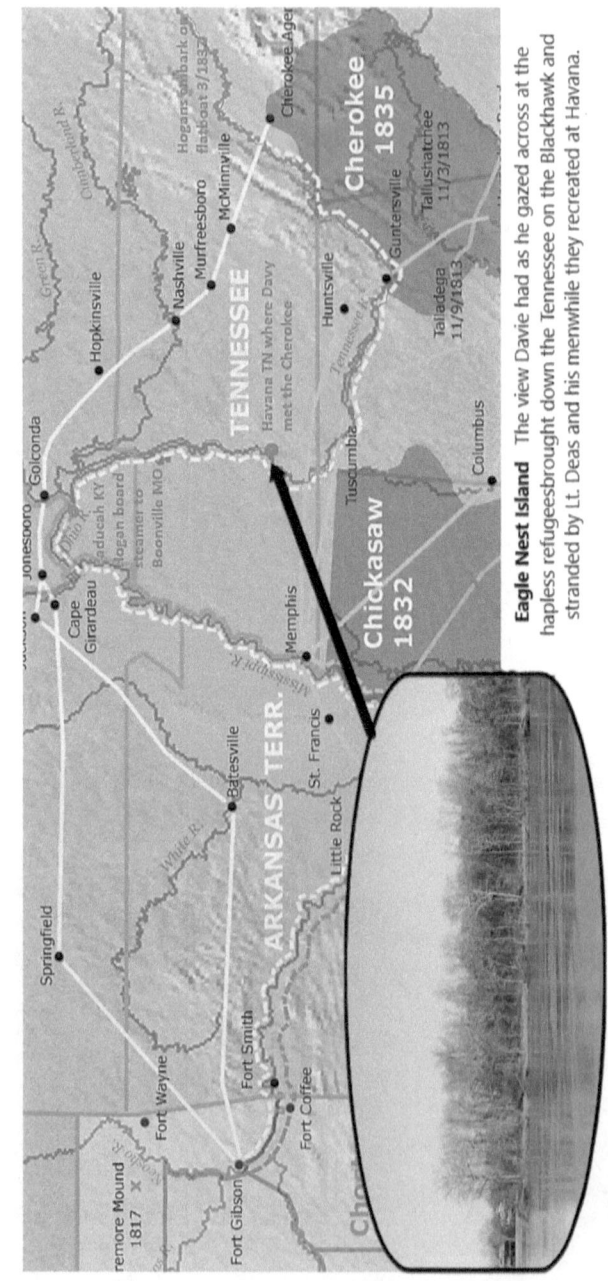

Eagle Nest Island The view Davie had as he gazed across at the hapless refugees brought down the Tennessee on the Blackhawk and stranded by Lt. Deas and his men while they recreated at Havana.

MISSOURI MINISTER (1838-1839)

Davie was a Circuit Rider again. In CPC parlance 'Uncle' was the term of endearment parishioners used for their preachers, though the ministers used "Brother" for one another. On the 18th of November, Rev. David M. Hogan – 'Uncle Davie' – licensed the month before, was ordained a Minister of the Gospel by the Cumberland Presbyterian Church in New Lebanon, its Missouri birthplace, where Davie had given his heart and life to Jesus Christ just over four years before. He passes over the mention of this big day in his autobiography.

> *That coming winter I served the Boonville, Cooper County congregation two Sabbaths in each month, and at Elkton[55] the same. I lived at Arator, Pettis County thirty miles from Boonville; the winter was severe, the travel horse-back, and I was several trips a little frostbitten.*

The restless Reverend was on the move again. Though still a Clerk for the New Lebanon Presbytery[56], Uncle Davie moved Elizabeth, their newborn son and his widowed mother-in-law, Polly Blackburn Hoss and her kids, sixteen miles west to Georgetown. David was becoming surrogate father to the Hoss kids. His sibling-in-laws ranged in age from nineteen to six. Sam, Julia, Edwin, Archie, and Emma kept the home from being too quiet. David had to pursue his Bible study mostly on horseback—tough with frostbitten fingers. He didn't neglect the discipling of this extended family. The Hoss tribe, including his new wife Elizabeth, converted from the Old (albeit New Light) Presbyterian faith they'd known in Tennessee to the Cumberland Presbyterian Church. A Cumberland Presbyterian

---

[55] Elkton was the original name of Otterville in Cooper County, just a mile east of the Hogan farm in Arator, Pettis County. This Elkton congregation was an easy circuit to ride.

[56] 21 April 1838 minutes of the New Lebanon Cumberland Presbytery.

congregation was soon gathered and meeting at the Hogan home (this church continued for years with Mrs. Hoss taking up the role of lady of the host home).

In March 1838, I moved my family to Georgetown, then the County-seat of Pettis County, however we only stayed a few months.

No preacher, who has faithfully, humbly, and lovingly delivered the message given him from Heaven to men on earth but has witnessed some remarkable conversions. I propose to speak of one or two such in my ministry, and the means used and the manner of occurrence. While living in Georgetown, a Mrs. McVey, from Baltimore, Maryland, died, whose husband had located in the new little town, hoping to live and raise his family by his trade, he being a carpenter. Mr. McVey came to me, desiring me to preach her funeral, as I had frequently visited her in her illness and talked much to her about her religious state of mind. She was devout and happy, and much blessed in her last days, and when death was cooling her body, her soul triumphed. She was a very bright intelligent lady of the Methodist Episcopal Church.

I asked Mr. McVey where would be the place of preaching, as there was neither school-house or church in the new small town; he replied that it would be in the Courtroom of the then unfinished Courthouse, upon which he was doing the inside carpentry. He said he could seat it well with the unused lumber: he did so. This was on Sunday, the day of his wife's death and the first death to occur in the town. On Sunday at 11:00 A.M. the corpse was brought into the unfinished Courtroom; there was a good attendance, and General George R. Smith[57] being among the number.

The order of a funeral service in that day and time was a regular sermon. My text was 1 Thessalonians 4:14[58]. The presence of the Savior by his Spirit was with me, the audience gave close attention, and there was a deep heartfelt presence of God. I believed at the time that good would result to some in that audience.

General Smith and two of my brothers, John D. [59] and William Hogan[60], were partners in a little store consisting of such goods as would supply the wants of the town and country. On Monday morning after breakfast, I had occasion to go to their store for some little article wanted. I stepped in the store, Gen. Smith, my two brothers and their bookkeeper, Robinson, was all that had gotten to the store that morning. I gave the usual courtesy of 'good morning'. Gen. Smith at once showed a deep state of feeling, expressing himself in the following manner. "Well! Davie Hogan, if I this morning owned the whole world, I would give it all to feel and enjoy what you felt and enjoyed yesterday while preaching Mrs. McVey's funeral."

By this time I discovered his tears. I feelingly replied, "General, I thank God for your desire; but let me say, if you owned ten thousand worlds like this, and would give them

---

[57] Founder of Georgetown and Sedalia, MO, and business partner of William and James Hogan. Smith built the Georgetown Courthouse.

[58] "For if we believe that Jesus died and rose again, even so them also which sleep in Jesus will God bring with him."

[59] Dr. John D Hogan (1810-2 Feb 1896 at Bastrop, Texas)

[60] William M. Hogan (1813-1895) 3rd Great Grandfather of the transcriber of this manuscript, Brian Hogan.

all, it would do you no good, you cannot buy it; but in one minute you can accept it as God's gift. 'Believe on the Lord Jesus and thou shalt be saved.' Accept Christ and it is yours." His streaming eyes turned up as toward Heaven, and he exclaimed, "Glory to God! I have got it! I have got it!" By this time my brothers had gotten away from the store, which way or where they went, I know not. Smith, Robinson and I were the only ones in the store. Robinson professed in a few weeks.

Strange as it may appear, all my brothers, except my oldest and youngest[61], would always run from my religious influence. Dr. John D. Hogan, two years older than I, and Dr. James M. Hogan, four years younger, never heard me preach, though they often had opportunity. (John D. died at his home in Texas five years since.[62] Dr. James still lives and visited me last June [1898] *in the home of my son in Vernon County. Neither of the two ever became Christians. I can only account for their avoidance of me that they would thereby escape the pain of conviction.)*

The funeral of Mary Edmondson McVey, wife of Absalom McVey (photo pg. 84) since 1825 and mother to their seven children was a significant event in the newly-minted burg of Georgetown. Her death on April 20th at 34 years of age occurred just as the Hogan and Hoss families were settling in. Since it was Georgetown's first death, the founder, George Smith was in attendance. Being in business partnership with Davie's brothers, he was already aware of the town's new preacher. Davie found the outcome of their meeting memorable enough to recount five decades later. Absalom McVey remarried the following year and died in Sedalia,

---

[61] Wilkinson Hogan (1807-1881) and Dr. Samuel Grant Hogan (1829-1852)

[62] 7 Aug 1890, Davie is writing his genealogical data 2 Dec 1894.

the next city founded by the newly saved and titled General Smith (in 1891).

One other occurrence of this year needs mention. On October 27, 1838, the governor of Missouri issued the Extermination Order, which compelled all Mormons to leave Missouri or be exterminated. We don't have any information on how Davie felt about this of how the conflict affected him, but we know that the neighbors in tiny Georgetown were mighty stirred up. It seems that both Mormons and "gentiles" had been responsible for the rising tensions that led to war on the frontier. The beliefs and practices of these "Latter Day Saints" were so odious to their neighbors in Missouri that, once conflict broke out, a wave of war enthusiasm swept the State. The call for volunteers was met with a huge response. In Pettis county, where Georgetown is located, a company of cavalry was raised, and George Smith enrolled as a private, refusing any higher post. The company had some hard marches around the state and missed out of any actual military action. The Mormons surrendered as soon as the Pettis county boys arrived in camp. After a watchful month they were disbanded. In the subsequent reorganization of the Missouri state militia, George R. Smith accepted the position of Brigadier General in command of the troops of Cooper, Benton, Pettis, and Saline counties. Though the feared Mormon resurgence never materialized, the militia organization was kept up for many years, meeting on regular "muster days," which not only served as occasions for drilling the troops, but also a social event among the farmers of the sparsely settled country. It was from this State militia commission that Mr. Smith, in accordance with Southern custom, was given the title of General by which ever after he was universally addressed, both in public and in private.

It's the beginning of 1839, and Davie's family is moving again. This time the distance is not daunting, just under 13 miles from Georgetown to Arator. I am sure Elizabeth felt keenly each mile put between her and mother and siblings back in Georgetown. Polly Hoss had surely been an immense help to the new mother. Now she would have to again find her place in General Hogan's huge family and plantation with its enslaved population complicating relationships. Rev. Hogan is unusually taciturn about the moves and motives behind leaving Georgetown.

The following January we moved back to Arator . . .
Whatever the reasons may have been, Arator proved little more than a way stop for the Hogans. After a four month stay, they were on the move again — over 70 miles northwest to Lexington. Only now, Elizabeth's vocation is providing the direction.

William Houx relates the following: In the forepart of the winter of 1838, George Houx and his brother Wm. Houx, originated the idea of establishing a high school. William Houx hewed cottonwood logs on an island in the river above Lexington, and floated them down to the town, and the same year erected a log house, 18ft by 20ft. He got the boards to cover the house from a large white oak tree that stood near where the Baptist church now stands, corner of North and Poplar Streets[63]. This was the beginning of high schools in Lafayette county. A number of ladies were principally educated here, who afterward became wives of prominent men of the state. The Messrs. Houx secured the services of Mrs. David Hogan, of Pettis county, to come and take charge of the school. The school continued in a flourishing condition for several years. The Messrs. Houx after a number of years, gave their interest to Rev. Robert Morrow. Mr. George Houx was leader in this enterprise and furnished all the means.[64]

. . . on the first day of May 1839, I moved again and located in Lexington. My wife being called to take charge of the Female Academy just having been erected in the new part of the town.

---

[63] Street names have changed: now Main and 12th Streets.

[64] From "History of Lafayette County"; Missouri Historical Company, St. Louis, 1881; "Cottonwood Academy"

Her credentials for qualification had been fully examined, and she was announced the most scholarly lady of the country, in that day. Here Mrs. Hogan won her great reputation as a scholar and educator. Whilst we were

Thomas Hart Benton

boarding with Rev. Finis Ewing in 1839, the Hon. Senator Thomas Hart Benton made Missouri a visit. He called two days at Lexington and was entertained by Mr. Ewing, to whom he remarked, "Mrs. Hogan is a walking library of history." He much enjoyed talking with her. Here was mine, and my wife's first personal acquaintance with him.

Senator Thomas Hart Benton visited Lexington in October 1839. He mentions it in a letter to Andrew Jackson dated October 14. Benton was a Jacksonian Democrat and huge backer of former President Jackson and President Martin Van Buren. Both Benton and Van Buren were moving toward an anti-slavery position. The conversations around the table were full of new ideas for Davie Hogan.

Uncle Davie is "without orders" from the Presbytery. However, he found himself in the denominational center as his small family moved into the spacious Lexington home of founder Rev. Finis Ewing and his wife, 'Aunt Peggy', who'd invited the Hogan family to live with them.

When I moved to Lexington, Spring Session of the Presbytery had passed. I was without orders. I however, sought work, and preached every Sabbath, sometimes as far as forty miles from Lexington. Rev. Finis Ewing had charge of the church at Lexington. Shortly after I arrived, Uncle Finis (as he was familiarly called) came to me on Thursday, and in his blunt way, said, "Boy, I want you to preach for me next Sunday at 11:00." I promised him to do so. I at once commenced preparation, for I felt my incompetency to occupy his pulpit. When the hour came for service, I took seat in the pulpit; he and Aunt Peggy, his wife, sitting nearby. I awaited his motion and preceded with hymn and prayer. I never felt more the need of the Holy Spirit's help, than at that time, and I may say, Its blessed anointing on that occasion. Aunt Peggy got happy and in the closing song many shook hands rejoicing.[65]

Finis Ewing

After the benediction Uncle Finis said to me, "Boy, get the madam, (my wife), you will take dinner with me today." After dinner he and I took seats in the back porch. After a little conversation he put his fingers into his vest pocket and drew out a five-dollar gold piece, handing it to me: "Take this, boy, I think your sermon was worth that much." (Let me say, this was large pay in those days.)

Two weeks after, he called me to fill his pulpit again. I consented; this time I made a failure. After services, as

---

[65] *'got happy'* and *'shook hands rejoicing'* both refer to manifestations of the power of the Holy Spirit, common features of revival. See footnote on "experiential religion" in 'Recapitulations' pg. 172.

before, he had myself and wife to dine with him. After dinner we took seats in the same back porch; in a few minutes his fingers were feeling in his vest pocket and he handed me a dime and said, "I think your sermon today was worth about that." I have related this to show the way of telling his boy, as he called me, the value of his preaching. I thought I had all I could bear before he handed me the dime, but the weight was doubled, as I received it.

Living with the founder of Rev. Davie's precious Cumberland Presbyterian Church must have been simultaneously thrilling and at times terrifying for the young minister. "Father Finis" was not one to withhold praise or criticism and seems to have dispensed both rather freely. It was also an opportunity for David's views on issues of his day to grow, mature, and change as he conversed with and listened to the great man hold forth on a variety of subjects with his many visitors. Coming from a family that ran large plantations with enslaved labor in Kentucky and Missouri, David had grown up in an atmosphere where human bondage was an unpleasant fact. Abolitionist views were simply not given oxygen in the home of General Hogan. Now Davie had a surrogate father perfectly suited to help him see the issue from a different viewpoint — and apply his faith to his conclusions.

Though himself a slaveholder, even before his move to Lexington, Finis Ewing views on slavery had altered to the point that he began agitating against slavery.

At some period in Mr. Ewing's life, but the precise period is not known, his mind became exercised about slavery. In 1835 he published a sermon in the Cumberland Presbyterian Pulpit, in which he took strong ground against at least some of the evils of slavery. The public mind was not so easily inflamed on the subject at that time as it has been since, and he expressed himself, to what has since been denominated a slave-holding Church, with great freedom. In the progress of the sermon, he gives the following as his own experience and purposes in relation to his slaves: "Lest some of my readers," says he, "should say, 'Physician, heal thyself,' I think it proper to state in this place, that after a long, painful, and prayerful investigation of the subject, I have determined. not to hold, nor to give, nor to sell, nor to buy any slave for life, mainly from the influence of that passage of God's word which says, 'Masters, give unto your servants that which is just and equal.' "

The result of his experience and resolution was, at his death all his servants were emancipated.

Ewing also was a pioneer leader of the temperance movement in Missouri. Once in Lexington he not only served as pastor but also worked for the Federal Government as registrar of the United States Land Office. This example of supporting himself while continuing in the ministry confirmed what Davie Hogan had been pursuing in his own ministry. Part-time ministry supported by honest labor provided an example for others and made it easier to urge disciples to "follow my example." He watched closely as due to Ewing's efforts, the Cumberland Church was greatly strengthened.

Missouri Minister (1838-1839)

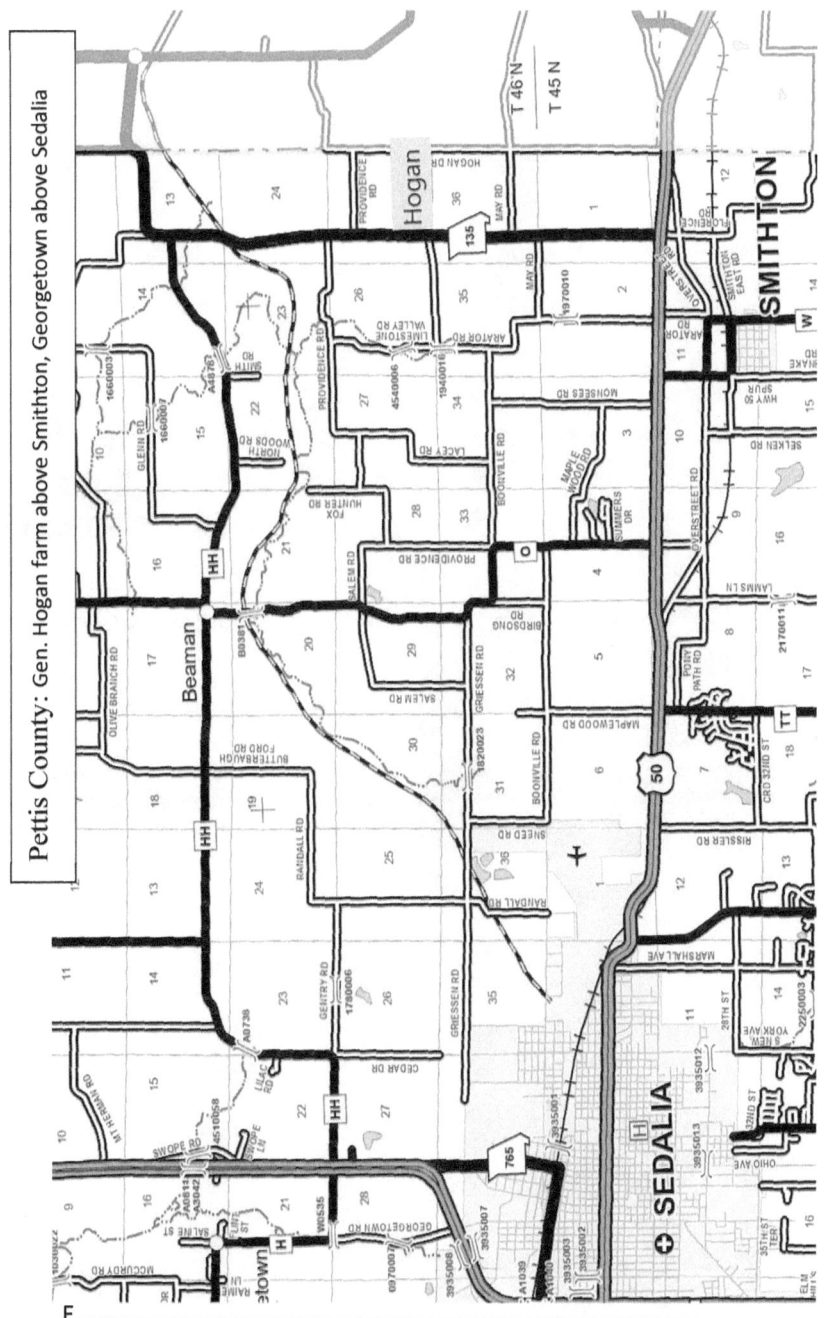

Pettis County: Gen. Hogan farm above Smithton, Georgetown above Sedalia

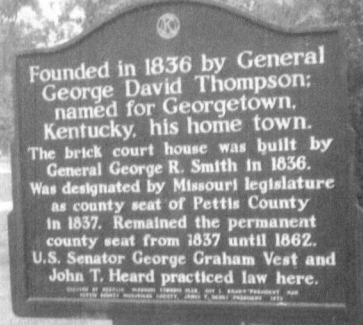

Clockwise from top left:
Gen. George Rappeen Smith, Davie's Georgetown convert, Sedalia founder.

Absalom McVey (1802-1891) whose wife's funeral was officiated by Davie.

Historic Marker: Mentions the 1836 building of the Georgetown Courthouse by Gen. Smith.

FINANCIAL RUIN (1840-1848)

The 1840 United States Census merely names heads of household. All others are simply numbers in columns sorted by gender and age. Nevertheless, we can track Rev. Davie Hogan and his relations through the data collected that year.

David Hogan was twenty-eight and had been married to Elizabeth Hoss for less than three years. Daniel McDowell, the census enumerator in Lexington found the young family living with Finis Ewing, founder of the CPC denomination. His name is recorded as 'Davin Hogan' and, in addition to his wife, the household includes five girls between 5 and 19 years of age (probably boarding students from Elizabeth Hogan's nearby Cottonwood Academy) along with Rev. and Mrs. Ewing. Their infant son Henry Hoss Hogan is also counted, but not David, Jr. who was born a few days after the census enumerator's visit.

Elsewhere in Missouri, the census netted Davie's parents, the General and Betsy Dorton Hogan, still living in Arator, along with their daughter Sarah, and sons Moses, Robert and Samuel. They also have a grandson under the age of five running around. The General owned 15 people in 1840.[66]

Across the county, in Georgetown, their children; William, George, and Elizabeth were living with Dr. John Hogan and his wife Hortensia and their two children[67]. John and George are preparing to move to new land opening in Texas. Brother Wilkinson's family with three boys and two girls are settled in Johnson County, Although the 1840 census missed him, brother Dr. James Hogan is

---

[66] Males: 3 under 10 years; 2 from 10-23; 2 from 24-35 and females: 3 under 10; 4 from 10-23; 1 from 36 to 54.

[67] and two enslaved persons.

an Allopathic Physician practicing as Pettis County's first Doctor.[68] Davie's mother-in-law, 'Polly' Blackburn Hoss also appears in the Pettis County census.

Meanwhile Polly's oldest child, Elizabeth Blackburn Hoss Hogan plunged directly into the work for which she carried both calling and passion — educating women. She was Director of a Female Academy that accepted boarding students, several of whom she arranged to house in Rev. Ewing's fine home. Amazingly, between her duties as wife to a minister, mother of a toddler, hostess for and caretaker to an old man, dorm mother for five young female students, administrator, and teacher at the Female Academy (the first west of the Mississippi), she managed to carry to term another pregnancy! In the first week of June of 1840, she gave birth to a second son — David Hogan III. There is no evidence that she slowed down at all. Indeed, in just nineteen months, Elizabeth would give birth again.

Living with his hero and mentor, Uncle Finis Ewing, was a sweet period in Davie's life. The comfort of a fine large home in a city and the ministerial opportunities afforded by being helper to the Cumberland Presbyterian founder were rewards for years of poverty and privation while searing or freezing on horseback. However, nothing lasts forever. In his 68th year of life, Father Finis Ewing died peacefully in his bed in their shared Lexington home. Though it was the Fourth of July there were no celebrations for the grieving Hogan family, though the noise of fireworks reverberated through the windows. At the end Uncle Davie was at the old preacher's side and was ever after famed among his church folk for: "*With his own hands he closed Finis Ewing's eyes when that hero of the Cross fell asleep in Jesus.*"[69]

Finis' widow moved to live with her offspring and Davie and Elizabeth were left with the task of tying up Ewing's affairs. They

---

[68] Dr. James Hogan, from Calhoun County came (to Pettis) prior to 1840. *citation in Directory of Deceased American Physicians, 1804-1929*

[69] *History of the Cumberland Presbyterian Church,* by Benjamin Wilburn McDonnold

seem to have inherited the house in Lexington and a fruit tree nursery in which Finis and Davie had partnered.

Sometime during 1841 the family made a visit back to Father Hogan's Arator farm and joined the tribe in celebrating brother George's marriage to Elizabeth Robb Rankin.

> *1842 and 1843 was the great bankruptcy of the United States: in 1840, the school had become so large, I determined to build an ample boarding-house (on credit) and in one year the oppressive times were such the school almost failed. In 1843 the builder pressed me, and the property was sold at greatly less than it cost. This left me out of a home and two thousand dollars in debt. I felt I was disgraced.*

Panics in 1837 and 1838 had rocked America's economy. In their wake Congress enacted a second bankruptcy law to enable both voluntary and involuntary bankruptcy. However, in 1843 the Bankruptcy Act of 1841 was repealed, amid complaints about expenses and corruption. Amid failing finances caused by these events far beyond their control, the Hogans brought a third child into the increasingly uncertain world. Placing their faith in Jesus, as they had always done and never once regretted, Davie and Elizabeth welcomed little Cyrus O. Hogan into their home, inherited from Uncle Finis, in Lexington. Facing the loss of everything they'd worked for, the pressure to find a more secure income must have been intense. The Enemy is a master of temptation, and he was ready to test David Hogan's principals and loyalties while he was financially vulnerable.

> *In my financial failure at Lexington, the idea was somehow put out that I was going to join the Methodist Episcopal Church. At that time there was no North and South. James Lapsly, D.D.[70] came to see me. He said the report had become public that I was going to join the*

---

[70] James Lapsley McKee, D.D., S.S., Presbyterian Minister of Kansas City.

Methodist Church on account of getting no support as a minister and asked if it was so. I answered, "No." He replied, "Well, I came here today specially to see you; if you have any notion of leaving your church on account of not getting a support, and will join the Old Presbyterians, I will find you a place in one week with a salary of not less than eight hundred or more than one thousand dollars. But understand, I am not wishing to proselyte." I replied, that doctrinally, my conscience would not allow me to join any other church while the Cumberland Presbyterian Church existed.

While the Academic School was running, I had been preaching in various congregations; among them were Rose Hill and Rock Spring, in Johnson County, and in that vicinity was a prospect for a good country school: so, on Christmas Day, 1843, I moved my family to Rock Spring, thirty-five miles from Lexington.

In spring my wife took charge of the Public School, and I, the pastorate of the congregation, which positions we occupied from 1843 to 1850.

Our greatest labor and success in those days were in camp-meetings, and the entire pay, or nearly so, was in the hat collections at these camp-meetings, which divided by the number of preachers in attendance, would vary from two to four dollars. This amount, you see, would not clothe the preacher. Hence, all preachers of the Cumberland Presbyterian Church had to have some secular business to support himself and family.

An article[71] by Floyd Shoemaker, Missouri historian and publisher, details the history of the Rock Spring Cumberland

---

[71] June 27th, 1942 issue of *Holden Progress*

Presbyterian church: *Rock Springs Church: In the year 1838 Robert H. White came to Johnson County and settled on a farm about two miles northeast of what is now Rock Spring.*
There was no church near. Mr. White started a Sunday school at his place and carried on the school for several years. Finally, he secured the services of circuit riders and had preaching services at his place. The Rev. W.D. Ware, F.E. Witherspoon and B.F. Thomas were among the ones who gave their services. Later John D.Morrow and the Rev. Jack Whitsett priest and gave their services. Camp meetings were held on the Grove on Mr. White's place in which R.D. Morrow, Edward Horne and Finis Ewing assisted. By this time more people had moved in and it became more thickly settled. This band of people organized into a church by the Rev R.D. Morrow in May 1837, as the New Hope congregation . . .
The congregation now held camp meetings at what is now Rock Spring. At this time a beautiful Springs poured its clear waters out from under a ledge of rock. But the overflows have washed in sediment filling up the spring until now no trace of it is found. On this Camp some had cabins built and some had tents . . .
Spring session of the Lexington Presbytery in 1843 the name was changed from New Hope to that of Rock Spring. In August 1848 James Gibbons was appointed trustee for the congregation and received the deed of trust, . . . containing 40 acres to hold for the said congregation. [Uncle Davie took up the preaching full time in Dec. 1843] *The first church to be built was of logs.*

During these busy years, even though running a school, Elizabeth made time for having another child. On April 2nd, 1845, she and Davie welcomed first daughter Mary Elizabeth Hogan into their growing family and home in Rock Spring (today's Holden, MO). This move made them near-neighbors to Davie's oldest sibling Wilkinson and his large family. Elizabeth's mom was a bit further away. Polly Hoss, still living in Georgetown with the CP Church meeting in her home[72]. Though the flock received a visit from an

---

[72] *The History of Pettis County Missouri, 1882 History*, DVD (Higginsville, MO: Hearthstone Legacy Publishers, 2006), pg.306.

ordained minister only once a month, they experienced the joy of house church life every week.

Uncle Davie had been stirred by other news from Georgetown, his brother Dr. John D. Hogan, who was living there, was being considered for a government post in the Powder River country of Montana where the Sioux Nation was centered. Davie couldn't help but be thrilled to think his older brother, already a physician, could be working with Indians. All of Davie's deferred dreams came rushing back with a pang when he read the letter from the editor of the Old School Democrat and a leading supporter of President Tyler in Missouri: (an excerpt) "*You can form no idea of the hurry and confusion I am in, trying to arrange my affairs to go East. I have fifty letters lying by me unanswered. I will see Dr. R. and converse with him on the subject of J. D. Hogan and Colonel Thomson as agents for the Sioux and Osage Indians.*" V. Ellis, St. Louis, MO, June 3, 1843.

For some reason this post did not materialize or perhaps Dr. John knew something about Montana winters and Sioux hostility, at any rate he'd "gone to Texas" before the year was out, settling in the Republic of Texas; first in Waco and later moving on to Bastrop.

> *In the winter of 1844 and spring following, I taught a six months school near Chilhowee, Johnson County, Missouri. The school was large, many young men and ladies were pupils. One prime object of the school was my teaching the young man of Lexington Presbytery who were preparing for the ministry, free of charge. They were the following: Finis King, W. D. Wear, Robert Wear and Samuel Thompson. This was a pleasant school, and the pupils*[73] *made fine progress.*

---

[73] STUDENTS: Finis Ewing King, 1819-1859, founding minister of Shiloh CPC in Ovilla, Ellis, TX until his death. Son of Rev. Samuel King, CPC Minister. Wear, William Duke 1821-1905 was the 1st Pastor of Cumberland Presbyterian Church, Baldwyn, MS. This church was first organized at old Carrollville (chartered 1834) in an early day, and moved to Baldwyn in 1860, when a frame house, 35x60 was built. At that time all Christian

Father Samuel King[74] and Rev. Robert D. King[75] lived in the vicinity, and well knew of my penury and want in my home at Rock Spring, fourteen miles distant. I had broken ten acres of sod on my pre-emption[76] home in the summer of 1844. I said to Father King one day, if I had my ten acres of broke land fenced, I could live. I had said the same to Robert D., his son, who was a patron of my school. The two soon had the arrangement made with the patrons of my school to go over to my home, with wagons, teams, tools and provisions, and camp on the place till they fenced the field. This was the greatest help for me that could have been devised. The tuition of my school was payable in meal and meat, which would enable the family to live till I could raise a crop. When they started for the work, Rev. R. D. King put his breaking plow in his wagon, and while his companions built a fence, he broke the ten acres of sod ground, and made it ready for planting.

In this same pre-empted home, my three youngest children were born; namely, Mary E., Julia P. and Edwin G. Hogan.

I'd owned a nursery at Lexington in which Rev. Finis Ewing and I were partners. I at once moved it, and planted

---

denominations of the community worshipped in it. [Biographical and Historical Memoirs of Mississippi, Vol. 2 Cities, Towns and Villages, Chapter 8, Pages 208 - 209]

Wear, Robert B. (?-ca 1875) was CPC Minister in Fort Worth Texas in 1902 and his brother, Rev. William D. Wear was also resident.

Samuel Thompson: possibly Thompson, J. S. (?-1887) later CP Minister.

[74] Rev. Samuel King 1775 - 1842 One of the three founders of the Cumberland Presbyterian Church.

[75] Robert Donnell King, 1801 - 1882, Cumberland Presbyterian Minister, the son of Rev. Samuel King, one of the church's founders.

[76] *Preemption* 1a: the right of purchasing before others especially one given by the government to the actual settler upon a tract of public land.

an orchard, which in a few years gave my family the luxury of good fruit. In the summer of 1845 Father King was complaining and not stout; he requested me to preach once per month at Shiloh, which I did, for one year; they treated me as they had ever treated him - they gave no temporal support. When Uncle Samuel died [1842], Aunt Anna (his wife) made me a present of his Polyglot Testament[77], having in it many manuscript notes for sermons, of his own making.[78] This was intended for a keepsake, and it is in my library today. I believe I never knew a husband and wife who were better suited in temperament, or more Godly, than Father and Mother King. He baptized my two first born children and impressed me for life."

Davie's brother, Col. William M. Hogan made the long journey east from his home in Texas. He spent time in the nation's Capital City. During his sojourn in the District of Columbia one of his main goals was to collect references from as many of Washington's leading men as he possibly could. William managed to obtain letters of reference from Henry Clay, future President James Buchanan, Sam Houston, and others. He didn't neglect the Washington social life though, since he was wooing a young woman from one of D.C.'s founding families, the Holmeads. Cornelia Virginia Holmead's great grandfather Anthony Holmead I had settled a large plantation in what would become the capital of the United States. Her maternal grandfather was German immigrant and folk portrait artist Samuel Endredi Stettinius whose family moved in 1798 to where the new

---

[77] Polyglot Bibles, in which the Hebrew and Greek originals are exhibited along with historical translations.

[78] *"I think it proper here to give a little explanation of the terms uncle and aunt, frequently used in connection with the names of the persons necessarily used in making this history. Cumberland Presbyterians, in this manner of address, aim doubtless, to show the reverence they feel toward the aged, and especially the fathers and mothers who lived and favored the organization of the Cumberland Presbyterian Church, in the year 1810. The address has become habitual."* – Rev. David Hogan

city of Washington, D.C. was under construction. They bought property and established a store at Seventh and Pennsylvania Avenue selling books, groceries, and general merchandise. Samuel painted portraits that were much in demand.

William was present at the inauguration of James K. Polk as the eleventh president of the United States in March of 1845. If nothing else, it provided access to all the men whose references he was collecting.

Col. William M. Hogan and Cornelia Virginia Holmead were licensed to marry on Tuesday, September 9, 1845 in Washington City[79] When Texas became the 28th state on 29 December 1845, William had to go back to where the action was. He moved his bride and their new baby to Navarro County, Texas in September 1846.[80]

The War with Mexico that roiled the United States and its neighbor from 1846-1848, seemed to have scant impact on the young Hogan family (though it would be much closer to two of his brothers' families). Uncle Davie was busy riding a circuit of ten miles around Johnson County and his main congregation at Bear Creek[81] in

---

[79] 9/9/1845 is the date of the marriage license itself. Sometimes these records show the date the license was issued and sometimes they show the marriage date specified by the applicants. Extracted from District of Columbia Marriage Licenses Register 1, 1811-1858, Dallas Public Library, Dallas, Texas.

[80] William and Cornelia's movements during their first year of marriage are unclear. It stands to reason that they stopped for some time in Missouri to allow Cornelia to meet the family before moving with brother George to Chatfield, Texas.

[81] "The Bear Creek Cumberland Presbyterians organized here at an early day, and worshipped at the Union church, and participated in the Union Sunday-school. . . .. It is said that Rev. David Hogan, one of the pioneer ministers, preached one year for $2.50, and rode ten miles to his appointments."

The History of Johnson County, Missouri, Johnson County Ministers pg. 559.

Warrensburg, He was tending flocks at Shiloh near Leeton, at home in Rock Spring, and conducting camp meetings in Chilhowee that would later organize as Pisgah CP Church[82], and possibly other locations as well. The entire year's labors netted the minister a grand sum of $2.50.

Warrensburg, despite being the seat of Johnson County, was more of a village in 1846. At the census in four years' time, it had only managed to grow to 241 residents. However, for Rev. David it was a practical pastorate for several reasons. Davie's grammar school in Blackwater was within the circuit and continued, along with his crops, to be the main source of income for the underpaid preacher. Several of their moves would be constrained by the need to continue this secular employment to put food on the table. The fact that family was — in the Wilkinson Hogan brood — nearby was certainly a plus.

In September, as Davie enjoyed community and family connections in Johnson County, three of his brothers were far from Missouri in the newest state of Texas. The Republic of Texas became the 28th state in February, triggering the war with Mexico. Having lived in the Republic of Texas town of Nacogdoches since 1844, and then going to Washington D.C. and getting himself a bride, Col. William M. Hogan moved to Chatfield in September, joined by his brother Col. George M. Hogan, Uncle Davie's brothers, were among Navarro County's earliest settlers.[83] Along on this 130 mile move through contested territory were two newborn baby girls with rhyming names: William and Cornelia's, Medora, and George and Ellen's, Isadora. Their toddler son, George, Jr. rounded out the party in their move by covered wagon. And their older brother, Dr. John Hogan had been in Texas for almost three years already.

---

[82] The first church built in Chilhowee township was by the Cumberland Presbyterian denomination in 1858 and known as Pisgah church. Camp meetings were held in this township as early as 1841.

[83] Col. William Hogan immigrated in September 1846 to Chatfield, Texas. "*Colonel George M. Hogan with his brother William came to Chatfield in 1846*"

There were many prayers said back in Missouri for these intrepid and possibly foolhardy relations.

Uncle Davie neglects to mention whether he was tapped to officiate at two weddings in 1847, but he attended each — they were his only two sisters after all! In late September he made his way back to his parents' home for the wedding of Elizabeth Grant Clay Hogan to Colonel Hiero Tennant Wilson. Davie's new brother-in-law was a fascinating character. This fellow Kentuckian was an Indian Trader for nine years at Fort Gibson on the Cherokee nation and was fluent in Osage, Cherokee, and Creek, before taking up the Post Sutler[84] role at Fort Scott in 1843. Davie was fascinated and his talks with Hiero only stirred the still glowing embers of his call to missionary work among the Cherokee. He wisely kept these conversations for when the menfolk would retire after dinner and Elizabeth was not around to throw him concerned looks. She knew how much Davie longed to cast off his pastoral role and go to these people to whom God had bound his heart.

When, at the reception following the ceremony, older sister Sarah Ann announced that Major Arthur Galbraith Young had proposed, the gathered Hogans discussed a return to the same spot before the year's end. The Hogan men, so replete with titles, military and honorary, gave Major Art some good-natured ribbing about joining a family that already boasted a General and, with new brother-in-law Hiero, three Colonels. Art countered that he'd be taking his orders from the same authority the Hogan boys had been answering to their entire lives, their older sister Sarah Ann. Davie laughed with everyone else and reflected inwardly that Sarah led him into the most wonderful experience of his life: surrender to his Savior Jesus Christ.

Five days after the signing of the Treaty of Guadalupe Hidalgo (2 February 1848) ended the Mexican War, the new peace was shattered in one household by the wails of another baby.

---

[84] The sutler was a civilian who was authorized to operate a store on or near a military camp, post, or fort. He could sell goods and items that were not considered necessary or supplied by the army. The sutler held a high social standing at the post and was on a par with the officers.

Davie and Elizabeth had a second daughter, Julia P. Hogan[85] at their home in Rock Spring. Elizabeth's sister-in-law was close by and provided her help with the birth and nieces and nephews to babysit. If Uncle Davie was traveling when the time came, we can be sure he hurried to Elizabeth's side as soon as word reached him. Julia would hold a special place in her daddy's heart for the rest of his life.

While their wives fussed over the new infant, Wilkinson and Davie proudly perused letters from brothers William and George pioneering in Navarro County, Texas, newly freed from the threat of reverting to Mexican authority. Each was making a name for himself and drawing fame to the Hogan name in that new state.

That year alone, they had built a bridge. The History of Navarro County[86] relates "Geo. and William Hogan also lived in Taos and when a road was opened from Chatfield to the south side of Chambers Creek, they built a bridge crossing the stream. The bridge at this point is still known as Hogan's Bridge." Not resting on these laurels, Col. William M. Hogan was elected as Navarro County Juror and served as road builder on the Taos-Corsicana Road.[87] On the 20th of April 1848 Col. George M. Hogan took up the well-worn family mantle of "Postmaster"[88] becoming First Postmaster of Muskete.[89]

In June both Johnson County Hogan households would rejoin to travel back to the original family homestead in Arator to attend the

---

[85] Rev. David Hogan, "Autobiography of David Hogan 1811-1899," Historical Foundation, Cumberland Presbyterian Church, Cordova, TN.

[86] *The History of Navarro County;* pgs. 193-194

[87] Samuels, Nancy T. (Fort Worth Genealogical Society).

[88] In this appointment George was joining his Grandfather Dorton, father David, brothers William and Davie, and Uncle Elijah Hogan, postmaster of Starkville, MS.

[89] (later Chatfield) in Navarro County, Texas (Navarro Co. Historical Society).

nuptials of younger brother Moses Dorton Hogan and Mary M. Wright on Monday the 12 day of June 1848.

Slowly Elizabeth and Davie, with help from their brethren, recovered from the setbacks they'd endured in their young nation's financial meltdown.

GOLD RUSH (1849-1857)

On January 24, 1848, James W. Marshall found gold at Sutter's Mill in Coloma, California. The news of gold brought approximately 300,000 people to California from the rest of the United States and abroad. Missourians were not immune to this Gold Fever.
The California Gold Rush (1848–1855) would be a life-changing event for both Davie and others in the Hogan and Hoss families.

> *. . except, I was in California two years, from 1850 to 1853, gold digging, of which I would like to give a full history. I was successful; at least, I was able to pay all my debts, and fix my home comfortably, and enter three hundred and twenty acres of land. Whilst I was in California, my wife by her teaching and saving economy, supported herself and two younger of the five children, and entered or paid for the ¼ section of land we occupied by preemption, ($200) and had fifty dollars loaned.*

Despite his stated desire "to give a full history", Davie never got around to putting his Gold Rush adventures on paper. What we know is Rev. David Hogan not only worked as a miner in and around the California gold camps of Mariposa County; he continued to preach the Gospel and act as pastor to his fellow miners.[90]

His overland route to California from his home in Missouri was known as the California Trail, an emigrant trail of about 3,000 miles

---

[90] Remembering this time, fellow minister N. J. Crawford, who'd heard the stories from Uncle Davie himself, wrote: "*He held this charge* (the pastorate of Rock Spring CPC) *until 1858, except two years while in California. While in California he was active and efficient among the miners, to whom he preached on every opportunity.*" --N. J. Crawford, Maysville, Ark. [Source: *The Cumberland Presbyterian*, June 16, 1904, page 764]

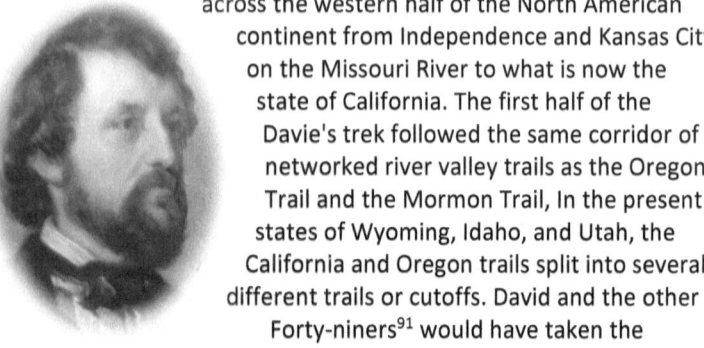

John C. Frémont (Nat. Portrait Gallery)

across the western half of the North American continent from Independence and Kansas City on the Missouri River to what is now the state of California. The first half of the Davie's trek followed the same corridor of networked river valley trails as the Oregon Trail and the Mormon Trail, In the present states of Wyoming, Idaho, and Utah, the California and Oregon trails split into several different trails or cutoffs. David and the other Forty-niners[91] would have taken the quickest route to the boom towns of the western slopes of the Sierra Nevada range. With early summer the best time for overland travel, Davie probably arrived just before California Statehood was declared on September 9th, 1850. The enumerator for the 1850 United States Census (a role David's brother William was performing rather haphazardly in Navarro County Texas) found Uncle Davie on November 17th, in the Mariposa County boomtown of Agua Fria[92], where John C Frémont had discovered gold in 1849. The Enumerator identified Davie as a 39-year-old Kentucky-born male. His occupation was left a blank, but the houses on the page were

---

[91] the high point of immigration was in 1849, so even those coming in 1850, like Davie, were Forty-niners.

[92] Agua Fria, today a true ghost town, was principally a placer mining camp divided into Lower Agua Fria and Upper Agua Fria. The name was derived from two springs of chilly water about a ¼ mile below Lower Agua Fria (the principal town). In 1850 it was a booming trade center and destination for many new arrivals in California. It was there, too, that James Burney, first county sheriff had established a log cabin which served as a jail of sorts. Burney also recruited men in Agua Fria for pursuit of the natives during the Mariposa Indian War, in 1850. It was Mariposa County's first Seat of Justice from February 18, 1850 to November 10, 1851. A post office was established October 7, 1851. In 1853 a 6-stamp quartz hill was established in Upper Agua Fria. The camp boasted a hotel, express office, assayers, billiard room, bowling alley, monte, and faro banks, about a dozen stores (one of which operated by Archie Hoss, Davie's brother-in-law), numerous tents and log cabins, and several houses of ill repute, by the Fall of 1850.

Gold Rush (1849-1857)

largely occupied by merchants, traders, lawyers, packers, and a baker. Most listed after Davie's house was counted were miners by profession. At the edge of this (slightly more genteel?) neighborhood, the Rev. Hogan is rooming with his wife's 25-year-old brother, Edwin Hoss, a packer, and another fellow, Edward Bell, a jeweler. In a boarding house next door, another brother-in-law, young Archibald Hoss,[93] twenty-three, is the sole merchant in a house full of miners.

On the rare occasions that mail arrived at the gold camp for Davie, he savored every detail of the doings of his family and relations back home. Elizabeth and their children were home next to Rock Spring Church, near Holden, in Johnson County, Missouri[94] The congregation made sure that Uncle Davie's family did not go without and Elizabeth continued do her best to provide education for girls and women in the area. David's 13-year-old eldest, Henry Hoss Hogan, is living over in neighboring Pettis County with his maternal grandmother, Polly Blackburn Hoss. Henry's Uncle, Samuel B Hoss, 32, is listed[95] as head of the family and is farming land valued at $1200. Henry is almost certainly there to work on the farm as there would be little productive work for him at home. Perhaps when David took two of the Hoss farmhands off to California, Henry was offered as replacement labor. Nearby were David's parents, Gen. David and Betsy, still living on Hogan Road in what once was Arator, and his paternal Uncle John and Aunt Ann Hogan are in Otterville, a town laid out by the General's friend, W.G. Wear, who was also first Postmaster of Arator. Otterville was in Cooper County, just east of Hogan Road (which served as Pettis/Cooper County line). Davie's youngest brother Sam had opened a medical practice in Bates County, MO earlier this year. The 21-year-old Doc Hogan was the pride of the family.

---

[93] Archibald, the youngest Hoss boy, spent the rest of his days in the gold camps and died sometime after the 1880 Census logged him in Fresno, CA.

[94] Somehow, they weren't counted in the 1850 Johnson County Census.

[95] 1850 Pettis County Census. Interestingly, census rules were broken, and Edwin and Archibald are listed in Missouri as "California miners" and so were counted in both states this year.

Several siblings had left Missouri and were pioneering new land opening in Texas. His brother Col. William Hogan was farming and, in 1850 was the U.S. Census Enumerator for Navarro County. He counted his own family, comprised of wife Cornelia Virginia Holmead Hogan and children: Medora, James and Eugene[96] on Thursday 19 September 1850 in Navarro, Texas. As William rode an undiscernible rambling route cataloguing his neighbors in Navarro County (roping in portions of two neighboring counties), he managed to include brother George Hogan, wife Elizabeth and kids:

Agua Fria, heyday 1850-1852. Where Davie lived, preached, and mined (1874

George Jr., Isa, Cyrus, and Fleeta. He did not make it over to Bastrop, Texas, where their brother Dr. John Hogan was practicing medicine. Even though historians and genealogists loathe the mess that William made of the 1850 Navarro County Census, he managed to impress (or fool) some powerful people and secured for himself an appointment to a government job in Washington D.C. William and Cornelia moved back to her home city in 1851. Cornelia Holmead Hogan's family was a founding-family and well-established fixture of capital society and probably another mark in his favor.

Out in California, young Edwin Hoss (25) was less than a year away from an unfortunate and untimely end. He had become a

---

[96] Eugene Hogan (1849-1908) is the author's great-great grandfather. Eugene begat Orville Eugene I, who begat Orville Eugene II, who begat Orville Eugene III "Gene", who begat Brian Hogan in 1962.

respected trader; packing goods between Agua Fria and Stockton, CA along the Merced River. One night in 1851, while staying at the ranch of a Dr. Lewis on the Merced, Edwin lost his life. The newspaper reported: "*Died February 22nd, Mr. Edwin Hoss twenty-six years of age. His death was caused by the accidental discharge of a pistol. He was asleep in an upper room and the pistol was discharged in a room beneath the ball passing through the floor and several blankets then through the body causing instant death.*" Another report names the shooter and ties the event to lawless and reckless violence common during the Mariposa Indian War. News of Edwin's death reached his brother and brother-in-law up in Agua Fria and they had the sad task of sending news to his mother and family back in Missouri. David was in anguish about how Elizabeth would take her younger brother's death. She'd charged Davie (the senior member of the trio by 15 years) when they set off, "Take care of Ed and Archie." After burying Edwin, Uncle Davie continued to preach the Gospel to the miners as well as seeking his own fortune. His burdensome debts were never far from his mind.

News of loss and grief traveled both directions. Sad news came to David Hogan in the post around Christmas 1852. Elizabeth wrote him that his youngest surviving sibling, Dr. Samuel Grant Hogan, had died suddenly on 10 November 1852 at the tender age of 23. Davie's tears soaked the letter as he read his wife's description of his family gathered around a plot his parents bought for themselves at Providence Baptist Church in Smithton, the nearest town to the family home.

Before his time in California was up, Davie had a third young relative — a first cousin — Samuel Lane Hogan, 28, living and mining with him[97].

---

[97] In 1852, Samuel Lane Hogan arrived and joined David in Mariposa. Within a decade, Sam had married a Native-American woman and they'd produced a dozen half-native Hogan children. Sam spent the rest of his life in Mariposa County, California.

In January 1853, having beat the odds and accumulating fortune enough to fully satisfy his debtors in Lexington and buy a home and acreage for his growing family, Davie bade farewell to Archie Hoss and California and made the long overland journey home to Holden, Missouri. It was a sweet long-awaited reunion for husband and wife. Nine months after Davie's return, on September 21 Elizabeth gave birth in their home to another baby boy. They named him after his uncle who had been shot in his sleep two years before while working in the gold camps with Dad. Edwin Grant Hogan was to be Elizabeth and Davie's final child.

> *The reader may know I was greatly relieved - out of debt and comfortable at home. I again took charge of Rock Spring congregation, and served as pastor until March 1858, when I sold my entire land possessions . . .*
>
> *Several years after the events above named (goldfields interlude). Rev. John B. Morrow moved and settled near Chilhowee, and he insisted on my teaching a winter school for the benefit of his, and neighbor families. I yielded. In this school were forty pupils. The two most advanced pupils (W. Benton Farr and Columbus Morrow) assisted me much in conducting the school. Uncle John B. Morrow said to me afterward, that that school had rendered the best educational service that vicinity had ever had.*

Rev. David Hogan was justly proud of the replacement of the log chapel at Rock Spring with a stone church constructed while he oversaw that congregation. However, forces were looming that would decimate buildings in Missouri — be they wood or brick. Storm clouds were gathering that would overtake the Hogan family, and indeed Missouri, with hurricane force. In 1854, Stephen Douglas' Kansas-Nebraska Act repealed the earlier Missouri Compromise. His idea was that new states could choose for themselves whether to be slave or free. This pleased the South creating a state that would have been free soil under the earlier law but now was able to choose to permit slavery. Though it created two neighboring states to the east and northeast of

Missouri, the Kansas-Nebraska Act effectively knocked the lid off the bitter slavery dispute and led to regional civil war followed soon by the division of the Union. Davie may have shared concerned talk with his congregation, neighbors, and friends about the doings in Washington. He would have gotten some inside reports from brother William, but he little realized the tornado of destruction that had been unleashed and was moving toward him. The duties of a pastor and school principal almost completely absorbed his attention during this time.

A painfully literal storm hit Davie's Chilhowee parish on Good Friday 1854. A bolt of lightning killed his newly married niece Elizabeth as she sat next to her husband in their home. Elizabeth Hogan Farr was the daughter of Wilkinson and had celebrated her first anniversary with her Uncle Davie's star pupil and helper William Benton Farr just two days before. As Uncle Davie (literally Uncle in this case) had performed their wedding and they attended his church, Jesus' crucifixion and the loss symbolized took on a new poignancy for the family and congregation. Davie strove to impart the glory and hope of Resurrection at the service Easter morning and the burial that afternoon. Elizabeth was laid to rest in the Hogan family plot at Shiloh Church in Chilhowee, next to her 11-year-old brother James, who'd died a decade before.

The Cumberland Presbyterian historical archives have more information on the Rock Spring congregation the Uncle Davie pastored before and after his California days:

In the year 1856 The Rock Church was built. The Reverend David Hogan being in charge at the time and donated two acres of land on the west of the present track already held by the congregation. The perishable part of the old Rock Church was burned in the year 1861. From the late 1850s until the end of the Civil War very few records of the church activities are found. Following this however on September 4th, 1866 the session met and admitted to the church 15 members. Two days later session again commenced and received 11 members and on a later date the same month 4 more were received as members.
In 1867 the congregation voted to sell 32 acres of land and use the proceeds to rebuild the church burned in 1861 . . . The church was

rebuilt and remained in use until replaced by the present building erected in 1891.

The following is a list of Elders serving The Rock Spring Church (shortened to only names of Hogan interest): Elders: James Givens, David Hogan[98], Phillip Givens, S.B. Hogan[99]; Trustees: James Givens, David Hogan; Deacons since 1896: W.E Hogan[100] . . . (at this writing the services are no longer held there, however the spot is beautiful and the cemetery is being kept up in appearance.)[101]

The Frémont Adobe in Mariposa, CA

---

[98] This David M. Hogan (1839-1927) is the son of Davie's brother Wilkinson. He married Mary Givens who is related to James and Phillip Givens. He served as both Elder and Trustee of the Rock Spring Church.

[99] Samuel Benton Hogan (1873 - 1967) is the grandson of Davie's brother Wilkinson Hogan through his son David.

[100] William Everett Hogan (1864 -1934) is another grandson of Davie's brother Wilkinson Hogan through his son David.

[101] June 27th, 1942 issue of *Holden Progress,* Floyd Shoemaker article.

War! (1861-1865)

PROSPERITY AND TRIBULATION (1858-1860)

> *... March 1858, when I sold my entire land possessions and moved to Vernon County. I located two and a half miles south of Deerfield."*

Uncle Davie sold his Johnson county real estate and invested in a large tract of land on Big Dry Wood Creek called the "Big Dry Wood Ranch." The road across his property afforded a shallow spot to cross the creek and is called "Hogan's Ford" or "Hogan's Crossing" to this day[102]. On April 20th, just a month after his arrival, Rev. David Hogan was appointed Postmaster of Deerfield, the nearest town. The Hogan home served as Post Office until 1863 when it was disbanded due to the Civil War.

> *It will not be out of place, I hope, to give some of the facts causing our move from Johnson to Vernon County. I had enlarged my land possessions in Johnson far beyond a profitable occupancy. The thought suggested to my mind that if I would sell my land in Johnson, I could go south, and for a small portion of what it would bring, I could buy a good home where the range was good and with the remainder of the funds, I could buy a fine start in livestock; and I could even get rich, if God would bless my efforts. Now mark this fact - I failed to observe the charge of St. Paul to Timothy (1 Tim. 6:9-11).[103] God apparently favored*

---

[102] Source: Johnson, Bernice E. "Place Names in Six of The West Central Counties of Missouri." M.A. thesis., University of Missouri-Columbia, 1933.

[103] *"Those who want to get rich fall into temptation and a trap and into many foolish and harmful desires that plunge people into ruin and destruction. For the love of money is a root of all kinds of evil. Some people,*

my every movement for three years, but destruction overtook me, as we shall hereafter see. Now I do not believe it is wrong to manage our business affairs, in temporals, so that we may even get rich, but the love of riches, God will not favor.

I succeeded in the purchase of a large tract of land on Big Dry Wood, in Vernon County, two hundred acres in cultivation; I also bought a good stock of cattle and hogs, twelve brood mares, and a fine Jack. This was the layout for a fortune. The purchases were made from March 1858 to 1860.

By 1860 the Big Dry Wood Ranch was valued at $9376 and in addition Davie had a personal estate of $4510 (livestock, ranch equipment, etc.).

Here I had an open field, being the only Cumberland Presbyterian Church preacher in the county. I soon made my appointments, embracing every important point in [Vernon] county, giving my entire time to the work. God's grace gave success, and soon I organized four congregations; - namely, Deerfield[104], Nevada, Badger Township and Montevallo. All these were broken up by the ruinous Civil War, as will hereafter appear in this history.

---

eager for money, have wandered from the faith and pierced themselves with many griefs."

[104] In Deerfield the congregation was called Ellis Cumberland Presbyterian Church. After the Civil War the Missouri Kansas & Texas Railroad connected Deerfield to Fort Scott and the rest of the region.

Prosperity and Tribulation (1858-1860)

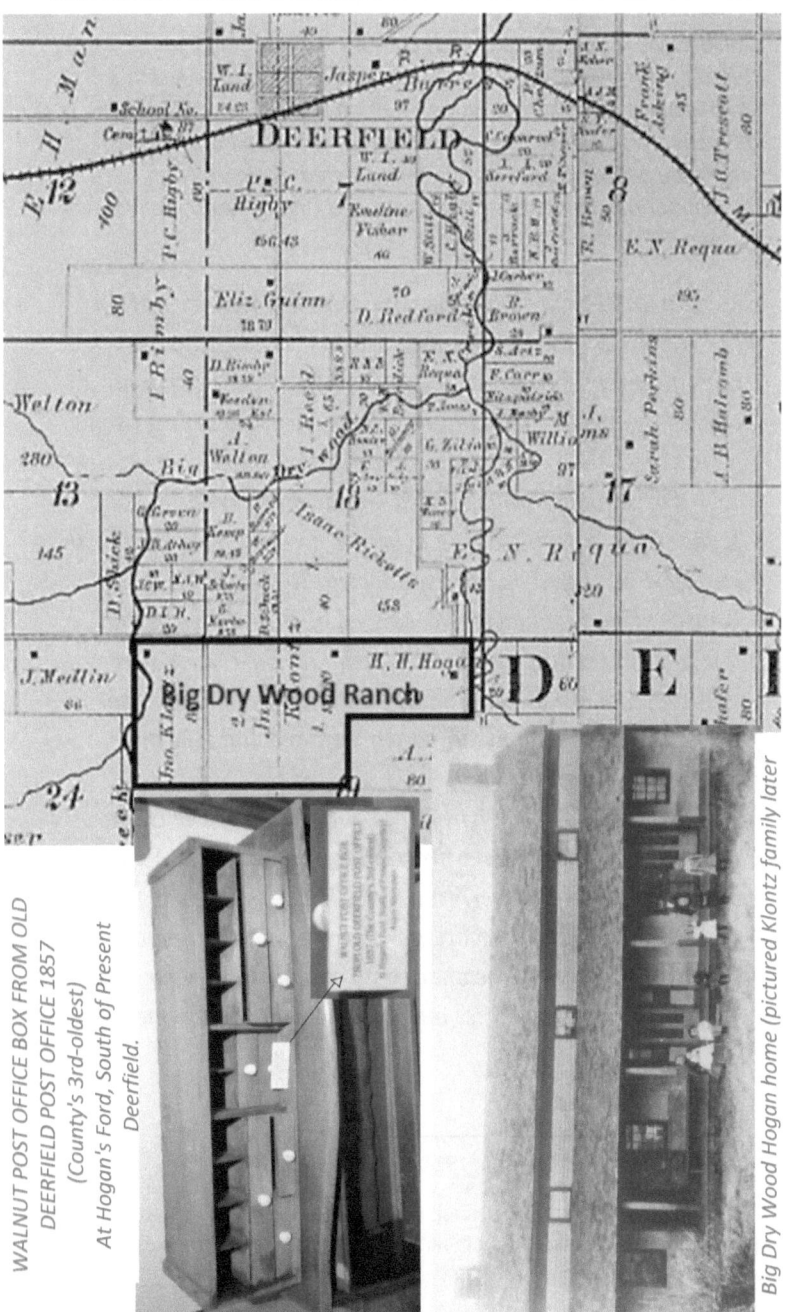

WALNUT POST OFFICE BOX FROM OLD DEERFIELD POST OFFICE 1857 (County's 3rd-oldest) At Hogan's Ford, South of Present Deerfield.

Big Dry Wood Hogan home (pictured Klontz family later)

Uncle Davie's pioneering church planting in the county seat, Nevada, finds mention in the *History of Vernon County Missouri*[105]: *"In this old schoolhouse a Union Meeting was held once a month by a Presbyterian minister from Deerfield by the name of Hogan in which the people became actively interested. Soon other denominations held meetings there and a Union Sunday School was formed.*[106]*"*

> In 1859 the troubles began over what was termed, in the North and East, "Bleeding Kansas", and the works ceased, though I tried at any time and place the opportunity offered, to preach. The congregations were broken up - some of our best ruling elders fell in battle, and many were slain.
>
> The state of things opened a wide door for the Jayhawkers, a people who had been colonized from the North and East by the Abolition Aid Society to the territory of Kansas. These Jayhawkers consisted of all the thieves and vile and low characters of the North and East, who were willing to be armed with Sharps rifles and sent to Kansas to rob and steal from and kill border ruffians and run their negroes into Canada.
>
> Now that I speak truly, it is only necessary to call to your remembrance one expression (out of hundreds) made by Henry Ward Beecher. In a tantalizing way he says to his great Plymouth congregation, "Talk about buying and sending Bibles to the heathen, your money will be far better spent to buy Sharps rifles and pay the way of such men as

---

[105] Vol. 1; editor: J. B. Johnson; 1911, C. F. Cooper & Co., Chicago.

[106] Union Meeting / Sunday School: these were ecumenical gatherings where several Protestant denominations would cooperate to hold services and educate children.

will go to Kansas and kill border ruffians."[107] *Now that these men possessed more of the thief and robber spirit, than the soldier spirit, they began wholesale robbery and murder in the border counties of Missouri in the years 1859 and 1860. Up to the firing on Fort Sumter their depredations were mostly under the cover of night, but after they were in broad open day, as well as in the night.*

Davie's memories here are certainly colored by his personal experience as a Missouri citizen receiving the attentions of Abolitionist raiders from over the Kansas border. The same depredations were being inflicted just ten miles west across the Kansas border by "Border Ruffians".[108] The only thing separating the two groups victimizing the border communities was their stance on the vile institution of slavery — whether it would expand or be contained. Davie's own views on slavery were complicated and evolving. His father, Gen. David Hogan was one of the largest slaveholders in the Cumberland Gap and later Pettis and Cooper Counties in Missouri. He had around 60 enslaved human beings

---

[107] (Wikipedia: Beecher's Bibles") The name "Beecher's Bibles" about Sharps carbines and rifles was inspired by the comments and activities of the abolitionist New England minister Henry Ward Beecher, of the New England Emigrant Aid Society, of whom it was written in a February 8, 1856, article in the *New York Tribune*:

"He believed that the Sharps Rifle was a truly moral agency, and that there was more moral power in one of those instruments, so far as the slaveholders of Kansas were concerned, than in a hundred Bibles. You might just as well. . . read the Bible to Buffaloes as to those fellows who follow Atchison and Stringfellow; but they have a supreme respect for the logic that is embodied in Sharp's rifle."

[108] In Kansas, Border Ruffians was the name applied to pro-slavery activists from the slave state of Missouri, who from 1854 to 1860 crossed the state border into Kansas Territory to force the acceptance of slavery there. Free-State settlers sometimes struck back. Free-State irregulars (known as Jayhawkers) attacked pro-slavery settlers and suspected Ruffian sympathizers. Most notoriously, abolitionist John Brown killed five pro-slavery men at Pottawatomie, Kansas.

and took great care as to whom should inherit each in his wills written in 1857 & 1860 (all for naught since enslaved Missourians were emancipated in January 1865, two years before General David's death and will reading.) The General took great pains to provide lifelong support and care for old and infirm servants of no monetary value. He also transferred ownership of people to his children before writing his will. This is where Davie and Elizabeth got the three females listed in the 1860 census. Esther and one daughter were a gift from Gen. Hogan and she had a second daughter (and after 1860, a son) while in their household.

By all evidence Rev. David Hogan was a reluctant slaveowner. His mentor, Finis Ewing had developed strong abolitionist views by the time Davie became his live-in caregiver. He had long promoted education for those enslaved; preparing them for emancipation and gainful employment. His views had continued to shift toward abolition. Elizabeth Hogan's friend and advocate, Senator Thomas Hart Benton also developed anti-slavery views and that was certainly a topic of conversation with Ewing and the young Hogans. Davie and Elizabeth were liked enough by Esther that she considered them her family, taking the Hogan surname, and staying with them, upon receiving her freedom. Most, if not all, Hogan slaves took the last name 'Hogan' as their own upon emancipation and continued their work for wages.

On the 3rd of April 1860, Deerfield Postmaster David Hogan thrilled to the news that a brand-new Pony Express mail service had set off for California from St. Joseph, Missouri. This meant that mail to and from his relations in the California gold camps could travel between Missouri and Sacramento in just 11 days. He would have letters waiting for the second Pony Express rider to carry.

1860 was also the year of the United States Census. Davie was sure that Vernon County (founded 1855), being counted for the very first time, would be numbered at just under 5000 souls. It would be of great interest to see how the state population had grown. In 1850 there were 682,044 Missourians and there had to be more than a million now[109]. The Enumerator's visit to the Hogan ranch

---

[109] 1860 Census Missouri population 1,182,012

Prosperity and Tribulation (1858-1860)

on Wednesday, July 11th, was an exciting event. The household reported: David Hogan, 49; Elisabeth Hogan, 44; Henry, 22; David Jr., 20; Cyrus, 18 (the three older sons were all listed as occupation: farmer); Mary, 15; Julia, 12; and Edwin, 6. There were two ranch hands living with the family: Joseph Collens, 35, and Joseph Tipton, 14. (Hollering "Joe!" would always bring some help.) The Enumerator had a separate book to record enslaved individuals, the Slave Schedule recorded a 25-year-old black female and two girls: 4-year-old black & 2-year-old mulatto.

The 1860 Census also preserves the locations of Davie's extended family that year: His oldest brother, Wilkinson Hogan and his wife Mary Margaret "Polly" Lane Hogan were living with their children in Chilhowee, Johnson County, Missouri. Wilkinson was also farming (he had 1000 acres owned and in cultivation at his death in 1881).

Brother Col. William and Cornelia Holmead Hogan and their five children were living in the nation's capital. William employed as a Land Office Clerk in Washington City, D.C.

Brother Moses Dorton Hogan Sr., his wife Mary Wright Hogan and their offspring lived at the original Arator homesite in Pettis County, Missouri, close by his and Davie's parents, Gen. David & Betsy Hogan who'd moved into town in Otterville, Cooper County. General David's brother Uncle John Hogan Sr. and wife Ann Beatty Hogan were also living in Otterville. Not far off in Elk Fork, Pettis County lived Davie's mother-in-law Mary "Polly" Blackburn Hoss is living with her daughters Julia Parke and Emma Arnold. Her son Sam's large brood (8 kids) is practically next door. Strangely, this is the last trace of Polly in the records. She is rumored to have died back home in Washington County, Tennessee, but whether the Civil War or something else was the cause, even her death date is unknown.

Just ten miles west of Uncle Davie's Big Dry Wood Ranch was his closest relation (in proximity) sister Elizabeth Grant Clay Hogan and her husband, Fort Scott's sutler, Col. Hiero Tennant Wilson.. The fort struggled to impose order on the border region as marauding bands of abolitionist Jayhawkers and pro-slavery Bushwhackers terrorized the region.

Davie's brother Dr. Robert Henderson Hogan and wife Mary Ellen Lewis Hogan had somehow wound up back at Tebo, in Henry County where the Hogan boys had tanned hides so many years before. There were two Hogan brothers doctoring patients in tiny Tebo in 1860, as Dr. James Hogan was also living there.

David's third doctor brother, Dr. John D. Hogan and wife Hortensia Gertrude Voris Hogan were away to the southwest in Bastrop, Texas. It was a point of family pride that the Hogans had sired no less than four medical doctors, though young Dr. Samuel Hogan had been in the ground a decade.

WAR! (1861-1865)

The awful Civil War came in 1861. From the time the first gun was fired at Fort Sumter, in one week or less, the minds of the people of the South (already prepared for) flamed with war demonstrations, and Missouri was crazed with the spirit of bloodshed.

[The Jayhawkers'] work was continued seven months after the war commenced, before they were mustered into the Government service; also, during the seven months of outlawry, they repeatedly and often helped themselves to arms and ammunition from Government wagons loaded for different U. S. Posts. **Mark well the fact**, *that the United States forces at Fort Scott, made no objection to the course of these miserable robbers and murderers, nor to them helping themselves as I have said from Government wagons. At this*

An illustration of Charles Jennison and the 7th Kansas Cavalry Infantry, aka "Jennison's Jayhawkers," launching a guerrilla attack in Missouri. [Courtesy the Library of Congress.]

time, I lived [with]in six miles of the line and ten miles from Fort Scott - was often there and know whereof I speak.

These Jayhawkers got fully one half of the livestock of Missouri. First, the larger share of such stock was on the borders of Missouri - Second, it is easy to see, why Missouri should suffer more than any border state. The Beecher Society had outfitted men for the work and sent them to Kansas. Now after the South foolishly struck the first blow at Fort Sumter, the Jayhawkers would drive off all the stock of rebels; they called it confiscation. It is impossible for me to believe otherwise, the Government winked at, and purposely allowed the Jayhawking for, by a special act of Congress they were granted pay for the seven months of Jayhawking done preceding their day of muster into the United States soldiery.

Suffice it to say, all my personal property was taken by the Union Army first and last, and some years back I instituted a claim for eight thousand dollars against the United States Government: sworn to and proven, the most of it, by the commanding officers. Said claim is just now to come before the United States Court of Claims. I have little hope of anything to myself or offspring.

In concluding this part of my history, I desire to say, so soon as I was fairly settled in Vernon County, and had bought this large stock, I became fully convinced there would be a civil war, and I fully anticipated the disastrous occurrences. With all this plainly before my mind, I can never cease to be astonished at myself for the want of exercise of better sense at that time. Every member of my family was with me in my Vernon home - consisting of three grown sons, two daughters nearly grown, and my youngest, a son of six years, also a colored woman and her two *children. My eldest son of twenty-one years, and my youngest not quite six. Thus, it is plainly seen, all my children could have been, at that time, put under an educational course.*

Here is where I made the greatest mistake of my life, and from the close of the war, till the present day, my thought has ever been, how foolishly and blamably I acted! I have a thousand or even more times asked myself, "Why did you not in 1860, when you saw the awful war coming, sell all your personal property (except the colored family) and get a fair distance north of Mason and Dixon's Line, and educate your children? The price of your personal property would have more than completed it." Now when all this comes up in my mind, even today, how badly I missed the mark, I feel to charge myself with being crazy at that time. Surely! Surely! Surely!! I must have been led by an unfortunate spirit, and not the spirit of God.

On the 12th of June 1861, Missouri Governor Claiborne Jackson called for 50,000 volunteers to stop Federal troops from taking over his state.

The War Between the States was, for General Hogan's family, a cause of division between family members. Some taking up Lincoln's call to defend the Union:

At Fort Scott, Dr. James M. Hogan enlisted with the 5th Kansas Volunteers[110], and Elizabeth Hogan Wilson, married to the fort sutler, stayed to defend the town when Union forces fled.

Moses D. Hogan kept working the plantation throughout the war but took an oath of allegiance to the United States.

---

[110] Serves one year until unit disbanded. James spent the next eight years in Europe.

War! (1861-1865)

In the Union Capital, Col. William M. Hogan labored for the Federal Government under five administrations[111] in various government posts (10 years clerking in the Land Office; then for William Seward in the wartime State Dept. His boss was an ardent abolitionist leader and Radical Republican member of Lincoln's Cabinet; William had to be a Union man.

Moses E. Dorton Jr., Davie's first cousin, was a Union soldier. As was his eldest son — Henry Hoss Hogan served in the Union Army with the 14th Kansas Volunteer Cavalry Regiment mustered in at Fort Scott.

Meanwhile, two of Davie's brothers joined the Rebel Cause against the United States. In Texas, Col. George M. Hogan served in the CSA military as a Private in Company B, 1st Regiment, 2nd Texas Brigade and Dr. John D. Hogan was Regimental Surgeon, 12th Texas Cavalry from 1861–1864. John signed an oath of loyalty to the C.S.A. in October 1861:

I Jn. D. Hogan, regimental surgeon, do solemnly swear that while I continue in the service I will bear true faith and yield obedience to the Confederate States of America, that I will serve them honestly and faithfully against their enemies, and that I will observe and obey the orders of the President of the Confederate States, and the orders of the officers appointed over me according to the rules and articles of war. —Jn D. Hogan, surgeon[112]

On October 3, 1863, expressing gratitude for a pivotal Union Army victory at Gettysburg, President Abraham Lincoln announced that the nation would celebrate an official Thanksgiving holiday on November 26, 1863. One can imagine the strained conversations and empty seats around the Hogan family table in Arator that year and for years to come.

---

[111] Presidents Millard Filmore, Franklin Pierce, James Buchanan, Abraham Lincoln, and Andrew Johnson.

[112] 4 Regt Inf 12 Co S Army, Subscribed and sworn this ___ day of October AD 1861; Jesse W Sparks, 12 Co. S Infantry Mustering Officer

War! (1861-1865)

The national chaos swirling around the residents of the contested State of Missouri just seemed to grow daily more dire. In August 1861, a famous son-in-law of the Hogan's friend Thomas Hart Benton, a man whose exploits had already impacted Davie and his family, issued a proclamation freeing all enslaved by Missourians. This came as a relief to Rev. David Hogan, who was extremely conflicted with the institution of slavery and his own entanglement in human bondage, but it served to turn up the heat under a community already boiling over. Davie remembered reading of John C. Frémont's discovery of gold at Agua Fria, California in 1849. It was this account that drew Davie to the Agua Fria digs to make his fortune the following year. He'd never met Frémont and it came as a surprise to have his life impacted once again by the flamboyant military man's Missouri Emancipation Proclamation.

General Frémont's move was not welcomed by his Commander-in-Chief, who was desperately attempting to keep the Border States in the Union and not drive them into the arms of the Confederacy. President Lincoln, though he shared the sentiment, knew the time was not ripe for emancipation and promptly rescinded Frémont's proclamation and removed him from his command. Maybe this was the situation Lincoln had in mind when he said, *"You can please some of the people all of the time, you can please all of the people some of the time, but you can't please all of the people all of the time"*.

Undoing this first attempt at proclaiming freedom for some (but not all) enslaved Americans lost Abraham Lincoln much support among Republicans and abolitionists and gained zero love from slave owners. Old Abe was in a no-win situation. John C Frémont would go on to run against Lincoln in the next Presidential Race.

Even if Davie was fine with the decision to extricate his family from the vile institution of slavery, Frémont's proclamation spelled financial disaster for his father and brother Moses and their large Arator plantation in Pettis County. The General had much at stake. In 1860 the United States census included a Slave Schedule providing an accounting of what he stood to lose. He had already given three persons each to sons Davie and Moses, and six to his other offspring as enumerated in his 1857 will.

Gen. David Hogan's August 1860 Slave Schedule[113] in Otterville, Cooper County[114] listed sixteen human beings in bondage:

[Gender Race – Name (extrapolated from Wills, later census, etc.) (Age)]

Female Black - Dinah (68)

Female Black - Sarah (6)

Male Black - James Hogan (49)[115]

Female Mulatto – name? (6)

Male Mulatto - Dick (45)

Male Mulatto – name? (5)

Female Black - Jane (40)

Male Black-David Hogan (3) [116]

Female Black - Mary (40)

Female Mulatto - Zilda (38)

Male Black – name? (30)

Female Mulatto - Hannah? (18)

Female Black - Catherine (15)

Male Black - James W Hogan (15)

Male Mulatto – Rob Hogan (10)

Male Mulatto - Jim Hogan (8)

---

[113] 1860 U.S. census, population schedule. NARA microfilm publication M653, 1,438 rolls. Washington, D.C.: National Archives and Records).

[114] Their plantation was on the Cooper-Pettis County line and administrative purview went back and forth between the counties, and towns, Otterville and Smithton over the years The elder Hogans were living in Otterville but the slaves were almost all still out on the plantation with Moses.

[115] By 1880 Otterville Census - James Hogan (b. ca 1809 KY) is married to Emily (ca 1825 KY) and living with children Laura (ca 1859 MO) and James (ca 1843 MO). On the 1860 *Slave Schedule* for Gen. David, we see James Sr (49), James Jr (15). Emily and Laura had been already given to Wilkinson Hogan ("negro woman and child").

[116] Also known as 'Eliot'.

War! (1861-1865)

Aug. 10, 1861. Following his Wilson's Creek victory near Springfield, Maj. Gen. Sterling Price led the pro-Confederate Missouri State Guard, which numbered about 10,000, north to capture Lexington. He detoured westward to attack Fort Scott, Kansas, where Brig. Gen. and U.S. Senator James H. Lane, a notorious Kansas Jayhawker, had gathered 2,500 men. On Sept. 1,

Brig. Gen. James H. Lane

Gen. Sterling Price, C.S.A.

Price concentrated in Vernon County south of Nevada. His scouts raided Fort Scott, which alerted Lane, who prepared to evacuate the fort and town. Early on Sept. 2, Lane sent Col. James Montgomery with 450 cavalry and a 12-pounder mountain howitzer to slow Price's advance.

The opposing armies were on a collision course. They would meet on the land of Rev. David Hogan — the Big Dry Wood Ranch.

That afternoon Price's rebels, mostly Missourians, swelled to 12,000 strong, marched on Fort Scott in a three-mile column. Around 4:30 p.m., their advance guard crossed Dry Wood Creek at Hogan's Ford 2 ¼ miles south of the village of Deerfield and collided

War! (1861-1865)

with Montgomery's Union troops from Kansas, who drove them across the creek and onto the prairie.

Price rushed his three-gun battery to a hill east of the creek and deployed infantry in support. The Union troops occupied the wooded creek bottom and opened a rapid fire with their Sharps breech-loading rifles. The Rebels replied with muskets and shotguns from the 6-foot-tall prairie grass. Montgomery's efficiently served howitzer soon silenced most of Price's guns. Another four-gun battery came to their aid but took losses and was in danger of being outflanked.

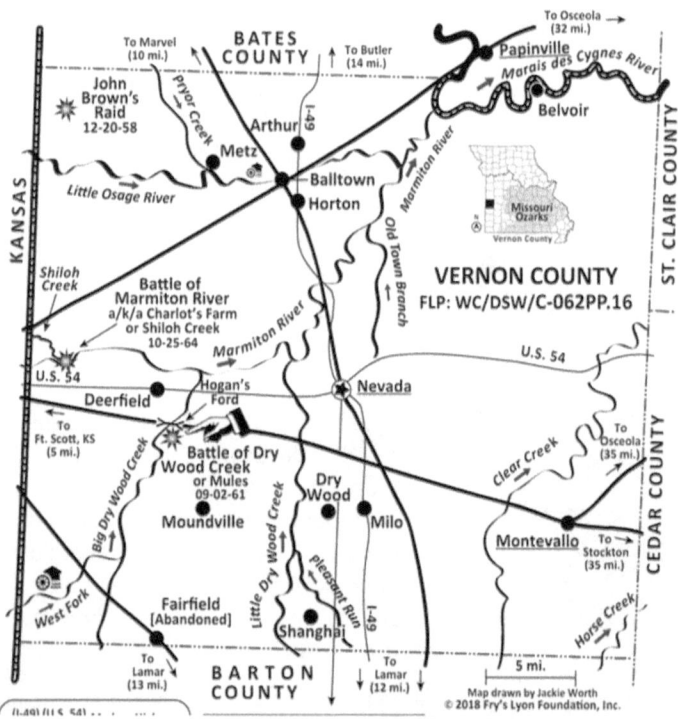

Price was forced on the defensive; the volume of enemy fire convinced him that he faced a larger force than he actually did. He reinforced his line, then advanced. Montgomery was low on ammunition, and he fell back, leaving their mules to be captured and retreated to Fort Scott as the sun was setting.

The fight had lasted less than two hours. Casualties had been light because of the thick woods and tall grass. Confederate casualties were two killed and 23 wounded; Union losses five killed and six wounded. The sight of these casualties had a moving effect on Robert S. Bevier, a major in the Confederate Missouri State Guard: "We passed some of the dead and wounded, the first sad results of real war I had seen, and the solemnity attending the awful mystery of mortal dissolution crept over my soul." The skirmish came to be known as "The Battle of the Mules" and "The Battle of Big Dry Wood".

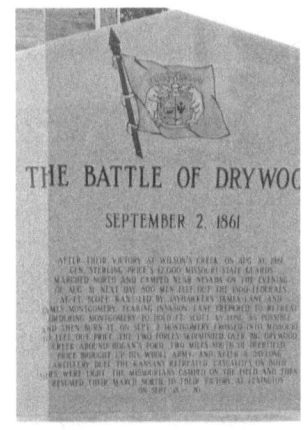

Battle of Big Dry Wood Monument in Deerfield

Following the Union defeats at the Battles of Wilson Creek and the Big Dry Wood, Fort Scott's citizens feared attack from Sterling Price's advancing Confederate Army. When James Lane's Kansas brigade, which included her brother Dr. James M. Hogan, evacuated, nearly all the townspeople fled. Davie's sister Elizabeth Hogan Wilson had other plans.

Elizabeth Wilson Saves the Town of Fort Scott From Destruction.[117]

September 3rd, 1861, at the outbreak of the Civil War, U.S. Senator and General James Lane ordered the town of Fort Scott to be burned to the ground. This extreme call was in reaction to the apparent impending invasion by General Sterling Price, leader of the pro-Confederate Missouri State Guard. Since Fort Scott was an important Union supply depot, the idea behind destroying the town was to prevent the supplies stored there from falling into rebel hands.

---

[117]Facebook.com for Fort Scott NPS "this day in Fort Scott history September 3, 1861 Elizabeth Wilson saves the town"

Several townswomen, including Elizabeth Wilson, stood firm on not evacuating until absolutely necessary and were able to convince the community to not torch the town. Elizabeth Wilson declared:

"You come here to my home tonight to say there is a chance that Price's Army will invade Fort Scott, pillaging and burning the town. Now you say that Lane has ordered you to burn our homestead and take our livelihood upon first sight of the rebels. It seems to me sir that either way the citizens of Fort Scott lose. It is Mr. Wilson's and my belief that if we stay in our homes, we can protect our property and I would say that everyone else staying would agree with me. I will not leave my home until my path is lighted by its flames."

Fort Scott, a reenactor portraying Elizabeth Wilson making her impassioned speech in front of the Wilson-Goodlander House.

Her influence paid off as General Price's forces never attacked Fort Scott. He declined to follow the retreating General Lane, since his goal was to free Missouri, not invade Kansas. He continued north and captured Lexington but was eventually forced from the state. During his desperate rout into Arkansas, Price and his troops again crossed Rev. Hogan's ruined ranch and left behind a greater number of corpses and supplies which were, for years thereafter, discovered scattered around the property.

On Thursday, the 28th of November 1861, Missouri was officially admitted to the Confederacy by the Confederate Congress in Richmond, Virginia.

Davie and Elizabeth and their family experienced a terrible loss on Christmas Day of 1862, when Cyrus, their 20-year-old son, died. No record has turned up as to what killed Cyrus, through the date suggests it is war related. There were constant depredations by Union and Confederate regular troops in addition to raiders from both sides (Bushwhackers and Jayhawkers). Cyrus' grieving parents and siblings buried the young man in a plot they bought for their family in the west end of Deerfield Cemetery[118]. Davie wept over the fresh turned sod of his son's grave. No parent should have to bury their child. Deerfield Cemetery was rapidly becoming the focal point of what remained of his ministry. Congregations hardly dared meet, but funerals had become commonplace.

Grave marker of Cyrus O. Hogan (1842-1862)

Elizabeth Grant Clay Hogan Wilson (1824-1895) Sister of Davie Hogan

Col. Hiero Tennant Wilson (1824-1895) Fort Scott

---

[118] Deerfield Cemetery; Section A19

War! (1861-1865)

Davie and Elizabeth's eldest, Henry Hoss Hogan, volunteered in the Union Army on April 3rd, 1863. He walked the ten miles west to Fort Scott, where his Aunt Elizabeth Hogan Wilson was the Sutler's wife, to enlist with the 14th Kansas Volunteer Cavalry. He was keen to defend the Union and free the slaves and wanted to strike a blow against the raiders of southern sympathies preying upon his family and farm. Henry first saw action at Cabin Creek on the Cherokee Nation, July 1–2, 1863. He must have enjoyed spending August chasing Quantrill and his raiders who'd been among the Bushwhackers preying on his family's Big Dry Wood Ranch. Various skirmishes and battles through the fall, followed by setting up a winter encampment in Fort Smith, Arkansas, kept Henry busy foraging and scouting in Confederate territory. His unit moved in February to Ozark, Arkansas and aside from a battle at Flint Creek, had mostly peaceful duty there until April 6th, 1864.

Whilst their oldest son was off chasing Quantrill and his raiders, the victims of these marauders were facing the effects of war again, quite literally in their front yard. *"Early in the summer of 1862 the population had in large measure disappeared, and in 1863 the northern portion of the county was entirely depopulated under the operations of Brigadier General Thomas Ewing's Order No. 11. The towns were laid in ruins by act of one army or the other, or of marauding bands who ravaged the country continually."*

War! (1861-1865)

"General Order No. 11" George Caleb Bingham.
General Thomas Ewing is seated on a horse watching the Red Legs.

The North suffered a massacre in Lawrence, Kansas perpetrated by Quantrill's Bushwhackers and in response retaliated on the residents of the Missouri border counties. On August 25, 1863, Brigadier General Thomas Ewing issued General Order No. 11, requiring all people living in Jackson, Cass, Bates, and northern Vernon counties to vacate the area unless their loyalty to the Union could be proven. In spite of the loss of his goods, livestock, and congregations, David and his family had managed to hang on in Vernon County, but Ewing's edict effected what terror and death threats had failed to do, and on September 20, 1863 he resigned his posts as Justice of the Peace and Postmaster and fled the region.[119] We are not told where Davie sheltered his family, but their logical course would be northeast taking refuge with Davie's parents on the Cooper-Pettis county line. The Battle of Pea Ridge in Arkansas had secured most of Missouri from Confederate depredations and they'd be safe away from the bloody border.

Just three days into his second year of soldiering, for a month beginning the 6th of April 1864, Henry's unit was plunged into a serious of heated battles during Steele's expedition against Camden Arkansas. Sometime during this baptism of fire, Henry Hoss Hogan took a "*gunshot wound in the groins*" and was put out of action. He became part of the company's wounded train and sometime in May transferred from the front to hospital care at Fort Scott. The care of his Aunt Elizabeth was surely a help and comfort, but his Uncle James, who earlier in the War had been Fort Scott's physician had scampered off to Europe to sit out the war over a year before.

It was a bittersweet homecoming when Henry came home from the war. He had been kept on the invalid list at Fort Scott, just ten miles west of the abandoned Hogan Ranch, from May through October. When the Union Army finally decided that he would not be able to return to the field of combat, Henry was sent home

---

[119] From Tuesday 20 April 1858–Sunday 20 September 1863 Rev. David M. Hogan was a Justice of the Peace & Postmaster in Deerfield, Vernon, Missouri

(though not formally discharged from his service until two months after war's end) to his family's home-in-exile. He was not the same lad that had proudly marched to battle the previous year. Joy over his survival was tempered by the doctor's news that his injury meant that he could never hope to father children.

Davie and Elizabeth's daughter Mary wed sometime around this period. Phillip Yelton Thomas, a Kentuckian eleven years her senior, and another displaced Big Dry Wood Ranch neighbor, tied the knot with the first of Davie's children to marry.

Wedding photo
Phillip Yelton Thomas (1834-?) & Mary Elizabeth Hogan (1845-1932)

At the start of the new year, slavery was abolished in Missouri by an ordinance of immediate emancipation. Missouri became the first slave state to emancipate; doing so before the adoption of the 13th Amendment to the US Constitution. This settled Davie's predicament (actually, four of them — Esther had given birth twice since and her daughter arrived from the General's place). They were free! Free to go or stay if they chose to. The three youngsters would eventually all leave to make lives and families of their own, but Esther felt that she was part of the Hogan family. While it was hers to choose, she would stay with them.

The dreadful and bloody Civil War came to an end at Appomattox Courthouse on a April Sunday in 1865 and a week later Abraham Lincoln, the President who'd saved the Union, lay dead across the street from a Washington D.C. theater. Davie's brother William Hogan was working as a translator at the State Department in that city. Booth's band of assassins not only killed Lincoln, but they also almost ended the life of William Hogan's boss, Secretary of State William H. Seward, who was viscously stabbed repeatedly while in his sickbed recovering from a carriage accident. In letters to his Missouri kin, William shared the terror of the days that followed and details of the largest manhunt in the nation's history. By the following year, William was done with government work and moved his family (wife Cornelia, five kids[120], and his father-in-law, James Beaury Holmead) to Iowa for a couple years and by 1868 they were back in Johnson County, Missouri living just north of Knob Noster city limits.

Uncle Davie had been greatly shaken by the war and the local impacts on his family and fortunes. During the course of the conflict, he'd buried a beloved son, lost his property to rampaging raiders, had two armies meet in battle on his Big Dry Wood Ranch, freed four servants (with a sense of relief), saw his congregations and all his neighbors killed or driven off by the violence along the Kansas-Missouri border that almost completely depopulated the border counties, and had to seek safety for his family and leave their home behind. He remembered thusly:

> *After the war, Vernon County was in such a ruined condition, as soon as I could, I obtained a letter of dismission from Ozark Presbytery, Vernon County and joined the Lexington Presbytery, and took work therein which kept me nearly all my time from my home in Vernon. All the people had been greatly deprived of preaching during the war and were now anxious to have the return of the blessed gospel of God's peace come to them again; hence, there were many precious revivals, and many souls were born to God."*

However, something drew him back to Deerfield. Slowly the survivors returned, and they craved Davie's loving and comforting ministry. Uncle Davie moved back onto his ruined ranch and reopened the Post Office that he operated out of his home. His neighbors, glad to have signs of order and law returning at last, elected him Justice of the Peace on 14 Nov 1865. He was busy in ministry as well as secular labors. Rev. Davie organized the first

---

[120] Medora, James, Eugene, William, and Susan. (Eugene Hogan is the author's 2nd great grandfather)

non-denominational Union Sunday School for the children of Nevada city in Vernon County. It was held in Nevada's only public building that stood in those days, the schoolhouse. He also led church services there once a month with other ministers filling the pulpit the rest of the Sundays.

Uncle Davie also circuited to Johnson County where he led Bethel CPC in Knob Noster. It was nice to get to know William's family again after their long sojourn in the nation's capital. Davie notes William continues to flee the scene if the subject of faith was broached.

Uncle Davie doesn't mention what his feelings were about the occupant of the White House, President Andrew Johnson. He certainly knew Andy from his college days at Greeneville, where he was the tailor and active in county politics. Not that this acquaintance proved any help to Davie in his lawsuit to recover wartime losses from the U.S. Government.

The Wilson-Goodlander House at Fort Scott, Kansas. This former Officers' Quarters was purchased by Heiro and Elizabeth Wilson and passed to their daughter.
Photo 2018 by the author.

RECONSTRUCTION (1866-1881)

In 1866, Davie and Elizabeth became grandparents when Harry Thomas was born to Mary Hogan and Phillip Thomas. As happens so often in life, grief comes in like a tide and attempts to erase the sandcastles of joy we build. On January 20, 1867, the patriarch of the Hogan family, General David Hogan, died in Otterville, just a few miles east from his Arator farm. He was buried in Providence Baptist Church Cemetery in nearby Smithton, beside his sons: Joseph and Samuel. His monument reads: "Aged 85 years 7 months 13 days".

A month later the family gathered for the reading of the patriarch's Will.

The Last Will and Testament of Gen. David Hogan[121]

In the name of God, Amen. I, David Hogan of the County of Cooper, and the State of Missouri, being of sound mind and memory, but being mindful of the uncertainty of this life, do make declare and establish this to be my last Will and Testament.

Item First, it is my will that after the expense of my last sickness, and funeral expenses are paid, that all my just debts shall be paid by my executors hereinafter named.

Item Second. It is my desire, that my executors so soon as they may deem it advisable, shall proceed to sell all my estate, real, personal, and mixed, it except as much thereof as is hereinafter specified, be devised or bequeathed, upon such terms as they may think best for the interest of the estate.

Item Third. Should my beloved wife Elizabeth P. Hogan survive me, It is my will and desire that she shall hold for and during her natural

---

[121] Transcribed from Record of Wills, 1818-1918; Author: Missouri. Probate Court (Cooper County); Probate Place: Cooper, Missouri Transcriber: Brian Hogan

life my following named Slaves to wit: Abram, Dick, Lucy, Rachel, Jane and Mary, and further that from the just proceeds of my estate, when sold or from money on hand at my death, it is my wish that --- my executors should invest --- the sum of four thousand dollars in a small and comfortable farm for the use and benefit of my beloved wife during her natural life, and that the further sum of two thousand dollars ($2000.00) shall be placed in the hands of a trustee, to be appointed by my executors, to be loaned out by said trustee, during the life of my said wife, and the interest on same to be paid annually to my said wife, during the continuance of said trust, and after the death of my wife said money is . . . to be distributed with what shall remain of my estate not disposed of. And I further desire that --- my said wife may have the entire and final disposal of my two old and infirm female servants to wit: the above-named Lucy and Rachel.

Item Fourth. It is my desire that my executors have tombstones placed over the graves of me and my dearly beloved wife, and that they are hereby directed to appropriate --- from my estate --- the sum of two hundred dollars for this purpose, that is one hundred dollars for each tombstone.

Item Fifth. It is my will and desire that my property should be shared equally by my children, not only that portion which may be subject to distribution in the event that my wife survives me, but also that portion which will remain undistributed at her death. And as I have given each of my children at different times property, differing in value according to the estimate --- which I have placed on the same and which I believe to be just and right . . . I have given to my son Wilkinson Hogan a Negro woman and child & cash which I estimate in all at $1200. I have given to William H. Trigg in trust for my daughter Sarah, a Negro girl, and to my daughter Sarah aforesaid absolutely some money, and I estimate the whole including the Negro girl at $1300. To my son John D. I have given in cash to $400. To my Son David I have given a negro woman and child, and cash, and I estimate the whole at $1300.[122] To William H.

---

[122] So, prior to 1857, the General gave Davie: Esther and her daughter Amanda and cash totaling $1300. By the time of the 1860 Census *Slave Schedule*, Davie held one 25 yr. black female (Esther) a four-year-old black

Trigg for the sole use and benefit of and interest for, the wife of and heirs of my son William[123], I have given one negro boy[124] and to my son William I have given cash, and I estimate the negro boy and cash at $1200. To my son James I have given in cash $300. To my son George M. I have given cash and do hereby bequeath to him and his heirs two small negro girls named Margaret, aged about eight years, and Elizabeth, aged about six years, all of which I estimate at $1300. To my son Moses D. I have given a Negro boy named Orange and cash which is all I estimate at $1300. To William H. Trigg in trust for the sole use and benefit of my daughter Elizabeth G. Wilson and her heirs I have given a negro girl, and to my said daughter Elizabeth G. I have also given money, all of which I estimate at $1000. To my son Robert H. I have given a negro boy named Westley[?] which I estimate at $1000. In order to carry out my intentions to divide my property equally, I desire that my executors, after providing for my wife as herein directed, and retaining the sum mentioned in item fourth for the purpose there specified, shall first - pay to those of my children or their trustees who have not been advanced, the sum of $1300 an amount sufficient to make up that sum. After that - it is my will and desire that - my property be equally divided among my children as follows. Whatever sum may be coming to my daughter Sarah A. Young as her distributions share of my estate I direct to be placed by my executors in the hands of William H. Trigg of Boonville or such other trustee as my executors may appoint, - for her sole use and benefit - and if she should die without issue, or intestate the same shall revert to my heirs. It is my will, that such trustee as may be appointed shall have power to invest, such distributions share from time to time and to change such investment by selling property or

---

girl (Amanda), and a two-year-old mulatto girl (born to Esther after coming to live with Davie and Elizabeth - she was probably already pregnant).

[123] specifically passes over William to inherit Cornelia and their five children.

[124] In 1879 William Hogan goes to the rescue of this former slave boy, John Hogan unjustly accused of murder in Sedalia and on trial for his life. The newspaper details William visiting John in jail, hiring him two lawyers, and providing witnesses from Knob Noster that gave him an alibi and acquittal.

otherwise, but to hold the proceeds at all times subject - to the limitations herein declared, whenever he shall be requested so to do by said daughter, and it is my will that my said daughter shall have the rents and profits of said trust funds to her sole and separate use while she is living. It is further my desire that any trustee who may be acting for my said daughter may at any time transfer his authority as such trustee to another person. It is my will that my daughter Sarah have power to dispose of said property by will. In like manner it is my will and desire, whatever portions of my property would be coming under the distribution to my sons John D. and Wm Hogan[125], may be placed in the hands of a trustee to be appointed by my said executors for the sole use and benefit of their wives and children begotten by their present husbands respectively, that is to say the share of John D. Hogan, for the sole use and benefit of Hortensia G. Hogan his wife, and his children by Hortensia G. Hogan, and the share of William for the sole use and benefit of Cornelia V. Hogan and her children by said William Hogan, and said trust to be subject to the provisions and limitations declared in the case of Sarah A. Young, abovementioned. It is my express meaning here, that all the property which might be coming to my said sons John D. & Wm. Hogan from my estate, be placed in and subject - to the trust -above declared. I give and bequeath to

---

[125] Here the General creates two very puzzling exceptions to the rest of his behests to children in his Will. He singles out two sons (one an Executor!) and basically gives their remaining inheritance (minus what was distributed while he lived) to their wives and their children. This would have made more sense if, at the time of the writing in 1857, these marriages had been in jeopardy, or the sons were abandoning their families. There is no evidence of this in either case. The families were intact and living under the same roof in 1850, 1860, and 1870. It feels like there is a personal axe being ground here. Since William is taken out as Executor in 1860's Codicil, it seems the issue(s) endured. What exactly it was remains a mystery. In 1857 the issue of slavery was at a boiling point. Perhaps Gen. David, a slaveholder, resents William's work for the Federal government (though under the Buchanan Administration the Washington "swamp" was more pro-slavery than not. Dr. John D Hogan and wife Hortensia were living in Texas at the time of the Will's writing, and he was later to fight for the Confederacy. Did he redeem in his father's eyes himself from abolitionist leanings with his rebel service? It is perplexing.

my son Robert H. Hogan after my death my negro woman Zelda & her child Catherine, and their increase to be valued to my said Son by my executors, and if their value be more than the equal share of my son Robert - he is to pay the excess to my executors. I give and bequeath to my son James my negro boys Jim and Elliott after my death, to be valued, and subject to the provisions of bequest of slaves Zelda and Catherine & increase to my son Robert. I give and bequeath to my son Moses D. my negro girl Hannah after my death with her increase if any subject to provisions of two last preceding bequests.

Item Sixth. In case my wife should survive me, it is my desire that, the property and its increase set apart- by my executors for her comfort and support after her death shall be equally divided amongst my children and their trustees, or the trustees of their wives and children. But it is my will that the slaves so reserved to my beloved wife for her life shall at her death be disposed of as follows. I give and bequeath to Hortensia G. (wife of John D. Hogan, my son) and her heirs, by my said son after the death of my wife, my negro man Dick. I give and bequeath to my daughter Elizabeth G. Wilson & her heirs after the death of my beloved wife, my negro girl Mary and her increase up to that time. I give and bequeath to Cornelia V. Hogan, wife of my son William Hogan, and her children by my said son after the death of my dearly beloved wife, my Negro girl Jane and her increase up to that time. It is my will and desire that my two old and very infirm slaves, Dinah and Abram be permitted to select one of my sons or daughters they may prefer to live with, and when this selection is made known I hereby bequeath the said old, faithful, and infirm slaves to said son or daughter selected, without a value on them and said son or daughter shall not account to my estate for said slaves but it is my bequest in this my last will that said slaves will not be exposed to hardships but that every exertion will be made to render them comfortable during the remainder of their lives.

Item Seventh. I hereby constitute, nominate and appoint Anthony Smith Walker of Cooper County Missouri and Charles S. Bohannon of Pettis County Missouri and my two sons Wilkinson and William to be executors of this my last will and testament, who may act jointly or severally in carrying into effect the provisions of the same.

In witness whereof I have hereunto subscribed my name and affixed my seal, this the 24th day of August, in the year of our Lord Eighteen Hundred and fifty-seven.

We attest the foregoing will by signing our names as witnesses hereto in the presence of the testator David Hogan this, 24th, day of August 1857.

Witness: Wm G Wear, H.A.B. Johnston, Harrison Homan, Samuel Wear

At the time of the writing of his Will, General David Hogan was among the wealthiest landowners in Cooper County[126]. Less than three years after the writing, David Hogan filed an amendment called a codicil for the sole purpose of removing two of sons from the Executor role he'd previously given them. No reasons are given, but it may have simply been a matter of practically in William's case. He was living in Washington, D.C. and could not be counted on to return to Missouri for probate, or there may have been an estrangement since his portion was given to his wife and children. The world had changed since he'd amended his Will in 1860.

Things began to move with Gen. David Hogan's passing. Probate was officially entered into on February 8, 1867. At some point early that month, the Widow Betsy Hogan and her ten surviving children, two sons-in-law and seven daughters-in-law, 39 grandchildren (5 had died), 6 step-grandkids[127], and eight great-

---

[126] The 1860 Census credits him with $25,000 in Real Estate, and $12,000 in Personal Property (including enslaved human beings, soon to be freed)

[127] Major Art Young, a widower, came into the marriage with Sarah Hogan already having six kids, though only five were still at home. The General words the Will in such a way to give Sarah's husband and his children absolutely no claim upon her inheritance and trust.

grandchildren[128] would have gathered for the reading of the Will. In hindsight, a second codicil was sorely needed, but never written. The General should have revoked the many behests involving human property as Lincoln and the defeat of the Confederacy had rendered all such odious clauses invalid. This would have changed the amounts going to each heir. Having these meticulous and irrelevant directives read out must have been both painful and awkward for the assembled Hogan heirs.

Moving on from the details of death, 1868 brought another new life. Orlando Thomas was born to Mary and Phillip. Davie had a second grandson to bounce on his knees!

Once again loss came on the heels of joy as the Hogan family mourned the loss of their mother and grandmother, Elizabeth Parmalee Dorton Hogan. 'Betsy' died on Wednesday, the 3rd of February 1869 at her home in Arator, Missouri. Once again the family found itself gathered in the cold wind on the snow covered grass of the Providence Cemetery. Betsy's casket was lowered in beside the grave of her husband of 61 years.

Five years postwar, the 1870 U.S. Census counted Hogans living across the disparate regions the disruption waves had washed them up.

David and Elizabeth, with their daughter Julia (22), were counted on Thursday, August 18, 1870 near Warrensburg in north Post Oak

---

[128] Seven grandkids from Wilkinson's line; three of whom were half Native American and lived in California. And one great-grandson, Harry, from Davie's daughter Mary Hogan Thomas.

The End of His Trail of Tears (1884-1893)

Township, Johnson County.[129] [130] Two formerly enslaved persons, emancipated in 1865, are still in their household. Both Esther, 36, and George, 9, have taken the Hogan name as their own. Though George's mom is illiterate, he can read, no doubt taught by Elizabeth (George Washington Hogan grew up to be first black policeman in Missouri — 1882 Sedalia Police Force.) Apart from Julia, their kids had mostly moved on in 1870. The boys, Henry, David Jr. and Edwin missed being counted and their whereabouts remain a mystery (through David Jr. was probably already in California). Mary Hogan Thomas and her family were living back in Vernon County, in a brand-new town called Moundville. Mary has hired household help. Amanda Hogan, 14, daughter of Esther is living with the Thomas' and helping with their two active boys. It was natural to have Amanda move in since she and Mary had grown up together under the same roof.

Uncle Davie was ministering at Bethel Congregation CPC to the northwest in Knob Noster, a town where brother William's family had located after leaving government service in Washington D.C. (with an unexplained sojourn in Iowa along the way). Knob Noster is at least a ten-mile ride mile ride from Davie's home, but the 58-year-old circuit rider was used to the saddle. He probably overnighted on William Hogan's farm at Knob Noster's north end. He and Cornelia and all five of their children, aged 16 to 23, have taken in Cornelia's father, James Beaury Holmead – a retired merchant and auctioneer from Washington D.C. who donated cane chairs to Congress in 1850. In addition to the eight of them, they have three Harte children (Cornelia's nephew and nieces) and two offspring of their former servants, John Hogan, 8, and Aaron Hogan, 1, who are being raised by Cornelia and William. Thirteen around the table must have made for a lively home.

---

[129] Post Oak is a historic township that no longer exists. It was just south of Warrensburg and the census lists the family as in the Warrensburg Post Office area of enumeration.

[130] *The History of Pettis County Missouri, 1882 History*, DVD (Higginsville, MO: Hearthstone Legacy Publishers, 2006)

The End of His Trail of Tears (1884-1893)

Their parents both having passed — the General three years ago, and Betsy just the previous year— Davie's generation are now the patriarchs of the Hogan Clan. Oldest brother Wilkinson and his wife Polly, now in their 60s, are Davie's neighbors, and still farming 1000 acres in Chilhowee. There is no lack of help. Their grown children have all established homes in the general vicinity. Three of Davie's brothers, John, James, and Robert, are practicing physicians and plying their trade in Bastrop, Texas; Fort Scott, Kansas; and Salem, Illinois; respectively. George is in Navarro, Texas and brother Moses is still on the original Hogan homestead in Arator, already a ghost town. Sister Elizabeth Hogan Wilson is also living in Fort Scott with her husband and one daughter. She must have enjoyed having her brother Dr. James so close. Davie's sister, Sarah Hogan Young, lives in the city of Lexington, Missouri.

Uncle Davie's 60th year began with two celebratory events. The second of Davie and Elizabeth's children to tie the knot tied it on Wednesday, the 25th of January 1871. The ceremony was in Lexington where the Hogan family had lived with Rev. Finis Ewing from 1839 to 1841. The "boy" getting married had been only a toddler when he lived in Lexington but was now 33 years of age. Ironically, he had been unable to attend his sister Mary's wedding because he was busy getting shot up in Arkansas during service for the Union. Now the whole family gathered to celebrate the union of Henry Hoss Hogan and Nancy Jane "Nannie" Fox.

On May 29th, Mary gave birth to Davie's first granddaughter, Julia Ethel Thomas. Now, surrounded by his wife, sons, daughters, son-in-law, daughter-in-law, two grandsons and a granddaughter; Davie felt like he was being given a taste of Heaven's bliss right here on earth.

In the fall of 1874, I received a call by the Argyle[131] congregation in Illinois, which I accepted, and took a letter

---

[131] The church had been called Beersheba while Davie pastored there. August 15, 1884 — a petition was made to the Rushville Presbytery to change the name Beersheba to Argyle. The average church attendance at

of dismission and recommendation from the Lexington to the Rushville Presbytery, McDonnagh County of Illinois.

Soon after Davie and Elizabeth began ministering up north, they received the joyous news that their daughter Mary had given birth to a healthy boy on November 16th in Parsons, Kansas. The Thomas family now had produced four grandkids for the Hogans, but the older two boys, Harry and Orlando sadly would not live much longer. Both are missing from the family in the 1880 census, probably carried off by cholera or another scourge of the frontier.

Living outside Missouri for the first time since 1837, Elizabeth and Davie, now in their sixties, found themselves craving news from home. They were riveted by news Jesse James had robbed the KATY train in Otterville on 7 July 1875. David's brother Moses wrote him about the exciting event that occurred just 4 miles east of his home (the original Hogan farm). Moses did his banking at Bank of Otterville, the closest town to his farm. Davie wrote back that although he had never knowingly met Jesse James, he was sure to have contributed more than his share to him when Quantrill's band (of which Jesse was a member) was raiding his old ranch in Vernon county.

A year passed and the invention of the Telephone was the talk of the home and congregation, but neither the parsonage at Beersheba Church nor any of Uncle Davie's Missouri and Texas family would have phone service for several years. Communication would remain limited to postal mail and occasional telegrams. The first Hogan to get a telephone was Davie's older sister Sarah, who was living a well-to-do life in Lexington with her husband Major Art Young. He had quite a bit laid by and had shelled out $10,000 for his church, First Presbyterian, to get a fine brick building. Davie had a softer spot for this "Old Presbyterian" congregation since it was the result of a merge of two congregations, one a Cumberland Presbyterian, whose first pastor was Finis Ewing. In fact, Davie had

---

that time was 60. Location of church: 5135 N. 1250th Rd. Colchester, IL 62326 (1 mile north of Argyle Lake State Park).

filled Ewing's pulpit and gotten to know Mr. Young, his future brother-in-law there.

Uncle Davie concludes his account on their Illinois sojourn with:

> Here I remained three years on a salary of $500 per year, the only years of my ministry I ever worked for a stipulated salary. I found I was losing, per year, nearly as much on my home in Missouri, as my salary, and in 1877, I returned to Missouri.
>
> On leaving Illinois, I took my letter from Rushville Presbytery, McDonnagh County and joined the Ozark Presbytery, Vernon County. During the time of my three year's stay in Illinois, Ozark Presbytery, Vernon County had wonderfully built up. Rev. E. E. Baker, an efficient worker, some two years before had located near Moundville, and become a member of the Ozark Presbytery, and was an active builder. Rev. R. L. Vannice, Rev. J. C. Allen, and other young men were licensed and placed in mission fields. They did an excellent work in organizing and reorganizing congregations; under their labors were many gracious revivals.
>
> On return from Illinois to Missouri, I began preaching all the time in the general bounds of Ozark Presbytery, and continued up to the 28th day of January 1882, . . ."

For the next four years, Rev. Davie Hogan was back in the saddle riding circuits again.[132] He ministered to Cumberland Presbyterian congregations in Vernon and Johnson counties; among them: Mary's Chapel, the CP Church in Montserrat and the one in

---

[132] From 1878 - 1882 (The Cumberland Presbyterian, June 16, 1904, page 764). Also: Billpenn@swbell.net, Wm. Hogan (1881; pg.791), 500.

Deerfield[133], along with returning to his old Rock Spring Church, where his elder brother Wilkinson and his family were stalwart members.

Davie began receiving exciting and troubling reports from his brother George in Navarro County, Texas. Davie's nephew, Cyrus Titus Hogan, was a lad of whom Uncle Davie was proud and took an interest in. Cyrus was an Elder in the CPC Church of Ennis, Texas. A revival had sprung up there and was causing quite a bit of consternation. Cyrus had invited the "Corsicana Enthusiasts" to do a meeting at his church. They, being mostly Methodist Holiness folk, had preached too hard (for some) against tobacco and worldliness. The Ruling Elders forced Cyrus to make them leave the building, but the meeting, and folks 'getting happy' continued outdoors. This Revival continued for years and bore the marks of the early Cumberland Presbyterian camp meetings. Healing, direct words from God, shaking hands and speaking in tongues were among the signs and wonders, as were hundreds of conversions. Apparently, Cyrus, his pastor and four other CP leaders became deeply involved. Other Cumberland Presbyterians and Methodists fiercely opposed the revival. By October 10, 1878 a Texas Holiness Association was formed with Cyrus T. Hogan as it's Secretary and Treasurer. Davie was thrilled at the signs that God was moving and concerned by the persecution and opposition the "Corsicana Enthusiasts" were stirring up. He was reluctant to sit in judgement on their beliefs (reported to him third hand) but felt they might be going too far in some of their methods of receiving Divine words and in setting a date for Christ's return. However, he remembered that God's moves were always accompanied by real manifestations that some inevitably took to ridiculous extents. Uncle Davie resolved to pray even harder for his nephew and the CP churches involved.

---

[133] David Hogan listed as a Minister in Deerfield, Ozark Presbytery in 1880 (Minutes of CPC 50th General Assembly, 1880.

The End of His Trail of Tears (1884-1893)

On a cold and snowy Sunday afternoon in January 1879, having ridden out the day before and preached in his old Rock Spring pulpit, Davie was relaxing in Wilkinson and Polly's comfortable parlor when A.J. Crutchfield, a cropper who worked Wilkinson's farm, rushed in waving a newspaper. "You Hogans made news up in Sedalia!" With that he threw down his copy of the *Sedalia Weekly Bazoo* which was already opened to page four. Davie picked it up and read the article entitled:

HOGAN

John Hogan, the colored man arrested by special agent Turner, in Webb City a week ago, for the murder of Robt. Fewell, was brought before Justice Clark yesterday, but his case was continued until Wednesday Jan. 23rd, Hogan of course persists in his innocence, and is confident that he can prove that he was not in Sedalia until Dec. 5th, two days alter Fewell was assaulted. He has been visited by Gen. Hogan, his former master, and has been furnished counsel to defend him. On the other hand, the testimony against him is said to be conclusive.

Davie finished reading and declared that the newspaper was living up to its usual standard of playing fast and loose with the truth. "My father, General Hogan, must've scared poor John to death when he visited his cell. In a fortnight Father will have been dead for twelve years!"

Once the hearty Hogan laughter abated enough to be heard, A.J. blurted in a torrent, "You're surely right that they get their facts snarled up. I got the whole story from the boy that sold me this paper in Sedalia Tuesday. This grubby kid knew more about the goings on than any newspaper editor. When I saw 'Hogan' I pumped him for details. The one visiting that murderer is your brother, Colonel William Hogan!"

With this intelligence the family fell into excited discussion while A.J. lobbed in fresh details like logs every time the conversational fire threatened to die down.

They all knew the unfortunate black man incarcerated in the Sedalia Jail. John had been owned as a boy by General David Hogan (the Bazoo had that part right). The General had made a gift of this

The End of His Trail of Tears (1884-1893)

"negro boy" to his son William and mentioned him in his 1857 Will as part of William's inheritance already bequeathed (in fact, Wilkinson and Davie had been gifted two slaves each at the same time and in like manner). Upon emancipation John had taken the surname Hogan and had remained remarkably close to Col. William and his family in the intervening years. He had been sent by Gen. David Hogan to William and Cornelia's home in Washington, D.C. and had returned to the Midwest with the family following the Civil War and William's leaving government service. John Hogan was about 23 years old. He lived in Knob Noster and helped on the Hogan farm there, but he had a bad habit of taking his wages and having a blowout with rough friends nineteen miles west in Sedalia. This wasn't his first run-in with the Sedalia police, though it was the most serious.

Apparently on December 3rd a fireman on the M K & T Railroad had been struck on the head and robbed. He lived long enough to identify his attacker as a negro loosely matching John Hogan's description. Police interviewed people in the black community, and several said that they'd heard John Hogan saying he'd hit a white man. John was identified as the prime suspect and a detective named Turner went on a prolonged manhunt that spanned three states before catching up with him just over a month later.

William had visited John in jail as soon as he'd heard he was locked up. Sam said that Sedalia was buzzing with the news that a white man of good reputation had spent real money and hired the two best lawyers in the city to defend the obviously guilty Negro.

Davie and Wilkinson had each known John since his birth and both declared that if John said that he was innocent and not even in Sedalia on the day Fewell was killed, then they believed him.

Davie was relieved that William had made sure John would have his day in court and not suffer the mob justice that seemed to be so much more common in cases like this. All the Hogans were anxious to hear how the trial played out. They wrote William for more details and asked him to send along newspapers mentioning the story to their home in Holden.

On February 4th everyone was thrilled to see in bold black text:

HOGAN ACQUITTED.

They already knew that the lawyers Col. William hired as John's defense team had subpoenaed several from Knob Noster to testify that, at the time that Fewell was robbed and murdered, John Hogan had been processing hogs on the Hogan farm — 19 miles away! John won a full acquittal, even it if did come with a mandate to leave Sedalia at once and never return.

June 1, 1880 — Census Day. Time for the tenth decennial census of the United States. The Rev. Davie Hogan had been around long enough to be enumerated in seven of these decennial counts. The Enumerator caught up with the Hogan family on the 12th of June at their home on the Big Dry Wood Ranch. David M. and Elizabeth Blackburn Hoss Hogan had re-occupied their old home in 1878 upon their return from Illinois ministry. Davie's occupation is listed as "Minister of the Gospel" and Elizabeth seems to have retired from active work in education. She is simply "keeping house". The sole Hogan offspring remaining with her parents is Julia P Hogan, by this time 30 years of age and probably viewed by the neighbors as an "old maid" or spinster. Julia's occupation was given as "At Home".

As for their other offspring, as previously mentioned, Henry and Nannie Hogan were on their farm adjacent to his parents' Big Dry Wood Ranch Henry is listed as "Farmer." They've been married for nine years and are still childless. They must blame Henry's Civil War groin injury.

David Hogan, Jr. has been out mining gold in California for at least eight years[134]. The census finds him in Shingle Springs gold camp listed as a "Miner". He is following his father's footsteps as well as carrying his name. He is still single and lives alone.

Mary Elizabeth Hogan Thomas is living with her husband Phillip and their two living children: Earnest Augustus (6) and Julia Ethel (9). Their first two boys, Harry and Orlando, having perished in the years since the last census. No account of these deaths has yet

---

[134] David registered to vote in Santa Rosa, CA in 1878.

The End of His Trail of Tears (1884-1893)

been discovered. The Thomas family has moved yet again. From Fort Scott, Kansas to Moundville in Vernon County, to Parsons, Kansas; they're now working the mines in a Colorado boomtown called Kokomo. Silver was discovered there the previous year and it already boasted 10,000 inhabitants. Today hardly a trace of Kokomo remains, but in 1880 it was in its heyday. Phillip Yelton Thomas has recast himself from clergyman to miner. They are housing another miner, Bill Sipple, a friend from their last home in Parsons, Kansas.

Edwin Grant Hogan missed being counted in 1880, but two years later he's in Kokomo, Brother Edwin had been there from the start, running his newspaper, the Summit County Times and probably living with Mary and her family. At an elevation of 10,618 feet, Kokomo is among the highest towns in the United States. The town had just burned to the ground (for a second time) this year and, though rebuilding was underway, it was entering its decline. Both the Thomas family and Edwin were probably weighing their options and looking for new homes. Edwin shut down his paper. It was too much to rebuild from the ashes and face new competition from two other newspapers. He quickly resettles in Vernon county.

Uncle Davie's elder three siblings are in their early seventies, and most are enjoying a slowing down of life and their grandchildren.

Wilkinson is still working his Chilhowee farm in Johnson County, Missouri. Wife Mary is listed as "bedridden" and they have a young A.J. living with them as a "cropper". Within 14 months both Mary and Wilkinson will be buried in Shiloh Cemetery, nearby their homestead.

Sarah Ann and her husband, Major Young are farming in Lexington, Missouri. They are comfortable enough to have hired a 17-year-old girl as cook. They have raised Art's six children from his first marriage and finally have an empty nest.

Dr John Hogan is practicing medicine in Bastrop, Texas and his wife Hortensia is "keeping house". Their children (the youngest is 30) have all moved on. They have an unrelated young family of three Jacksons living in their home. The father is listed as "Farmer" as is every near neighbor, so it seems that William Jackson is cultivating John's land for him.

That accounts for Davie's elder siblings, now what about his younger brothers and sister, now in their fifties and sixties?

Col. William Hogan, four years a widower, is still on his farm just outside the north city limit of Knob Noster, not very far from Wilkinson. He seems to be retired from active labor, but his home is a hive of business activity. Only one of William and Cornelia's five kids moved out of the family home. Eugene, his wife Jennie Rouch, and their three small boys, are living in Knob Noster — an easy walk between the homes. Of the other children, only James has married — three months before — to Miss Maggie Fisher. The newlyweds are living with James' dad. James and his brother William have gone into the Fruit Tree business in a large way. They are both listed as "Fruit Tree Dealers" and their brother Eugene as a "traveling fruit tree salesman". The home and headquarters even have a "fruit tree salesman" boarder in Mr. Everett Miller, who, within a year will be wed to his bosses' sister Alice. Medora "Dora" Hogan remains the unmarried "Music Teacher" but wedding bells are soon. Next door to the bustling Wm. Hogan place is another William Hogan and his 20-year-old daughter, Alice "Ally" Hogan. This William is first cousin to Col. William and Rev. Davie through General David's brother John.

Dr. James Hogan is still caring for patients at Fort Scott, just 10 miles west of Davie's Big Dry Wood Ranch. Fort Scott is no longer a military outpost and the city of over 5000 has become a premier city of the frontier, one of the largest in eastern Kansas and a competitor with Kansas City to become the nation's rail hub. Dr. James, a bachelor, enjoys the cooking of his sister, Elizabeth Hogan Wilson, most nights at her sumptuous home on the old fort's parade ground — the former Officer's Housing that her husband, Heiro Wilson, bought at the fort's decommissioning auction. Heiro and Elizabeth's three girls are all married, and one, Elizabeth Wilson Goodlander and her husband, lives with her parents in the Wilson-Goodlander house (photo pg.130).

Col. George and Elizabeth "Ellen" Hogan are also "empty nesters" except for a non-related 12-year-old girl living in their home. He is

The End of His Trail of Tears (1884-1893)

listed as a "gardener" and Ellen "keeps house" in Ennis, Ellis County, Texas.

Moses D. Hogan and wife Mary have three of their daughters and two sons all unmarried and still living with them at his parents' old homestead and farm in the ghost town of Arator, above Smithton, in Pettis county. Moses and his boys are all farming.

Dr. Robert Hogan is six years a widower and still practicing medicine in Marion County, Illinois. He is boarding in the home of the Edes, an illiterate tailor and his sister. One of their most prominent neighbors is William Jennings Bryan, a 20-year-old college student in 1880 but whose parents were already locally famous. Robert's married daughter Alice Norris has moved away. Robert is the farthest afield of General David's offspring. He will be dead in four months at just 54 years of age. He is buried at East Lawn Cemetery in Salem, Marion County, Illinois under a large obelisk. Strangely, his wife of 20 years, was laid to rest in a different section of the cemetery, though she has an inscription on his monument.

The only other relative that warrants a mention is Samuel Lane Hogan, 48, Wilkinson's eldest, Uncle Davie's first nephew, and first Hogan born in Missouri (1832, at the tannery at Tebo Grove, just before the rest of the clan arrived from Kentucky). In 1880 Sam had a ranch on Magoon Creek in Mariposa County, California. This ranch had been the scene of a battle in the Mariposa Indian War of 1851: *"The Battle of Hogan's Potato Patch."* In 1860 Sam married a native woman, a Mariposa Band Ahwahnechee named Mary Ann Austin and the couple had produced nine children by the time of this census, with another "in production". He'd almost certainly come to prospect gold, but the boom was already fading, and he quickly decided that the real money was indeed underground, but in taters! Sam's cousin, David Hogan, Jr. (son of Uncle Davie and now 40) was also in California's gold country, but 125 miles north. They probably didn't see much of each other.

Julia married A. J. Bass, a butcher from Virginia City, Nevada (another silver boomtown. Had Mr. Bass come to check out the Kokomo diggings only to meet Julia's siblings and hear of a different undiscovered precious ore living in southwest Missouri?).

The End of His Trail of Tears (1884-1893)

The couple wed at Davie and Elizabeth's Deerfield home on the 6th of October 1881. David proudly walked his daughter down the aisle for her nuptials ably performed by CPC colleague R.B. Ward. Joining the happy parents on this proud and joyful day were most of their Hogan and Hoss siblings and their families:

From David's side — Wilkinson and Polly Hogan and some of their 10 offspring came from Chilhowee (88 miles); Sarah Ann and Maj. Arthur Young traveled by train the 134 miles from Lexington in Lafayette County; Col. George (newly-minted Justice of the Peace) and Elizabeth Hogan came north by train 440 miles from Ennis, Texas; brother William M. Hogan, a widower, came with his five kids from Knob Noster in Johnson County (112 miles); Mary and Moses D. Hogan were living on the original Arator homestead (120 miles) and came via the Missouri-Kansas-Texas Railroad (MKT or Katy), Dr. James Hogan and sister Elizabeth Hogan Wilson were just 12 miles away at Fort Scott, KS where the Wilsons were living in the sumptuous former Officers' House they purchased when the fort was decommissioned. The only brother to miss the celebration was Dr. John D. Hogan who not only lived the farthest in Bastrop, Texas, but was still bitter about being passed over in General David Hogan's will. John's unreconstructed Southern sympathies made family gatherings a bit of a minefield.

From the Hoss family (Elizabeth's siblings) — Widowed Aunt Julia Hoss Parke, came the 80 miles south with her daughter Cousin Mary Parke Chaney and her "Old Presbyterian" minister husband, Rev. Chaney, with whom she lived in Pleasant Hill, Cass County, Missouri. Julia's uncles Sam and Archie Hoss live in far-off California and could not have come, but her Aunt Emma Hoss Arnold along with husband Finis and twelve-year-old Cousin Katie would have been there to share in the celebration[135].

The new couple seem to have moved to Kokomo to join Julia's siblings in the silver mines. Sadly, the marriage was over almost before it began. In under four months, Mr. Bass was out of the

---

[135] By 1900, Davie, Julia, and Uncle Finis Arnold were all widowed and living together at her Central Hotel in Cambridge City, Indiana. Julia was obviously close to her Aunt Emma's family, the Arnolds.

picture and Julia's life. There's scant trace in the records of what may have happened, whether annulment, or abandonment.[136].

---

[136] Aspen, CO put out a $7.50 warrant for A. J. Bass in January 1893. This indicates that he was living and had committed a petty crime in Colorado 12 years after the ill-fated marriage to Julia Hogan. In 1905 he may be living in Gove, KS. This Alexander Jasper Bass died in Parsons, Kansas in 1918.

BEREFT (1882-1883)

As January 1882 wound to an end, Rev. David Hogan was dealt a severe blow. His beloved partner of 45 years, Elizabeth Blackburn Hoss Hogan, died suddenly of heart attack. Davie was almost completely alone in his grief. The only person sharing his loss and lonely home was Esther, the 47-year-old black woman he'd emancipated years before who'd become part of the family. The eldest son, Henry, lived nearby with his wife Nannie. They'd failed to produce children due to Henry's war injuries. David, Jr. was far away in Sacramento, California, striving to duplicate his dad's gold mining success. The other three surviving children, Edwin, Julia and Mary were all living in a Colorado mining boomtown. Julia, recently separated after less than four months as Mrs. Bass, was living in Kokomo, Colorado with her sister Mary's family.

". . . the 28th day of January 1882, which is the day of the death of my dear, beloved wife, on which event, not a soul was left in the house, but myself and an old colored woman whom I had owned up to emancipation by the war. After her emancipation, she ever refused to leave her home. My children were all grown: two daughters and the youngest son in Colorado, second son in California, and eldest son on his farm one-mile distant, who was the only child that could accompany me, in sorrow and grief, at the burial of the mother. He was not present to see her breathe her last, on account of the peculiarity of instant death by heart failure. He could have no warning.

This mother's mortal remains are deposited in Deerfield cemetery, beside the grave of her third son, Cyrus O. Hogan, who died in his twenty-first year, on the 25th day of December 1862.

Bereft (1882-1883)

Uncle Davie and Henry laid Elizabeth to rest on the first day of February 1882. Davie had carved upon her monument:

ELIZABETH B.

WIFE OF REV DAVID HOGAN

BORN DEC. 16, 1815

DIED JAN 28, 1882

Rev. R. B. Ward composed contained a moving obituary:

> HOGAN — Died, Jan. 28, 1882, Mrs. Elizabeth B, wife of Rev. David Hogan, of Ozark Presbytery, in Vernon County, MO. She was the daughter of Henry and Mary Hoss; her father having been chosen president of Greeneville College, East Tenn. , moved to that place — there she received a large portion of her education. She was indeed a lady of learning. She professed religion in her 13th year, and afterwards joined the Presbyterian Church. Nov. 16, 1836, at Greeneville College she was married to Rev. David Hogan, in 1837 they removed to Georgetown, Pettis County, MO. ; here she joined the Cumberland Presbyterian Church. She immediately began an important school, but in 1838 was called to take charge of the first Female Academy of Lexington, MO. , which was the antecedent to the present Elizabeth Aull Institute. A sizable portion of her life was spent in teaching, and numbers of the mothers and grandmothers of our country received instruction at her feet. Her religious life was very exemplary; she was indeed a helpmeet for a minister; and I have heard Uncle Davie say for twenty-five years she almost supported himself and family. And as I say this allow me to say I feel ashamed of calls I have seen in the paper for ministers without wives or families. She was ever ready to encourage him in his work.
> Her sympathy for the minister was great. When I have been at her house, I found her as a loving, tender mother. She had, perhaps, no warning of her death, as it was from heart disease; but in her life she left the marks of a godly walk. But she has gone—left behind her weeping children and a loving husband. To father Hogan I would say—your days of sorrow cannot be many; your three-score years and

Bereft (1882-1883)

> *ten have already been numbered, and ere long you will meet again in "the sweet by and by."*

The Cumberland Presbyterian, *March 23, 1882*

My two daughters, on learning of the death of their mother, came as quickly as possible to their bereaved father and the old servant woman[137], who felt they had lost all that had constituted the earthly light and happiness of the humble home.

After a stay of several weeks, the eldest[138] returned to her family, but the youngest,[139], having no family, stayed with me, endeavoring to give all possible comfort by helping me to bear my severe load of grief. Here was the lonely home of grief for myself, daughter, and old servant, from January 28 to October 2nd, 1882, when I gave possession to a gentleman who had bought the farm and home in all this proceeding.

The dream of being a rancher had been knocked out of Davie by the war, and the loss of Elizabeth completed what war began. On October 2nd, 1882, he sold the Big Dry Wood Ranch to a neighbor named John Klontz. It is unknown whether the Deerfield Post Office he had operated from the lower story continued or was moved elsewhere. The pigeonholes from the desk (see illustration pg.109) used by Postmaster David M. Hogan are still on display in the Bushwhacker Museum in nearby Nevada, Missouri.

Uncle Davie, Julia and Esther stayed four nights with Henry and Nannie, on their farm, which he'd given to Henry from the Big Dry Wood property years before. On October 6th the three loaded up their possessions into Henry's buckboard and made their way eight

---

[137] Esther, 47 years old.
[138] Mary Elizabeth Hogan Thomas
[139] Julia P. Hogan Bass, now single again.

miles east to the KATY station in Nevada. As Henry started the drive back to his farm, there were further tearful farewells on the platform.

> On the 6th day of October 1882, myself and daughter boarded the M.K.&T. train for Ennis, Texas; and on the same railway, to her daughter's home in Clinton, Missouri, the old servant journeyed. This was a painful parting with all three.

'The old servant' Davie from whom parts in tears was Esther (hardly old at 47), the 22-year-old woman with a girl infant General David Hogan had bequeathed him in 1857[140] and mentioned as part of Davie's inheritance in the General's Will. Soon after joining David and Elizabeth's household, Esther gave birth to another daughter. This child was listed as a two-year old mulatto female in the 1860 Census Slave Schedule and appears likely to have been fathered by a white man before her mother came to live with Rev. Davie's family. She gave birth to a son, George, a year later. In any case, it seems that soon Uncle Davie found himself the reluctant owner of four human beings. He had imbibed anti-slavery values both in his education[141] and from his mentors and faith. He never purchased a human in bondage; his father gifting him these and their increase, and he only owned them for eight years. In 1865 all slaves in Missouri were emancipated. It is telling that all four took the surname Hogan and stayed with the family as free family members; in Esther's case, for 17 years! Both daughters eventually married and moved away, and George Hogan joined Sedalia's

---

[140] 1857 Will of Gen. David Hogan: "To my Son David I have given a negro woman and child, and cash, and I estimate the whole at $1300."

1860 *Slave Schedule* for Davie Hogan: 25-year black female and two girls: 4 year old black & 2 year old mulatto.

[141] Greeneville College was an anti-slavery institution. In 1806, freedman John Gloucester became the first African American student to attend Greeneville College. He was the first African American to graduate from college in Tennessee and later helped found the First African Presbyterian Church in 1807, in Philadelphia.

Bereft (1882-1883)

Police Department, but Esther only left her adopted family when the home she loved was dissolved in the wake of Elizabeth Hogan's passing. The familial love between former servant and masters was real - a grief to tear apart.

The choice of Ennis, Texas was due to an invitation from his brother, Col. George Madison Hogan, seven years Davie's junior. George, his wife Elizabeth and their three-year-old son, George, had moved to Texas in 1846, accompanied by brother William Hogan and William's wife Cornelia, and her father. They'd all settled in Navarro County, and in 1848 George had become the first Postmaster (a family tradition) of Muskete (later Chatfield, TX) and he and William worked hard to tame the wild country — building roads and bridges among other endeavors of settlement. But, in 1851, William's family moved to Cornelia's hometown, Washington D.C. for a government post, and stayed on for sixteen long years.

The Civil War drove wedges between brothers. In 1861, George was hauled into court to answer for William, Cornelia, and her father James Holmead. The plaintiff was a first cousin, John B Hogan, from the Mississippi branch of the family. The cause was an unpaid $70 debt, but rebel bitterness over William serving in the Lincoln Administration was almost surely why the debt was suddenly due and payable. George testified that all three were non-residents of Texas and a "citation to appear" was issued (and never answered). Two and a half years later George joined the rebellion and enlisted in the Confederate Army as a Private. One can just imagine the simmering family hurts this conflict brought. After the war, George and his family stayed on in Navarro County where he was Justice of the Peace until an 1880 move to Ennis in Ellis County. George listed his new career as "gardener" in the 1880 census. It was to this new home that the grieving Davie and daughter Julia made their way — to move in with a brother David had rarely laid eyes upon for three and a half decades. The adjustments proved to be too formidable, and they lasted only five months in George's home. As Davie admits, his deep grief made him less socially flexible than he'd been throughout his long life. George and Davie were far apart in matters of faith, politics, and opinion ("the environments in Texas ") though they'd grown up in the same family. George's estrangement from others dear to Uncle Davie must have been a strain as well. It became clear that another move would benefit all concerned.

Myself and daughter lived in Ennis from October 1882 till the 1st of March 1883. My extreme grief over the loss of my wife still seemed at times, unbearable, whilst I know I fervently and earnestly prayed to God for submission; also, the environments in Texas were not favorable to the relief of my state of mind. Hence, during my stay in Texas, my physical strength was greatly reduced, and I determined to leave, as soon as I could so arrange.

Deerfield Cemetery, Elizabeth Blackburn Hogan monument and detail

THE END OF HIS TRAIL OF TEARS (1884-1893)

Although zealous Cumberland Presbyterian preachers have often visited the Cherokees and held meetings, yet it was but recently that the board sent permanent missionaries to that field. The first of these was the Rev. N.J. Crawford, in whose veins there is some Indian blood. He determined in 1876 to cast his lot among the Cherokees. More than 400 conversions were reported as the result of his meetings prior to 1885.

. . . The first Cumberland Presbyterian Church among the Cherokees was organized by N.J. Crawford in 1877. It is in the eastern part of the Cherokee country and is known as the Prairie Grove congregation. There was a great revival among the Cherokees in 1880 and 1881.

In 1874 a Cherokee boy came to Cumberland University, Lebanon, Tennessee, to prepare for the ministry. He was graduated in 1879 and is now in his native land preaching Jesus. His name is R.C. Parks. His churches now number over a hundred members. [142]

Davie was always very alert to the doings of his precious Cumberland Presbyterians and the Cherokee Tribe had been a special interest for over five decades. We can be confident that he was thrilled hear to Rev. Crawford's reports of this revival from the field. Did he have a sense that his dream to be part of God's move among this people was just a few years in the future?

> *While in Texas, I had earnestly prayed our Father in Heaven to direct my work and my mind to the right field: in*

---

[142] McDonald's History of the Cumberland Presbyterian Church, 4th Ed. Nashville. Board of Publication of Cumberland Presbyterian Church, 1899.

this submission, I was more inclined to go among the Cherokees than elsewhere.[143]

How amazing to witness a call to ministry that God planted in the heart of a twenty-two-year-old seminarian, long nurtured and watered, joyfully fulfilled fifty years later. "Great is Thy faithfulness, Lord God Almighty."

At the General Assembly at Austin, Texas, in 1881, I had made the acquaintance of Rev. N. J. Crawford, who had charge of the mission work in the Cherokee Nation. I had determined to write him about my being his fellow helper in the work among the Cherokees; he gave a quick reply, urging me to come as soon as possible. I determined to do so if all things favored. My daughter[144] *had consented to go with me anywhere that would restore my former and happy cheerfulness.*

I wrote to Ex-Chief Col. William Potter Ross, a Cherokee, who had been a classmate at Greeneville College.[145] *He politely and quickly replied that his people would rejoice to have me; also, urging me to be sure and get a commission from the Mission Board of my Church. This demand gave me trouble in mind; you ask how? Answer: I am now in my seventy-second year. Will the Board commission a man of that age? I fear it will not.*

---

[143] Davie here relates his meeting schoolmate John B. Jones and the impact on his call to the Cherokee. This has been included chronologically on page 33.

[144] Daughter Julia was living with her widower dad as he grieved.

[145] Another 'God Nod' in Davie's long calling to the Cherokee Mission.

*I, however, wrote to the Board referring them to Rev. J. H. Hacey, Dr. G. L. Moad. and S. Finis King[146] of the Lexington Presbytery, in regard to my capabilities of still doing work, even at my advanced age. Yet, I somewhat begged the question, saying, if they would commission me, I would serve the best I could, without salary. I got the commission, and in its wording it said, "without **salary**". I worked 12 years and the Board never gave me one cent. Thank God! The work was done for Him, and the Books will balance correctly."*

"In coming to the Nation, my stopping place, as directed by Rev. N. J. Crawford, was Gibson Station, the nearest point to his residence on the M. K. & T. (Missouri-Kansas-Texas) Railroad[147]. The station is just inside the Creek Nation[148] and is settled by both Creeks and Cherokees.

"Tiny Gibson Station was the terminus for the railroad and "it was not uncommon for several dozen area residents to descend upon Gibson Station whenever a train was scheduled to arrive. Many came to send out freight or welcome travelers, but just as many

---

[146] Rev. S. Finis King. Born 1848 near Warrensburg, in Johnson County, MO. Born-again at 17. Pastor at Mt. Hebron, Harrisonville, Shiloh, Mt. Zion, Shawnee Mound, Pisgah, Columbus, Odessa, Warrensburg, Urich and Walnut Grove. Secretary of the Board of Missions and Clerk Treasurer of Lexington Presbytery. Died January 24, 1902.

[147] The Gibson Station was the first passenger and freight station built in Indian Territory, now Oklahoma, constructed in 1872 by the MKT Railroad.

[148] The Creek (Muskogee) are the people, marooned on Eagle Island during The Trail of Tears, Davie viewed from the roof of his flatboat cabin. Fitting his arrival on the field is in their Nation.

came to enjoy the spectacle of the smoke-belching steam engines pulling into town."[149]

> My daughter and I had only to walk a few steps from the depot to the tavern. The proprietor had our trunks and luggage brought to the tavern. I directly asked him if he knew where Rev. N. J. Crawford lived, and how far from this; he replied, "Eight miles." I said, I wished to get word that evening to Mr. Crawford, if possible. He replied, "I think Miss Belle Cobb is in town. I will see if she is here, and if so, will have her come in. She can take any information to Mr. Crawford you may wish." He at once sent out for Miss Cobb, and politely introduced us. While Miss Cobb and I were in conversation, he was giving an apparent unnoticed attention. Miss Cobb was expecting me there soon but did not know the exact day. Our conversation gave the proprietor a good knowledge of who I was, and what my business to the Nation was. Ms. Cobb was, and is today, one of the prominent, if not the most prominent, Cumberland Presbyterians in the Cherokee Nation. She is highly accomplished; she is an M.D. from the Medical School at Philadelphia, Pennsylvania.[150]
>
> Under Superintendent Crawford, I was located at Chouteau in Cooweescoowee District, and my field of labor appointed. There was a good deal of traveling to do, yet not equal to our first circuit riding. I had charge of two

---

[149] *Muskogee Phoenix*, Jun 28, 2015, by Jonita Mullins.

[150] *Isabelle Cobb, M.D. studied medicine in some of the best colleges in the East and locating at her hometown, Wagoner, Indian Territory, she is still pursuing the duties.* Online at archive.org: *An Illustrated Souvenir Catalog of the Cherokee Female Seminary Tahlequah. Indian Territory 1850 To 1906.*

organized congregations and two outposts. I found the people kind and hospitable wherever I went; appointments well attended, and a listening ear given to the gospel. We were soon able to organize churches at the different outposts, and so extended the work for the Master.

The Cumberland Presbyterian preaching force at this time consisted of Rev. N. J. Crawford, Rev. R. C. Parks[151], myself and licentiate.[152] And from facts I shall hereafter state, perhaps the Cumberland Presbyterian Church would be stronger today in the Cherokee Nation, if there had not come to the territory another Cumberland preacher till now.

[At this point Rev. Hogan includes a section of exposé on the mission field characters who caused great consternation. To facilitate the narrative flow this portion of his *Autobiography* is in 'Recapitulations'.]

Uncle Davie and Julia had scarcely unpacked at their new home on the mission field when they got news from Vernon County the youngest Hogan offspring, Edwin, had finally married. At a small private ceremony at the Rockwood Hotel[153] in Nevada, Missouri, Edwin Grant Hogan and Elizabeth Esther Palmour Smith of Moundville were married by Rev. McClure on Tuesday, May 8, 1883. The wedding and reception were over before Davie could think about attending. It would have been nice to gather the children and grandchildren. All could have come, except for David, Jr. out in Sacramento, California starting a mining supply business.

---

[151] Rev. R.C. Parks, a Cherokee, recent Cumberland University grad who joined Davie after two months.

[152] Rev. J.H. Kelly of Arkansas Presbytery, was this licentiate, later an early pastor of the CPC of Prairie Grove,AR and CPC Fayetteville, AR.

[153] this Italianate building still stands at 126 W. Walnut in Nevada. Right across the street from the Bushwhacker Museum that houses a letter box from Uncle Davie's desk (picture pg.94).

The End of His Trail of Tears (1884-1893)

Only he, of the five surviving siblings, remained a bachelor. Julia's marriage to Mr. Bass was over, but at least she'd married.

Having missed his son's wedding, Davie was cheered to learn the newlyweds would be making a honeymoon stop at his mission station. They intended to make their home in Indian Territory so Edwin could break into the cattle business. Uncle Davie and Julia hoped Ed and Lizzie would be frequent visitors.

Further background on the C.P. Cherokee Mission work:

*"There are curious items about some of our missionaries in that field. The **Rev. David Hogan** had been preaching fifty years before he determined to become a missionary. He has preached along with Finis Ewing in other days. With his own hands he closed Finis Ewing's eyes when that hero of the Cross fell asleep in Jesus. A most interesting thing it is to hear Hogan talk of his early experiences. He says: "My church is better known and held in higher esteem in heaven than it is on earth." When he was seventy-one years old, he said to the Board of Missions: "If you will commission me as missionary to the Cherokee Indians, without salary, I will spend the rest of my days preaching to that people." The commission was given him, and now for more than three years he has been laboring in this mission field.*

*The Cherokee Presbytery was organized in February 1884, at the residence of the Rev. R.C. Parks, Canadian District, Indian Territory. N.J. Crawford, **David Hogan**, and R.C. Parks were the original members. J.H. Kelley, licentiate, placed himself under the care of the presbytery at its organization. This presbytery now has five ordained ministers, two probationers, and seven congregations, with nine out-stations. The aggregate number of communicants is four hundred and fifty.*

*One of the schools in the Cherokee country is partially under the care of our Woman's Board of Missions — that is, this board has been giving it assistance. This school is known as **Hogan Institute**. Our native members and preachers have also aided in various other schools among the Cherokees. An item of interest connected with this presbytery is that a consecrated Christian young lady, Miss Belle Cobb, is its stated clerk. In the manuscript history of this presbytery, prepared by this lady, the work of N.J. Crawford, R.C. Parks, J.H. Kelley, **David Hogan**, Laman Carter, and J.H. Pigman is described with a fullness of detail which cannot be repeated here. This interesting narrative closes with some statements which are brief enough to be quoted:*

In May 1886, the Rev. Joseph Smallwood, of the Methodist Episcopal Church, South, a full blood Cherokee Indian, was, by a commission

The End of His Trail of Tears (1884-1893)

appointed by the presbytery, received as a minister in the Cumberland Presbyterian Church. All the ministers in this presbytery are now in the field and identified with the Cherokee people, and, under God, and by the help of his Holy Spirit, intend to maintain and advance the church's work among them. The Board of Missions has three missionaries in the Cherokee Nation: Rev. N.J. Crawford, with a salary of $25 per month; the Rev. R.C. Parks, with a salary of $8.33 per month; and the Rev. David Hogan, without a salary. The presbytery has one missionary in the field, the Rev. Joseph Smallwood, with a salary of $12.50 per month.

We predict a bright future for the Cumberland Presbyterian Church in the Cherokee Nation. The intelligence of the people, the self-sacrifice of the ministry, and the leadings of the Holy Spirit all point to the success of the church and the glorification of God in the salvation of this people." [154]

Uncle Davie must have sensed the glowing pleasure of his departed educator wife Elizabeth as he founded a school for education of students from the Cherokee, Choctaw, and Chickasaw Nations in the town of Locust Grove. In 1884, the Board of Directors met and named the school *Hogan Institute* in honor of its founder and senior minister of the Cherokee Presbytery.[155] Tuition for the Hogan Institute — free to "any indigent or orphans" — was set at $2.00 per month discounted over time to a top lifetime rate of $500 (a 33 $1/3$% discount). The Cumberland Presbyterian Women's Mission Board served by subsidizing teacher salaries. The school was dedicated *"to the Honor of God in the education of the youth . . . The object shall be to disseminate a knowledge of Literature & Science & to impress the mind with the importance of an experimental knowledge of Jesus Christ as a Personal Savior."*[156]

David Hogan his mark on the Nation. In addition to his school there is the small town of Hogan, the Hogan Cemetery which adjoins the

---

[154] *The History of the Cumberland Presbyterian Church;* Benjamin McDonnold.

[155] WEB: cumberland.org/hfcpc/schools/HoganInstitute.htm

[156] Source: "Session Records of Locust Grove Cumberland Presbyterian Church. Saline District. Cherokee Nation. Indian Territory. (Now Locust Grove, Mayes County, Oklahoma). January 2, 1887 to February 21, 1890.

grounds where the Institute once stood, and dozens of Cherokee boys given the first name 'Hogan' in honor of this much-loved missionary educator.

> *At the end of the year, my daughter went to Oswego, Kansas, and lived with her youngest brother[157] till she married Frederick William Fraunberg. This you see, left me to live and home, in the homes of the Cherokees, which I ever found welcome, and quite pleasant.*

Having settled into his missionary labors with a growing school to run, David was happy and busy enough for Julia to think again on her own future. Having been married for such disastrously brief time might have posed obstacles to entering another relationship, but Julia was plucky and resourceful. She figured she'd meet more eligible men living with her brother in his new Kansas home, than in the role of "Old Maid Missionary" on the Cherokee Nation. Edwin, ever restless, had given up cattle trading having discovered that only Cherokee could own cattle on the Nation. Most whites got around this by partnering with locals to lend their name to make the enterprise legal. The preferred method was to marry a Cherokee woman. Edwin was hampered in following prevailing business practice as he was already married. Soon the ever-restless young man moved his bride north into what he hoped would be better opportunities in the Labette County, Kansas town of Oswego.

Canny Julia was right! After only a couple months she was engaged to a successful German immigrant landowner, Fred Fraunberg.

Frederick W. Fraunberg (1838-1899)

---

[157] Edwin Grant Hogan (1853-1940)

The End of His Trail of Tears (1884-1893)

On Thursday, 15 May 1884, Julia P. Hogan Bass married for the second time. Frederick William Fraunberg had managed to wear many hats since coming from Germany with his father at the age of six. After being schooled on the "Queen of the Rivers", the Ohio at Cincinnati, he went to work on a Mississippi paddle wheeler at the tender age of twelve. Afterwards he ran a dry goods store, Chicago hotel, wholesale liquor distribution, and a pork packing plant, before moving near Parsons, Kansas where he bought one thousand acres. This was going to be a great spot for a cattle ranch because Parsons was the third largest railroad hub in the United States![158] Here, he met the lovely Julia Hogan Bass and, being a man who knew a good thing when he laid eyes on it, quickly proposed.[159] Davie was thrilled that Julia had at last found a man worthy of her. Though he'd performed almost 1000 weddings, Rev. David demurred from being the officiant. Rather than wade through the mine field of doctrinal problems with performing a second wedding ceremony for his youngest, coupled with fresh memories of celebrating her first nuptials with a vibrant and healthy Elizabeth at his side just three years before, Uncle Davie asked a Methodist Episcopal colleague to officiate, while he enjoyed playing 'Father of the Bride'.

Having discovered that he was not cut out for hands-on cattle ranching, Fred Fraunberg left his ranch to be managed by capable folks and built Julia a town home thirty miles southeast in Baxter

---

[158] The location for the town was chosen because it was where the two branches of the railroad being built from Junction City, Kansas and Sedalia, Missouri would meet and was on a ridge between Labette Creek and Little Labette Creek, which were soon dammed to provide a water source. The railroad commenced building a massive rail yard, foundry, and locomotive shop at Parsons, which was the third largest railroad facility west of the Mississippi River with only Kansas City and Los Angeles being larger. Settlers from nearby towns uprooted and moved to Parsons, and new settlers arrived on every incoming train. Parsons soon became a major hub for several railroads including the Missouri Kansas & Texas Railroad, Parsons & Pacific Railroad, Kansas City & Pacific Railroad, and the Memphis, Kansas & Colorado Railroad. (Wikipedia.org)

[159] Memoirs of Wayne County and the City of Richmond, Indiana: Vol II.

Springs; where she was somewhat closer to her father's mission station. This loving concession to wife and father-in-law is a precious window into Fred's character. Davie would have a child to visit only 70 miles along the railway to the north.

> *Soon after my work began with the Cherokee Indians, I became acquainted with Red-Bird Six-Killer, a full blood, a man about my own age, judging from facts of history. (No record of his birth.[160]) He remembers the first treaty made between the Cherokees and the United States Government in 1819, and thinks he was ten or twelve years old at that time. He has always since a mature man been a prominent character in his Nation, filling responsible offices in the tribal government. From our first acquaintance a warm attachment has existed between us. He professed religion in 1840 under the ministry of John B. Jones[161] and lived a consistent member of the Baptist church until the time he joined our Church at Locust Grove, N. J. Crawford having charge. A short time after he was elected a ruling elder of the congregation and was ordained. He was fervent in prayer, and always prayed in the Cherokee language. There are some living today who well remember his fervent prayer in the General Assembly at Sedalia, Missouri - the hearty Amen in the tears of many, the only way they could Amen, for they understood not his words.[162]*

---

[160] No record that Redbird knew of. He was about four years Uncle Davie's senior. His recollection to have been 12 when the Cherokee Treaty was signed was accurate.

[161] Bunkmate of Davie Hogan at Maryville, see page 46

[162] Davie's friend Lt. Redbird Sixkiller served as an elder of the Hogan Institute from the school's founding.

My mind was impressed that there was a historical meaning in his name. In an enjoyable talk one day, I asked him how he got the name Red-Bird?

He replied, "Oh! Way back, my grandfather was Chief Red-Bird."

"And how came the Six-Killer part?"

He replied, "In war he killed six white men when mad at one another - don't know when. Way back."

Now his replies presented a probable occurrence in the lives of our grandfathers, given to me in my boyhood by my grandfather Dorton.

In 1779[163] Daniel Boone made his third trip from North Carolina to Kentucky; in that emigration trip were both my grandfathers, Dorton and Hogan. Grandfather Hogan, a few days before the emigration started, married a young Betsy Fullington[164]; she was in the emigration. My grandfather Dorton was in his twenty-second year, and single; before he left his home on the Yadkin River, North Carolina, he became engaged to Miss Dicy Robinson[165], whom he married

---

[163] Davie remembers it as 1780 in his memoir, but history places the events a year earlier when Moses was 21 years of age.

[164] The adopted daughter of Daniel Boone, also known as Sarah Elizabeth "Betsy" Grant Hogan.

[165] She comes from a curious parentage. Dicy (whose full name was Laodicea Robinson was born in 1768 of the union of William Robertson, a North Carolina planter and a Native American woman, Charity Kennedy. In court he was charged that he "*On 10 January 1769 with force and arms did commit heinous crime fornication upon one certain Charity Kennedy*". The puzzling thing is the timing of the charge since the couple had already had three children (Nelson & twins Dicy & Billy) during the four years *before* this offence (The first birth when Charity was 14 yrs. old!). After the trial they got on with things and had another four little Robinsons. Since one could not be charged with rape of a lawful wife (at that time) they must have made their common law union official sometime between January

The End of His Trail of Tears (1884-1893)

sometime in the year 1781. When Boone's company had passed through Cumberland Gap and came to the ford of Cumberland River[166], Boone thought it proper to leave what was then termed a spy guard at the ford, as other emigrants would be on in a few days, and would be in great danger without a guard. My grandfather Dorton was left commander of the spy guard. I have often heard him tell the following story:

A few days after they were left, one mile from his camp at a place called the Narrows, a pass with only room enough for a wagon to pass between the mountain and the river, the Cherokee Indians attacked a little company of emigrants, and as I remember, killed six of the emigrant men, and took off with them a white woman and babe. The spies pursued the red rascals, as grandfather called them, up a creek into the mountain. He afterward named the creek Strait Creek and the mountain, in which it headed, he named Log Mountain[167]. There had been a hurricane or cyclone a brief time before, and it had felled the timber to the

---

1769 and March 1775 when they are recorded working out complicated land dealings as a married couple. (Charity later lived with her daughter Dicy and son-in-law, Moses Dorton in Kentucky by 1810).

[166] Since 1792, Moses' future father-in-law, Wm. Robertson had been running a fort, *Robertson's Station*, at this location on the Wilderness Road, located at Cumberland Ford, across the river from the present town of Pineville, Kentucky. It is quite probable that Moses obtained Dicy's dad's permission to wed his daughter on this very trip, having already obtained her consent before leaving North Carolina. It also seems likely that Moses' relationship with Robertson is what persuaded Boone to bring him along and entrust him as Commander of the Emigrant Spy Guard. *Robertson's Station* at the Fords of the Cumberland would become *Hogan's Tavern* and later *Dorton's Mansion Tavern*.

[167] Strait Creek and Log Mountain are both in today's Bell Co., KY.

ground so that the path had to surround it. They followed the Indian trail to the top of the mountain, and down on the opposite side twelve miles to a creek, on which the Indians were camped. He said he afterwards named this creek Red Bird. The Indians were taken by surprise, and number of them were killed, the Chief was taken prisoner, and the woman and child rescued.

The evergreen holly trees grew thickly on Strait Creek. On their return down said creek, many red birds were flying among the hollies. Their prisoner Chief pointed to the birds and then to himself, giving his captors the idea his name was Red-Bird, which was afterwards so proven. Hence my grandfather gave the little stream on which he captured his Chief the name of Red Bird, and that is its familiar name to this day. Captain Campbell[168], of

---

[168] Colonel (or Captain) David Campbell *(1753-1832)* founder of Campbell's Station, TN. He was a Scotsman from Virginia. Campbell and Moses Dorton would meet again, the following year, as comrades-in-arms at the

The End of His Trail of Tears (1884-1893)

Campbell's Station, Tennessee, obtained of grandfather, Chief Redbird[169], to exchange with the Indians for one of his men the Indians had taken. The exchange was made, and that was the last heard of Chief Redbird.

When I was a small boy riding on horseback behind my grandfather through the Narrows before spoken of, he pointed to a rather oblong heap of earth with some stones laid on its top, and said, "Under that heap of earth grandfather buried six men who were butchered and tomahawked here by the Cherokee Indians. I took the Chief prisoner and killed most of the red rascals."

Now, it is not only possible, but probable, and almost certain, here is the Red-Bird and the Six-Killer in the foregoing history, given by my grandfather and his grandfather. It is a strange occurrence, that their grandsons, after they had passed their three score and ten years, should meet - be in the same church communion, and his peculiar name so develop the history as to place it beyond doubt.

Battle of King's Mountain where Moses and his brother William served with him.

The Battle of Kings Mountain was a decisive victory in South Carolina for the Patriot militia over the Loyalist militia in the Southern campaign of the American Revolutionary War. In *The Winning of the West,* Theodore Roosevelt wrote of Kings Mountain, *"This brilliant victory marked the turning point of the American Revolution."* Thomas Jefferson called it, *"The turn of the tide of success."* President Herbert Hoover at Kings Mountain said, *"This is a place of inspiring memories. Here less than a thousand men, inspired by the urge of freedom, defeated a superior force entrenched in this strategic position. This small band of Patriots turned back a dangerous invasion well designed to separate and dismember the united Colonies. It was a little army and a little battle, but it was of mighty portent. History has done scant justice to its significance, which rightly should place it beside Lexington, Bunker Hill, Trenton and Yorktown."*

[169] *Dotsuwa* (Cardinal, a red bird) was is his Cherokee name.

When he accompanied me to the General Assembly at Sedalia, Missouri, all this history was clear to my mind, but I had not written it out at that time.

Time passes from 1780 to 1885 and the two grandsons of these hostile grandsires, meet and count that they have met in Christ Jesus the Lord, by faith and love. And I am fully persuaded we shall soon meet in Heaven above.

The encounter described between Moses Dorton and Red-Bird took place in 1779. Davie heard the story about four decades after the events happened. As an eyewitness participant in the events he described, Moses Dorton provides a remarkable window into a period of American history often obscured by lack of written accounts and sheer number of casualties and remote locations of settlers during these tumultuous years. References are few when it comes to the characters and events related in Moses' story. I have been able to piece together supporting evidence to identify 'Chief Red-Bird.'

The original Cherokee Chief named Red-Bird (Dotsuwa) was brutally murdered in 1796 by two whites from Tennessee. He can be ruled out as the Red-Bird captured by Dorton in 1779. The captured Chief Red-Bird related the identical story to his grandson — a boy not born by the date of this first Chief Red-Bird's 1796 murder. The most likely antagonist for Moses' account is the son of this Red-Bird, later known as Six-Killer.[170] Given the language gap existing between Dorton and his hostage, it would have been an easy mistake to understand a reference to the hostage's father as his own name. The honorific and descriptive name Six-Killer was still in the future for the 30-year-old Cherokee. It is possible that he was already a chief in his own right and had been named for his famous father — a second Chief Red-Bird.

---

[170] Sixkiller (1749-1864), son of Chief Red Bird (d.1796) and the father of Rufus Sixkiller (1776-1856). Rufus fathered Redbird Sixkiller (1807-1893). The name given the grandson is further evidence for the veracity of Moses Dorton's and Sixkiller's accounts and his heritage.

The End of His Trail of Tears (1884-1893)

David Hogan was seventy-three and starting to feel the years. Julia used the excuse of the birth of her first child to force him to take time off from the demanding Cherokee work. Davie came to the Fraunberg home in Cherokee County, Kansas for an extended visit to welcome his newest grandchild.

Frederick and Julia Fraunberg appeared in the Kansas State Census on the First of March 1885 in Neosho Township. David Hogan was also counted — listed as widowed and living with the family. If Davie told him it was only temporary, the Enumerator failed to make note of it.

Two days later Julia gave birth to a strong baby boy, Roy Humboldt Fraunberg. Holding his grandson in his arms eased David's grief, as wise Julia had known it would.

> *One salvation that came with my ministry occurred around this time. In the Tebo congregation of Henry County, I had an old friend, Uncle Jimmy Munday, who had passed his three score and ten and, who seemed to have no interest whatever in religious conversation. During a revival meeting I went to his home and being nearly equal in age, I thought I would talk to him in a very plain way about his eternal interests, and the little time he had to secure them. I said, "Uncle Jimmy (the way everyone addressed him) can I get you to think this evening that God tells you the truth when he says, 'Behold now is the accepted time; now is the day of salvation', and that you will accept it as your time and God's opportunity, and that you will accept salvation this day? He gave me his hand and showing signs of softening.*
>
> *I said to him as I felt, "This is your last call of mercy, the close of opportunity, and God will save you this instant if you will accept Jesus by saying in your heart, 'Thou art my Lord and my God.'" In one minute he embraced the offer and cried out "He is my Lord and my God" and for some*

months, even till he came to cross the cold river, he astonished his friends by every day rejoicing.

I will now tell a rather ludicrous anecdote on myself which happened to me in 1888, in the Cherokee Presbyterian Church, and to give it zest, I will relate one that Roger Sherman, one of the signers of the Declaration of Independence, used to tell of his brother, who was the old-style Baptist preacher. I came across it twenty years since in some old Boston journal. He (Roger) said that in the colonial days the church houses were log buildings and much of the men's wearing apparel was buckskin; his brother often wore his buckskin pants in his pulpit. His appointments were monthly. Now at his July appointment when he mounted his pulpit which had been vacant a whole month, all eyes were turned up looking to their good preacher. He read his 'hime' (as they termed it) it was sung, then a prayer, then another hymn, and he arose and announced his text, and in an instant was slapping the sides of his leather trousers first on one side and then on the other. They being a little dry and hard, the sound of his violent slaps fairly echoed. His audience began to look wild; some of them rose up as though they might have to hold him. He perceived their alarm and said to his audience "Don't be alarmed brethren and sisters, the Lord is in my heart and mouth, but the Devil is in my breeches."

Now the case developed, in vacation of the long summer month, the yellow hornets had built under the floor of his pulpit, and his step and stir on the floor had stirred the hornets, and they came through a knot hole, just under his feet: his breeches being a little stiff and sitting out from his legs, they had gotten inside his leathers to his naked legs *and were stinging him severely. It is said, Roger often told this, saying, "The hornets took the church that day."*

I had related this anecdote to N.J. Crawford. and other brethren of the Cherokee Presbytery. You will now be able to see the aptitude of the anecdote happening myself.

In 1889, a licensed preacher, R.C. Grace, came to the Cherokee Nation from Round Rock, Texas, holding a letter of dismissal as a licensed preacher, and was received under the care of the Cherokee Presbytery. He had married a young lady in Texas, one-quarter Cherokee, and she wished to live in the Nation. She was a great acquisition to our Sunday School work. In March 1890, at a regular session of Cherokee Presbytery, in the town of Chouteau, the committee on education recommended the ordination of R.C. Grace, which was approved, and I was appointed to preach the ordination sermon on the next day, Tuesday, at 11:00 A.M. The young man had preached his trial sermon Monday night.

When it came to the performance of my duty, to preach the ordination sermon, I went on the rostrum which had nothing on it but a chair and a small table. I numbered and read the hymn, the music was well rendered, the house was crowded to witness the solemnities of the ordination. I prayed, then the singing of three stanzas. Just while requesting the singing of the three stanzas, I thought I felt something crawling up my right leg inside of my pants.

As soon as I could, I sat down in the chair; the sensation increased, and I began grabbing at different points on my pants leg, hoping I could catch whenever it might be. My grabbing caused it to run down into my boot leg; I jerked the boot off quickly, but it instantly was again up the pants. All who were near the rostrum (Crawford in the midst), were looking with astonishment at my actions. The Sherman anecdote had come to Bro. Crawford's mind, and he could not restrain laughter. I put on my boot as the third stanza closed, but the crawling and scratching was still inside my pants leg. While announcing my text (1 Timothy 2:7a), many who had heard the Sherman anecdote could scarcely keep from laughing; by the time I was ready to say the first sentence, it ran down my pants leg, jumped off the rostrum, ran across the floor in front, and not thinking of the result on those who had been watching, I pointed my finger at the poor little church mouse as it ran across the floor and remarked, "There goes the thing that has been troubling me!"

A general laugh for one minute took place, whilst I took my chair. When I arose, I said, "Solomon said, 'There is a time to laugh and a time to cry.' Now if all are through with present laughter, I will go on to preach the required discourse." Repeating the text, Paul says, "Where unto I am ordained a preacher," the blessed Lord who ordained Paul, helped me to preach, and the service was truly solemn, and the time came for many to cry. Perhaps a mouse had never before, or ever will hereafter, trouble a Cumberland Presbyterian preacher, as this one did me. I have often thought since, it was alone in the Grace and power of God, to give the sudden turn in the mind of the audience that day. No preacher, who has faithfully, humbly, and lovingly delivered the message given him from Heaven to men on earth but has witnessed some remarkable conversions.

In 1886, at the Cumberland Presbyterian Convention in Sedalia, Missouri (a city founded by a man Davie had led to Jesus and baptized!) Rev. David M. Hogan was formally affirmed in his mission to the Cherokee Nation by the Board of Commissioners,

The End of His Trail of Tears (1884-1893)

CPC Synod of Arkansas. He gave a report of the remarkable progress of the work on his field and enjoyed his Church's recognition of his calling from God, so long delayed.

As so often happens, a high point was merely the prelude for devastating lows to come . . .

Just months after receiving the approbation of his peers in Sedalia, Uncle Davie faced another personal grief and a humiliating financial predicament. He had received crushing news from California about the death of his son, David, Jr. A newspaper clipping from Placerville's *The Mountain Democrat* of December 11th had accompanied the post carrying the news to the bereaved father. On December 3, 1886, David, who'd emulated his father in prospecting the California goldfields, was *"'drifting for gold' [with a partner] and had a dig of 6-8 feet deep when the side gave way and crushed David Hogan. Mashing his right leg and breaking his back, killing him."* This fresh loss, without even the closure of a burial service he could attend, overwhelmed Davie — at just the time he was again facing that familiar old enemy, financial ruin.

The Hogan Institute was struggling. Heavy taxes on the school and land were outstripping the income generated by paltry tuitions. Davie realized, due to his advanced age and grief-stricken state of mind, he was not going to be able to turn things around as he had with the Lexington debts and his Gold Rush success (even with encouragement from brother Moses of Otterville who blessed Davie with a donation of fifty dollars that year — the only recorded financial support from his family). Rev. Hogan was forced to hand over the school that bore his name - so loved by the Cherokee parents and pupils - to the administration of the Chouteau Presbytery who could subsidize it, effective January 2, 1887.

The impact of the Hogan Institute among the Cherokee was profound. Testifying to that, the Cherokee boys born during that period who were named for him. There was an Eastern Cherokee named David Hogan Gaylor who was born just after Davie's birthday in 1885 in Wagoner, just south of the Hogan mission station.[171] Below is a partial transcript of an interview with Hogan Markham (b. May 1891), Cherokee:

> EARLY DAY TOWNS AND SCHOOLS AND MISSIONS
>
> (Well, what towns were in existence at that time?)
>
> Well, Chouteau was in existence and Pryor was in existence. 'Course Locust Grove wasn't anything. It was just a school and a post office and a little old store there. We all went to school at Locust Grove. And then right down west of us there on Highway 33 there was a place that they call Hogan. And it was called Hogan Institute. And my name Hogan is from the preacher who was there. Brother Hogan, we called him. Preacher. It was established by the—mission. this Hogan Institute was. And just a few—a year or two ago they tore it down. But the cemetery, the Hogan cemetery is still there. And a lot of the old-timers are buried there of course.
>
> (Right where the cemetery is now? I know where that is.).
>
> That was the school right there. It was a boarding school. My oldest sisters went to school there. Joe Ross is living up there—you probably know Joe. Joe still went to school there. I guess he was one of the oldest—
>
> (What kind of building did they have there for that—)
>
> Frame building. And a dormitory for the girls.
>
> (What year was that in use?)
>
> I'd say 1885 to about 1904 or '05.
>
> (Well, that's the first time we've ever heard of that.)
>
> Informant: Hogan Markham, Cherokee; Interview date: May 23, 1968

S.S. Cobb, another Cherokee interviewed, remembered: "One of my sisters taught school at what was known as the Hogan Institute, started by a Presbyterian preacher. This school was a frame building and was located some five or six miles east of the present town of Chouteau. Meetings were usually held in the schoolhouses and in this part of the Cherokee Nation the predominating faiths were Cumberland Presbyterian and Methodist. During the summertime, usually after all crops were laid by, arbors were

---

[171] https://catalog.archives.gov/id/56537136. The WPA taped interviews in Indian Territory in the 1930's.

constructed under which meetings were held. These arbor meetings lasted from one to two weeks and people brought their provisions, camped out, and when not engaged in church services, enjoyed visiting.

*I remember one of these arbor meetings was held east of what is now Chouteau and was conducted by **Reverend Hogan** each year for many years. Some four miles' southeast of Wagoner and as near our home was another arbor meeting held annually by Reverend N. J. Crawford and Reverend Bryant. At these arbor meetings the faith preached made little difference as all denominations participated. The church near the arbor grounds southeast of now Wagoner wee a one room log church and was built by the Cumberland Presbyterian members."* [172]

His Master did not fail to send Davie encouragement during trials. A grandson was born just eleven days later. James Bailey Fraunberg was the second son of Fred and Julia Hogan Fraunberg in their home in Chetopa, Kansas. Julia was almost 40 and, with her first failed marriage and advanced age, there must have been times when David had thought she'd never produce grandchildren, but he was thrilled to have another from her in just two years. The fact that they were just a short train ride north of his home on the reservation, enabling frequent visits, was a source of even greater joy. Holding Julia's boys lifted much of the pain he was feeling. As he traveled north to meet his new grandson, he remembered earlier trips along this route to meet daughter Mary's children (Harry, Orlando, Julia and Earnest) as they were born. The memories were bittersweet. Harry and Orlando had died in childhood in the 1870's, and Julia and Ernie, now in their teens, lived far away with their parents, Phillip and Mary Hogan Thomas in the Colorado mining boomtown of Kokomo, almost 800 miles further west. Rev. David's surviving sons, Henry and Edwin were both still childless. Henry and his wife Nannie were still in Deerfield, but because of his Civil War injury-induced sterility they were trying to adopt, and Edwin and his bride wouldn't reproduce for another three years. David praised God for the family he did have nearby.

---

[172] COBB, S. S. INTERVIEW. 12833; Journalist, L. W. Wilson, January 27, 1938. Interview with S.S. Cobb, Wagoner, Oklahoma. Western History Collections, University of Oklahoma, Norman, Oklahoma.

The End of His Trail of Tears (1884-1893)

Uncle Davie's son-in-law, Fred Fraunberg, would regale Davie and Julia with stories from his days of running a Chicago hotel. It was clear the German immigrant fit much better in the urban world than in dusty rural Kansas. In May 1889, Fred traded his acreage outside Parsons, Kansas for *Stahr's Central Hotel*[173] at Cambridge City, Indiana. Julia proudly wrote Davie that her family was moving north to become hoteliers of the City's finest hotel June 1st! Fred and Julia renamed the establishment *The Central Hotel* and began at once on a feverish renovation program.

While Davie knew the move was a needed one for his daughter and her family; he bravely hid his own disappointment and fear of loneliness at the thought they'd be so far away.

The loneliness Davie feared steadily increased as, beginning with the death of older brother, Dr. John Hogan in August 1890, his beloved siblings "crossed the river' ahead of him.

The Central Hotel, Cambridge City, Indiana in 1906

---

[173] Often incorrectly remembered as *'Star Central Hotel'* in later histories. Built in 1875 by William P. Stahr.

KEEPER OF FAMILY LORE (1894)

Davie spent the holiday season of 1894 visiting the Fraunberg family up in Cambridge City, Indiana. While he was staying with them in the *Central Hotel* Julia persuaded him to write out some family history for her to pass on to his grandsons, Jimmy and Roy. On his 83rd birthday he sat down to write out a gift for the Fraunbergs. The following is what he presented to Julia:[174]

December 2, 1894, Cambridge City, Ind.

I, DAVID HOGAN, being eighty-three years old today, at the request of my affectionate daughter JULIA P. FRAUNBERG, do make for her the following sketch and notes of ancestry, as my recollection serves me.

Of the HOGAN ancestry: Your great-grandfather (WILLIAM HOGAN), was of Irish decent and his wife SALLIE FULLINGTON (Nee HOGAN), was of Scotch decent. They were both born and raised in North Carolina.

These great-grandparents being a young and newly married couple in 1780 emigrated to Kentucky with Daniel Boone on his second trip to Kentucky, and settled in Bryans Station on the first day of January, 1781.

Your grandfather, DAVID HOGAN, was born in said Station, and it is said he was the second white child born on Kentucky soil. So, you see he was born and raised among the first pioneers of Kentucky.

I will now give the names of your great-grandfather HOGAN'S family and in the order of birth,
  DAVID (your grandpa)
  PATSY, nee BATY ['née' signifies change of name by marriage]
  NANCY, nee HERNDON
  WILLIAM
  JAMES

---

[174] Sadly, minus info on Hoss side omitted by transcriber Clara Hane.

ELIGAH
JOHN
SALLIE, nee GRIDER
LUCY, nee CONNELL
SAMUEL

All lived to ripe years, but have all passed over the river, and are on the distant shore.

Your grandpa and grandma HOGAN were married in 1805 near Cumberland Ford, Kentucky. Of them were born the following children:

1. WILKINSON (b. 1807)
2. SARAH A., nee YOUNG
3. JOHN DORTON
4. DAVID (b. 1811, writer of this letter)
5. WILLIAM (b.1813)
6. JAMES
7. GEORGE MADISON
8. MOSES DORTON
9. JOSEPH WARREN
10. ELIZABETH GRANT, nee WILSON
11. ROBERT HENDERSON
12. SAMUEL GRANT
13. a son died at birth.
14. a daughter died at one year old.

Of this list, the following numbers have passed to the invisible World 1, 2, 3, 9, and 12. The remaining part are all above seventy (70) years of age.

Your great-grandfather on my mother's side was MOSES DORTON, of Scotch descent. Your great-grandmother was DICY ROBINSON, Nee DORTON; her extraction was Scotch, Irish, and Indian, She was a relative of Pocahontas and of JOHN RANDOLPH.[175]

---

[175] The author has uncovered no evidence for the Pocahontas connection. However, Dicy's mom, Charity Kennedy was described as "*a dark complected woman named Kennedy in the Cumberland Gap area, said to have been possibly of 'Portuguese' blood*". Melungeon is a term traditionally applied to one of a number of "tri-racial isolate" groups of the Southeastern United States, mainly in the Cumberland Gap. Tri-racial describes populations thought to be of mixed European, sub-Saharan African, and Native American ancestry.

These two great-grandfathers were in the same emigrant train with Boone on his second trip to Kentucky (1780), and DORTON with a number of men was stationed at Cumberland Ford as Indian spies, for the safety of emigrants; and when the protection was no longer necessary, DORTON started back to the border of Virginia, near Abingdon, and there married DICY ROBINSON in 1784, and immediately settled in one mile of Cumberland Ford, his old spy station in Kentucky.

To them were born the following children:
1. *BETSY PALMER, born 1785.*
2. *JOSEPH*
3. *WILLIAM*
4. *SALLIE, nee WOODS*
5. *PATSIE, nee PATTON*
6. *CRISSIE, nee TAYLOR*
7. *JAMES B.*
8. *DICY, nee WILSON*
9. *NANCY, nee WOOLUM*
10. *MOSES*
11. *LUCINDA, nee GILBERT*
12. *EMILY, nee HIBBARD*

Of this list, none are now living. You also see your two great grandsires were emigrants to Kentucky in Boone's second trip, and that your grandpa and grandma HOGAN each were a first child. You will see I have written many names herein after the familiar way of calling them in days of yore.[176]

---

[176] *Comments by Mrs. Clara M. Hane, transcriber:* "My source of this letter is a typewritten - copy of the original. I have never seen the original, nor do I have contact with any of the descendants of the writer, who was a brother of my great -grandfather, Wilkinson Hogan, and a son of David and Patsy (Dorton) Hogan. You will notice that he was 83 when he wrote the letter -- he lived to be 92 - - and he writes "as my recollection serves me," so there are doubtless some mistakes (other than the incorrect use of 'nee'). He was an intelligent man - a Cumberland Presbyterian minister - and was writing about his own grandparents, so his account is probably mostly correct." *At the end of her typewritten transcription, Mrs. Hane notes,* "There follow two paragraphs about his wife's parents,

Though Davie listed just five siblings who had passed, that was about to accelerate. His older sister Sarah Hogan Young had died in October, two months before David Hogan typed out the preceding history, and the deaths were just beginning.

David remained in the saddle of active ministry. He returned to his former home, the Big Dry Wood Ranch, on January 14, 1894 to perform the wedding for Calvin Klontz, son of the man who bought the ranch. Maybe the incessant funerals nudged Rev. Davie's thoughts to retirement. He couldn't avoid reminders of the fleeting nature of life and experienced a growing desire to live out his days surrounded by children and grandchildren.

---

whose name was Hoss - - mother, Mary Blackburn - - I assume would not interest you, so I'm not copying them." *David Hogan 's Letter;* Knox County, Kentucky Kinfolk, Vol. V, No. 2, April 1961]. *Author's note: Davie also errs with the name and birth of "Betsy Palmer" should read Betsy Parmalee Dorton, born 1787.*

RETIREMENT (1895-1899)

Retirement from ministry after 60 years in the saddle (much of it literal) did not come easily to Uncle Davie, even at 83 years of age. The biggest enticement was the opportunity to live with his daughter Julia and her family. He'd always been closest to Julia of all his children, and she to him. And now, in addition, a fine son-in-law who loved and respected him and the opportunity to get to better know his Fraunberg grandsons, Roy and Jimmy, sealed the deal. Davie made his goodbyes to those he'd poured his heart into for the past twelve years and took the train north to Indiana. He was soon settled into his own rooms in Cambridge City's *Central Hotel*, which the Fraunbergs owned and managed. He had just three months to adjust to retired life and the enjoyment of daily contact with family when sorrow again knocked at the door of his suite at the Central. On the 3rd of June 1895, barely five months after burying Sarah, Davie received a telegram that his younger brother, Col. William Hogan, had died in his home in Knob Noster.[177] Davie immediately set off for Missouri and conducted

---

[177] *William Hogan, P. O. Knob Noster, Missouri; was born in Kentucky in 1813. His father was a native of Kentucky. His grandfather was a native of North Carolina and made his second trip into Kentucky in company with Daniel Boone. William's father was a farmer and lived in Kentucky till 1832, when he came to Missouri and settled in Howard county. He afterwards lived in Cooper County, then Pettis County, then moved back to Cooper County, where he died in 1867. William spent his youth on a farm. He attended the Western Theological Seminary for three years. In 1822 he came to Missouri with his parents where he taught school for one year, and then engaged in the mercantile business, which he followed until 1844, when he went to Texas. He remained until 1851, when he went to Washington, D.C., where he remained until 1866, during which time he held various responsible positions under government employ. In 1866 he returned to Missouri (after a couple years in Iowa), and in 1868 he came to Johnson County and located near Knob Noster. He was married in 1845 to Miss C. V. Holmead. His family consists of five children: Medora, James, Eugene, William and Alice S.*

the June 5th funeral, bringing comfort to his ever-shrinking band of siblings and his hordes of nieces and nephews.

Five months and one day after William's demise, Davie's sister Elizabeth Grant Clay Hogan Wilson[178] died at her home in the old officers' quarters within old Fort Scott. She'd been widowed three years before and had her daughter Lizzie Wilson Goodlander and family to keep her company in her grief. Davie got the news from his brother, Dr. James Hogan, who still lived at Fort Scott. This resulted in the second trip back to the region in the year of his retirement.

Finally, in March 1896, brother George died down in Ellis County, Texas. Even though George had proved a difficult housemate, Davie remembered gratefully how he'd reached out to a grief-stricken brother and welcomed him into his Texas home. By the spring of 1896, only three of General David and Betsy's thirteen offspring remained alive: Rev. David, Dr. James, and Moses.[179]

Davie bore the grief and, ever frugal, seized these opportunities and his unplanned proximity to visit his Cherokee disciples and encourage them, as mentioned in the memoirs. He made another trip in June 1898 and his brother Dr. James met with him at the home of Davie's son Henry.

---

[178] *Mrs. Col. Wilson Dead. — Has Lived in Fort Scott Since 1847. - The Historic Female Character of this City. — Mrs. Elizabeth C. Wilson, wife of the late Col. H. T. Wilson, died at the home of her daughter, Mrs. C. W. Goodlander, at No. 2 south Crawford street. She was 71 years old and died of stomach trouble. Mrs. Wilson came to Fort Scott immediately after her marriage to Col. Wilson at her home in Pettis county, Mo., thirty miles from Booneville, on September 28, 1847. Her maiden name was Elizabeth C. Hogan. Her funeral services will be conducted by Dr. W. C. Porter at the home of her daughter, Mrs. C. W. Goodlander, Wednesday, Nov. 6th at 2 p. m., and interment will take place in Evergreen cemetery.* --Obit of Mrs. Elizabeth C. Wilson, 3 Nov 1895

[179] Moses Hogan would outlast Davie by little more than a year. Last survivor of Davie's siblings, Dr. James Hogan, lived to age 92 and died April 12, 1907.

In February 1899 one war ended and another broke out. A peace treaty between the United States and Spain ended the Spanish-American War and the Philippine–American War began as hostilities broke out in Manila[180]. That same month Rev. David Hogan began work on his memoirs at the urging of his daughter Julia Fraunberg. Mostly unaffected by these far-off wars, the household at the *Central Hotel* enjoyed a period of happy and busy enterprise.

I went to Chouteau last July to dedicate a new church built through the energy of Rev. D.B. Bryant.[181] While there, I learned the work was generally prosperous, though they scarcely ever let us hear from them through the church papers.

If I were in the Cherokee Nation today (too old as I am to do active work) there are several fine homes, in which they would be glad to have me live and die with them. Yet I prefer to live with my children, and at death, my mortal remains to be laid to rest beside their mother.

---

[180] Davie's nephew Eugene Hogan (son of recently deceased brother William) lost a son, Willie, to "friendly fire in this conflict the following year.

[181] Cumberland Presbyterian minister who pastored a church at Pryor Creek and later Chouteau, both in Indian Territory (OK).

The timing of this July 1896 trip to the Nation was timely. Uncle Davie and his old friend Redbird Sixkiller had one more opportunity to enjoy each other's company. On October 21st, at the age of 94, Redbird died in his Locust Grove home. His wife Elizabeth followed him in death less than 36 hours later. Davie was grieved to not be able to travel down again and perform their joint funeral. They were buried in the Sixkiller Cemetery in Locust Grove which still

Lt. Redbird Sixkiller   *Sixkiller grave marker, Locust*

exists on a small, wooded knoll behind the Kolsch farmhouse.

David M. Hogan, pioneering minister, and missionary of the Cumberland Presbyterian Church, having finished both prayers and morning coffee, sat down at his desk, and stared at the stack of blank sheets of paper mocking him next to his 1890 Underwood 1 typewriter as they had for the past five years. He'd promised his daughter Julia to write out his life story for her kids and later descendants. He had been visiting her family in 1894 at *The Central Hotel* they ran in Cambridge City, Indiana. With every story he'd told his two grandsons, Julia prodded, "You should write a book." Realizing that his stories were beginning to induce eye-rolling responses (to be fair, the boys and their folks had heard them all numerous times over the years), Davie had decided to make her happy and agreed to write "a little something up". Before heading back to Indian Territory he'd left Julia with a letter laying out the Hogan and Dorton branches of her family tree. That short work had failed to do the trick. Julia had continued to press him to put down the events of his own remarkable and extraordinary life in written form, especially when he retired from active ministry and moved north to take up residence with her family. After half a decade of excuses and no longer being pulled in every direction by the demands of running a mission station among the Cherokee Tribe, he was staring the task in the face. Finally, heaving a sigh, Uncle Davie Hogan summoned up the determination and grit that had propelled him forward for more than eight decades and set his finger to the keyboard . . .

> *I propose on this the 16th day of February A.D. 1899, in the 88th year of my life, to continue the work of writing a biographic sketch of my life, from a very imperfect, or partially kept diary. I will here state, this work is only intended as a manuscript for the information of my children, grandchildren, and those who in the future may be interested in the history this writing may afford. I have tried to keep as far from self-laudation as possible. I therefore pray that whosoever may consult or read it, if they think they see a spirit of exultation, they will account for it, on other grounds than intention of the writer.* [182]
>
> *. . . In conclusion, I may never meet with you in this world again. May you ever be under the baptismal influence of the Holy Ghost in all your deliberations and administrations, till we meet, in the grand convocation above, where Jesus Christ will ever preside. Amen.*
>
> *David Hogan*

Uncle Davie pulled the page out of the typewriter and sighed. It had proved as much work as he'd anticipated, but the

---

[182] David M. Hogan's words from his hand-typed autobiographic narrative are presented throughout as he wrote them excerpted and rearranged chronologically in *italicized Palatino Linotype* form]

Retirement (1895-1899)

remembering of all his losses had worn him out. Still, something about the recounting of a life's worth of accomplishments and the evidence of faithful obedience lifted the old preacher's spirit. He gathered up the account, his autobiography, and slowly walked downstairs to present it to his beloved daughter Julia. She wanted him to read it aloud to her family and any hotel guests who had any interest, but Davie was going to insist she do the reading herself or pass it around and let a variety of voices tell his story. It would give him pleasure to hear his grandsons' clear voices reading out portions of the life the Lord had given Elizabeth and him. Besides, his wife would have never passed up a chance to have children practice reading aloud. His pace picked up. This was going to be fun.

Just four months after setting down his memories on paper, Davie's home in retirement was the scene of fresh grief. His wonderful son-in-law, Fred Fraunberg, died suddenly (cause not recorded) on June 17, 1899, and the family's rooms in *The Central Hotel* were covered in black crepe while Davie consoled his widowed daughter Julia and his grandsons, Roy (14) and Jimmy (12) . It is unknown, though likely, that he performed the funeral service. Fred had been an able landlord of a popular and successful hotel, to which he'd made vast improvements. This weighty task now fell to Julia; and David was determined to provide his bereaved daughter all the help and comfort he could in the difficult days to come. She needed the help. Julia is raising Davie's teen grandson Roy (James, her 13-year-old, is spending his summer with Uncle Edwin's family in Kansas), and taking in widowed male relations. In addition to Davie, Julia has welcomed her mother's sister's husband, Finis Sloan Arnold, recent widower of Emily Hoss Arnold (died 1898).

Davie has three other surviving children and growing broods of grandchildren. Henry is still farming his land below Deerfield, which these days is providing as much income from oil (discovered there in 1888) as he makes from crops. Though they are in their sixties, he and Nannie have adopted a child. Their nine-year-old daughter Ollie M. Hanley is a welcome addition to a house that longed for the laughter of children for far too long. Henry's father is filled with gratitude to God for giving them this gift and him another granddaughter. At 88 years of age, the rigors of travel hold little appeal, but Davie is planning another trip to visit Henry's expanded family. He has yet to share his thought but he is actually thinking of moving back to Deerfield when grandson Roy reaches his majority in three years. His daughter Mary has recently lost her husband, Phillip Thomas, and has only one child still at home with her in Albion, Idaho. Her daughter Julia is engaged to Edwin Holden[183] and the couple will marry within the year. (By 1920 Mary will be living in the "widow's quarters" at the hotel with Julia.) Julia's brother, Edwin, now an attorney, is married with two children, David and Julia. He's hosting his nephew, James Bailey Fraunberg for the summer. The boy now goes by "Bailey". Both Davie and Julia must have been held in high regard considering the number of children named for them. Edwin and his wife Elizabeth are making their home in Baxter Springs, nestled in the corner of Kansas near the Oklahoma and Missouri border. [184]

Of the twelve offspring of Gen. David Hogan who survived infancy, only three remained by the 1900 Census. Davie's brother Dr. James Hogan's exact whereabouts are lost to history, though he's certainly still around. He is most probably still doctoring patients in Fort Scott, Kansas, though within a few years he will retire to live with his nephew and namesake James E. Hogan in Knob Noster, Missouri. Moses Dorton Hogan Sr. and his wife Mary are still farming his father's original farm, now annexed to in Smithton in Pettis County, Missouri for Census purposes — the hamlet of Arator existing only in memory. In a family of pioneers and 'rolling stones' Moses is the stable and solid one that never moves. His son and namesake, Moses D. Hogan, Jr and his family live and farm with his mom and dad.

---

[183] In 1940 Edwin Holden becomes a Justice on the Idaho State Supreme Court.

[184] Baxter Springs was experiencing a boom due to discovery of lead deposits. Edwin was still in the mining game, but had concluded the real money was in law rather than ore excavation.

FINISH LINE (1900-1904)

I may say, perhaps no years of my life were more blessed and useful, or more agreeably spent, than those among the Cherokees; and if souls won to Christ Jesus by the minister, give stars to his crown, I may hope my crown will have many from the Cherokee Nation. I labored for this people from March 1883 to March 1895. Since my retirement from active labor, I have visited the Nation several times and have done some work for the Master.

As I have already indicated, I have kept a very imperfect diary of my ministerial life work. Hence, the numbers of sermons, conversions, baptisms, churches organized, etc., are only partial. The marriages being of legal record, I have one thousand and six, I desire here to advise young preachers to keep a full diary, it may preach when they shall be silent in their graves.

Upon retiring from the aggressive work, I have made my home with the daughter[185] who lived with and kept house for me, my first year with the Cherokees.

Now, at this time, having my home at Cambridge City, Indiana[186], it requires a long journey to visit my Indian brethren, yet, since 1895, I have several times visited them in the interest of the church.

---

[185] Julia Blackburn *Hogan* Fraunberg

[186] With daughter Julia Fraunberg and family, 2 Dec 1894 - 19 Aug 1903

Rev. David M. Hogan, after a lifetime of near constant movement, was looking for a place to settle down. Even though the pool of old friends and relations still living was a rapidly draining one, the western Missouri town of Deerfield was home to most of them and the closest place to a permanent home Davie had ever known. The plot at the Deerfield Cemetery held those dearest to his heart and he longed to escape the Indiana winters. Henry and Nannie Hogan were 65 and 67 years old and, since 1893, raising Olive, a 13-year-old adoptive daughter. Davie decided that he could achieve worthy ends by moving back to Vernon County and living with his son's family. On Thursday, the 20th of August 1903, Uncle Davie made his last move.

His ministry was not over, in addition to informal pastoring of his neighbors, Uncle Davie performed his final wedding[187], the 1007th of his long career, for the daughter of the family that had purchased the Big Dry Wood Ranch from him years before. It must have felt strange officiating the ceremony on his former ranch in the home he'd shared with Elizabeth. The Klontz family were still next-door neighbors to Henry, and now Davie. On November 1st, Versailles, Missouri newspaper printed the following:

Rev. David Hogan, of Vernon County, must pretty nearly hold the belt in Missouri as a marrying parson. He wedded his 1007th couple near Deerfield last week. Rev. Hogan is 92 years old. He first came from Tennessee to Missouri in 1832 and has lived in this state constantly since 1859. He has been a minister in the Cumberland Presbyterian church since 1835 and delivered the first sermon ever preached in Vernon County in an old building which was used for several years as a schoolhouse, church, and courthouse.[188]

For Uncle Davie, time now seemed to fly by faster than he could ever remember. He was still able to get around and alert as ever but was surprised by the 92nd birthday celebration held for him at his new home with Henry, Nannie and Ollie. He felt like he'd just unpacked and here it was almost four months later. Ninety-two

---

[187] 18 Oct 1903. Wolfe.

[188] *Morgan County democrat.* (Versailles, Mo.), 06 Nov. 1903. *Chronicling America: Historic American Newspapers.* Lib. of Congress.
Web: chroniclingamerica.loc.gov/lccn/sn90061782/1903-11-06/ed-1/seq-6

didn't seem like something that folk should excite themselves over, though he loved that Edwin and Elizabeth and their kids joined the party. Two weeks later, while reading the newspaper, he declared that this was something to get excited about! He read aloud to his granddaughter the news that, on December 17th, Ohioans Wilbur and Orville Wright made four brief flights at a beach called Kitty Hawk with the first-ever powered aircraft. Then putting down the paper, Davie led Ollie in a prayer of praise to the Creator of the marvelous mind of man.

Two months after his species broke the bounds of Earth and leapt into the skies, David M. Hogan, peacefully let go of Earth himself and leapt into the arms of his Savior.

1904. He was born in Harlan County, Ky., in December 1811. With his father he moved to Missouri in 1832 and settled near New Lebanon. Here he professed religion and joined the Cumberland Presbyterian Church in June 1833. September following, he was received by the Lebanon Presbytery as a candidate for the ministry. In March 1834, he entered a theological seminary at Maryville, Tenn. October 16, 1835, he was licensed to preach by the Knoxville Presbytery, but remained in school at Maryville until August 1836. In September 1836, he entered Greeneville College, with an arrangement perfected to complete his course of study. October 27 of the same year he was married to Miss Elizabeth Blackburn Hoss, daughter of Henry Hoss, then president of said college. October 21, 1837, he was ordained to the full work of the gospel ministry by Lebanon Presbytery in called session at Elkton. Soon after his ordination he became what was then called a "circuit rider," in which he served until 1843, when he was called to the pastorate of Rock Spring church in Johnson county, Mo. He held this charge until 1858, except two years while in California. While in California he was active and efficient among the miners, to whom he preached on every opportunity. In the fall of 1858 he moved to Deerfield, Vernon County, Mo., and was the only Cumberland Presbyterian minister in that county at that date. Between the years 1858 and 1874 he did much building work in the state of Missouri and was the pioneer Cumberland preacher in many important centers of the church's work at this day. In 1875 he was called to Argyle church, Rushville Presbytery, Illinois. Here he served for three years on a salary, which was the first and only salary of his long ministerial life. In 1878 he returned to Vernon County, Mo., and, as formerly, did what he could for the cause of Christ until 1882, when his wife was taken by death. In May of this year, he attended the General Assembly at Austin, Texas, and it was here the writer first met him. Having the

Obituary from the Kansas City Star.

REV. HOGAN IS DEAD.

Was the Oldest Resident of This County.

Preached the First Sermon and Organized First Cumberland Presbyterian Church Here.

Rev. David Hogan, Vernon county's oldest resident and one of our very best men died Saturday night at Deerfield, his death being due to the infirmities of old age. The deceased was 92 years of age and for the past sixty eight years had been a minister of the Cumberland Presbyterian church. He was one of nature's noblemen, faithful to his duties as a citizen and to the work of his choice. He was identified with the early history of this county and few are there of the old settlers who did not know and love this good man. He came to Missouri during the year 1832, but soon left for Greenville, Tenn., where he entered college. In 1837 he returned to Missouri and in 1858 located in Vernon county, where he spent the remainder of his life.

Rev. Hogan preached the first sermon ever delivered in this county and organized the first Cumberland Presbyterian church of this county. During his life as a minister he married 1007 couples, the last wedding he performed being on October 18, 1903, when he united in marriage Mr. Frank Wolfe and Miss Maud Kion's both of Deerfield. On October 18, he visited Nevada and while here met many of his friends.

This good man and faithful worker in his Master's vineyard has gone to his eternal home of rest. He leaves behind the results of a well spent life, deeds and an influence that will live longer than the life of the giver.

The good man will be missed by many friends as well as the relatives who now mourn his death. The remains of the deceased now rest in the quiet peaceful graveyard at Deerfield.

supervision of the work among the Cherokees, he applied to me to ask the Board of Missions to commission him without salary. The commission received; he entered the work in March 1883. He was active in mind and body, and these he gave wholly to this mission work until about the close of 1892. During these years he was self-sustaining aside from small gifts by the natives, who loved him dearly. He was sent to save a struggling cause, and he was the strong prop upon which it rested to gather strength to stand. Self-depreciation was his chief characteristic, and he would never claim what I have claim for him. When God calls him from the Deerfield cemetery, methinks much fruit will be revealed as his, which he never claimed in life. He was God's man, which means more than a finite mind can conceive or tongue or pen express.

— N. J. Crawford, Maysville, Ark; The Cumberland Presbyterian, June 16, 1904, page 764.

Later, friends and family gathered at the Hogan plot in the Deerfield Cemetery. The Rev. David M. Hogan was laid to rest next to his beloved Elizabeth and their son Cyrus, lost 42 years previously. There's no record of the mourners gathered in the Missouri wind that cold February day in 1904, but Henry and Nannie Hogan would have been taking care of the arrangements since they lived in Deerfield and it is reasonable to assume that Henry's sisters and brother, Mary, Julia and Edwin (with his wife) also made the journey home to bury their father. Of their 13 Hogan uncles and aunts, only Moses and James remained. They would have come right to Deerfield by the KATY train from Knob Noster (110 miles) and Otterville (124 mi), probably meeting at the Sedalia station and traveling together (as their towns were only separated by thirty-two miles), the old men helped in their journey by Davie's nieces and nephews. According to Davie's beliefs and wishes, those who gathered around his coffin were celebrating a life well lived — for the love of others, and beyond all else, for Jesus Christ. One can only imagine the laughter and tears shared by the group as they rode together to Henry's house for the reception.

The obelisk that marks the resting spot of David and Elizabeth Hogan has their names and dates carved into opposing sides and, for David, a crown with olive branches (symbolizing victory over death and the peace of God, with the following words:

REV DAVID HOGAN
BORN
DEC 2 1811
DIED
FEB 20 1904

On the face between Davie and Elizabeth's epitaphs is a poem and a scripture passage, Colossians 3:4.

True Worth will live beyond the grave,
'Twill pierce Death's shadowy mist
And near the throne of
God on high eternally exist.
When Christ who is our life shall appear
Then shall we also appear with him in glory.

Henry, the eldest of Davie and Elizabeth's six children, had less than three years left himself as he hosted his father's funeral reception. Henry's wife, Nannie, would die from a stroke and be laid in the same cemetery little over a year after Uncle Davie. Less than two years after burying his beloved Nancy, Henry contracted a

The obelisk that marks the resting spot of David and Elizabeth Hogan

fatal case of nephritis and died at the General Hospital in Jackson, Missouri. He joined his wife, his parents and younger brother in the Deerfield Cemetery, just months before he would have given his daughter Ollie in marriage.

Of Henry's siblings; Mary Thomas died in 1932 in Idaho, Edwin Hogan in Topeka, Kansas in 1940, and last to leave was Julia who outlasted the Axis Powers and died on the very last day of 1945 in Indianapolis at 97 years of age.

The Hogan family plot, Deerfield Cemetery

Rev. David M. Hogan grave monument

'RECAPITULATIONS'

New Lebanon Cumberland Presbyterian Church, Cooper County, MO
Constructed about 1860, Photographed in 1933.

David Hogan included in his memoirs a sort of appendix he entitled "Recapitulations". Having integrated all items of more general interest from this section into the main body of the preceding narrative, the author has included these notes for any interested in greater detail about the Cumberland Presbyterian cause for which Uncle Davie labored so long and so well. The following remaining 'Recapitulations' contain his feelings, convictions, and concerns about the denomination and mission and memories of certain characters with positive and negative impacts. Because these passages didn't serve to move the narrative along and may not be of high interest to all contemporary readers, they have been presented in this "Afterword".

Uncle Davie's Beloved Church

I am sometimes called an old fogey. And so I am, as it regards old fashioned experiential religion.[189]

I think the young preacher of this day or any subsequent day of our church, if his eye could fall on these very imperfect sketches, would certainly feel that he owed a debt of eternal gratitude to the set of grand heroes who have lived in continual battle, on less than half or no rations, but have fallen victorious, leaving to them a heritage of the richest fruits of which our heavenly Father gives to his children here on earth. Standing on the bank of the Jordan, as I regard myself today, I find myself every passing day, filled with the spirit of praise to our blessed Father above for the use he has made, and the place he has given to the Cumberland Presbyterian Church in this world. I am less than the least.[190]

I was once young. Now in my eighty-eighth year, let me deliver myself upon the former effective work, and of the later effectiveness of the Cumberland Presbyterian Church. The question may with some propriety be asked, "Has the Cumberland Presbyterian Church outlived, or rather lived out her great revival spirit?" I recall to mind the spirit and manner in which I have heard two of the founders, Samuel King and Rev. Finis Ewing, preach; also the Morrows, R. D. King. and other Missouri preachers, and the host who were converted in the great camp-meeting revivals. These men were not scholarly, never having taken a course at the Church University, Lebanon, or Yale or

---

[189] "Old fashioned experiential religion" refers to personal manifestations of the Holy Spirit's presence common to camp meetings and revivals including ecstatic handshaking ("a sort of wagging that appeared like dancing at a distance"), shouting, jerking, trembling, falling to the floor insensate ('slain'), etc., often in a circle around penitents who would at some point "get happy" (in Davie's words: "profess religion") and join the circle of praising celebrants.

[190] Added in handwriting to the manuscript by David Hogan.

Princeton, even never having been a student in any college, which may or may not have been their misfortune. Their power seemed to move the power of God and the power of God, as we know, physically and morally moves the world. It appeared that the convicting and regenerating power of the spirit was in force with their preaching. They relied on the power of the Holy Ghost; this power they regarded to be the sum of the promise of the blessed Savior, the answer to the call and commission of the Savior (Matt. 28:19,20) "Lo I am with you always even unto the end of the world. Amen."

History of the great revival of 1800 has been written and often spoken of by the best scholars and writers of the Cumberland Presbyterian Church, by way of indicating the revival spirit which has ever been maintained by every minister true to our newborn Presbyterianism. Its true history has never been written: the scope of its worldwide influence will only develop in the unfolding of eternity. Years and years anterior to this great awakening by the Holy Spirit, a dead formality pervaded the church, and the Presbyterians strenuously maintained the form of Godliness, but denied the power. Men found a place of retreat in joining the church while their souls were unregenerate, and they were strangers to pardoning mercy and saving grace.

Praise God! A remnant was left. The Holy Spirit gave it the full size of the robe of righteousness, in that of the height and depth, length and breadth, of the love of God in Christ Jesus, to be put on for the wedding feast. In this revival and for fifty years, the style of preaching was and has been vastly different in all the evangelical denominations; and even today, in an important measure, dead formality has given way to spirituality. The idea that a great supper is prepared, and all are bidden and the larger portion must perish because of the decree of the provider, and a merciless inability thereby, to be partakers, is nearly lost in all the reformed pulpits. This constitutes a reform from hyper-Calvinism.

As above stated, for fifty years, and even today, the Cumberland Presbyterian Church has preachers who are, the most of them, "spiritual and mighty through God to the pulling down the strongholds of the enemy." Yet they seem not to have that special anointing of the Holy Ghost which the first and second fathers of the church possessed. The truly called and sent ambassador of the present day is empowered of the Holy Ghost, as the environments of the subjects of his embassy require. This is the only way I can, in the least, account for the apparent difference of power shown in the first part of the history of the Cumberland Presbyterian Church, and that part now forming. God can suit his instruments to do his work as seems good to him.

The early ministry had a hard and discouraging time, not so much on account of the poverty of the new organization; true it was poor in means, and numbers, as a failure to carry a true scriptural financial policy. I remember well how it discouraged many, myself among the number, when Scott[191], Ogden[192], Ford and Scotch Smith[193] left with a number of lesser lights, and went to the Old Presbyterian Church. I then believed, and still believe, the salary was the proselyting force. I do not know that they suffered any in conscience, but I know I should. I will here give an instance of the preventing of my conscience.

In my financial failure at Lexington (before indicated) the idea was somehow put out that I was going to join the Methodist Episcopal Church. At that time there was no North and South.[194]

---

[191] William Anderson Scott (1813-1885) CPC preacher and missionary who went over to the "Old" Presbyterian Church.

[192] John W. Ogden

[193] James "Scotch" Smith (1798-1871) First historian of the CPC. The Rev. James Smith served as a Cumberland Presbyterian minister through October 1844, at which time he went over to the Presbyterians. He pastored First Presbyterian Church in Springfield, IL (where Abe Lincoln's family soon began to attend) from 1849-56.

[194] "North and South" reference to the division of many denominations along the fault lines of the American Civil War.

John Lapsley Yantis, D.D. [195] came to see me. He said the report had become public that I was going to join the Methodist Church on account of getting no support as a minister and asked if it was so. I answered, "No." He replied, "Well, I came here today specially to see you; if you have any notion of leaving your church on account of not getting a support, and will join the Old Presbyterians' Church, I will find you a place in one week with a salary of not less than eight hundred or more than one thousand dollars. But understand, I am not wishing to proselytize." I replied, that doctrinally, my conscience would not allow me to join any other church while the Cumberland Presbyterian Church existed. After I went to the Cherokee Nation, Rev. R. J. Crawford was offered a salary of eight hundred dollars if he would join the Old Presbyterian Church.

All honor and praise to our heavenly Father for his supporting grace to such men as Cossitt, Beard, Bird, Burrow, Blake, Bell, T. C. Anderson,[196] and a host of others entirely worthy

---

[195] JOHN LAPSLEY YANTIS, D.D. was born September 14, 1804, in Lancaster, Kentucky. His sought to become a physician and studied medicine for nearly two years. A change occurred that resulted in his . . . studying for the ministry of the Presbyterian church. He was . . . ordained in 1832. The next year he moved to Missouri, [eventually settling in] Lexington, in 1841. Dr. Yantis is the oldest Old School Presbyterian minister in Missouri. [extract from *Biographical Sketches, Salt Pond Twp., Saline County, Missouri History of Saline County Missouri,* Missouri Historical Co, St Louis, 1881]

[196] Franceway Ranna Cossitt (1790-1863) Pres. of Cumberland College. Beard: There were two prominent Beards in the CPC Ministers List: Richard Beard (1799-1880) Pres. of Cumberland College and John Beard (1800-1866). John rubbed shoulders with Davie in Illinois' Rushville Presbytery and in Missouri in the Lexington Presbytery. Reuben Burrow (1798-1868) "one of the oldest and most useful of the CPC preachers. Thaddeus C. Blake (1825-1896) author of doctrinal books, editor and publisher of denominational newspapers, Board of Missions chairman. Thomas C. Anderson (1801-1882) President of Cumberland College.

of mention. By their sacrifices great victories today belong to the Cumberland Presbyterian Church. Thank God! The fathers, even to the third occupancy, never advised the members of our church to join some other church, when, through circumstances of removal, or otherwise isolated, they should be deprived of the word and ordinances by our ministry. No; indeed, they were encouraged to "pray the Lord of the harvest to send more laborers into his vineyard" and to work for the building up of the church wherever they might be. They did not say to such, connect with the Presbyterian Church till we come and organize. No, for they knew such advice, in almost every instance, would obstruct the way to organizing. They could worship with others, without joining them.

I wish now to present some of our grand advances and victories. This I will attempt by comparing what was once the condition of the Cumberland Presbyterian Church in her educational capacity, and what now. When I, a candidate for the ministry in 1834, sought educational qualification, we had no Board of Education, no Presbyterial Societies, only one college (situated at Princeton, KY) and that in such a deplorable condition for want of funds as to cause many injudicious changes in its management, and it finally floundered and fell through, as our church history states.

In March, 1834, R. C. Ewing[197] from the Lexington and myself from the New Lebanon Presbytery, aiming to educate ourselves for the ministry, set out our journeys, he to Princeton, Kentucky, and I to the Southern and Western Theological Seminary, East Tennessee. We kept up a correspondence while he stayed at the Cumberland College, Princeton, Kentucky, about

---

[197] Judge R.C. Ewing, son of Rev. Finis Ewing. Author of *Historical Memoirs: Containing a Brief History of the Cumberland Presbyterian Church in Missouri, and Biographical Sketches of a Number of Those Ministers who Contributed to the Organization and the Establishment of that Church, in the Country West of the Mississippi River (1874)*.

eighteen months, I think, but he changed to Center College, Kentucky, and our correspondence ceased.

I promised a comparison by which I hope to demonstrate that with all the adversities attendant upon the Cumberland Presbyterian Church, God's great abundant favor has crowned her with success in every department of her work. I bless God I have lived to see this happy day of success. See our grand Cumberland University at Lebanon, TN; our Lincoln University, IL; our Trinity College, TX, our Waynesburg University, PA, our Valley College, MO, and a number of others too numerous to here mention, with the Education Board general, and all her schools and colleges backed up and helped by Presbyterial and Synodical auxiliaries or Educational Societies. Right here, I will say the young man who was called of God to preach, under the facilities of today, if he will not appropriate and thereby educate himself for his life work, the Presbytery should drop him from her roll. This applies to all young men, I care not how poor they may be. The man advanced in years and having a wife and children, may be the exception.

I cannot close this hasty desultory sketch of my life, so deeply involved in all the interests of the Cumberland Presbyterian Church, without a word in her behalf. As a natural born son would love a tender and affectionate mother, so do I love the Cumberland Presbyterian Church, my spiritual mother. I knew it was a young and weak denomination when I joined it, but little as I had habitually thought of churches and church relations, I was simple enough, or wise enough, to believe a child would likely be treated as well by a true mother, as it would by a stepmother; and this simple reasoning determined my destiny of life and labor. I bless my heavenly Father today; all my sympathies are with her.

The Kingdom of our blessed Savior is spiritual, and all who are members of his Kingdom are one in Him. I am not so far prejudiced as to lose sight of the fact that all the truly regenerated are one in Christ and in the various denominational or human organizations are found the members of his mystical body - the invisible Church. If a man is a conscientious Christian, he will adhere to that formula of Christian faith which he believes is taught in the scriptures; and the fact that those who believe as he does are few in number, fall and are poor and cannot worship God in so grand an edifice, as in other organizations, should not cause him to lose sight of his moorings and despise the company of the few and the poor, and follow the pride of his evil nature seeking the company of the rich and stylish. A man really Christian must be true to his own conscience, without which, I do not see how he can be true to God. A proud Christian is an absurdity. That blessed Savior and the scriptures recognize no such being "Pride is an abomination in the sight of God."

Humility is the essence of Christianity. There can be no genuine Christianity without it. Pride and piety are antagonistic. The idea that a man is too proud to worship God with his fellow creatures on account of their poverty or popularity with the world is absurd. All in the life of humility and words spoken by Christ give especial prominence to humility "Humble yourselves under the mighty hand of God and he shall lift you up." It therefore behooves all persons who prefer to be Christians to examine themselves, that they may see the motives which have actuated them in forming their church relations. We may shamefully ignore our human obligations to a fellow man, but God requires a pure heart in his worship.

I have for nearly sixty-six years lived a member of the Cumberland Presbyterian Church. The Church was about twenty-three years old when I became a member; hence, I have lived a member about two-thirds of the whole time of its existence, and am familiar with the days when the mother church[198] refused to fellowship, or allow our preachers to preach in their houses of worship by such regulations or resolutions adopted in their Presbyteries or church sessions, which forestalled the action even of the few who felt a more liberal Christian spirit.

---

[198] The "Old Presbyterians" of this account.

After I entered the Southern and Western Seminary, I concluded to go to Nashville to see what the General Assembly of my church would look like. It met on the 20th day of May 1834. F. R. Cossitt was moderator and Milton Bird, Clerk. At that time, I think Cossitt was the only D.D. of the church; at least, I heard no one else addressed as such. The number of commissioners was forty-five. The statistics I got from the appendix of our last General Assembly. The showing and principles speakers in that assembly are as fresh in my mind today, as are the members and discussions of 1898, the last assembly I attended, and perhaps the last I shall ever attend. The whole number of General Assemblies I have attended is ten. At several of these assemblies my attendance was only as a visitor.

It may not look comely or be pleasing to look on, by some of the present day, but I will here give a special observance I made at Nashville in 1834. The commissioners were (most of them at least), dressed in Janes. I do not recollect to have noticed but one or two broad-cloth coats in the assembly. Kentucky Janes[199], however, was good enough dress in that day.

I suppose it has often been said by some fettered in mind by prejudice, that the Cumberland Presbyterian Church is a failure. Let us see. I have no way of the ascertaining the number in communion when I joined the church, but her greatest Presbytery now outnumbers the sixth General Assembly in 1845. I do not know her number of preachers at that time, but judging by a Presbyterial representation, it would be about four hundred. Today she has near two thousand ministers, eleven thousand ruling Elders, and two hundred thousand in communion.

At the meeting of the General Assembly in 1856, there was a warm discussion on the propriety of having the statistics of the church reported. Milton Bird favored and Ruben Burrow opposed. At that time, we had no statistics, and today they are far from full or perfect. In these, my last days, I am made to rejoice, when I

---

[199] A type of fabric (historical).

think of the army of young men God is calling and our colleges are educating to enter the field in the coming century, at the close of which, I believe the gospel will have been preached in all the world for a witness. "Then cometh the end." [Matthew 24:14]

A few words about missions and financial matters:

In my first work, as herein already stated, mission work was the circuit or district work, to which the Presbytery would send a man to preach. If an ordained man, he was authorized by his Presbytery to organize churches and do all the work of an ordained minister. If only a licensed man, he was required at the different [preaching] points to give opportunity to all who wished to join the Cumberland Presbyterian Church to come and give him their hand and he would enroll their names and report to the Presbytery. These missionaries had no Board to give them a salary or support. The mission had to give the support, or the missionary did without.

In the third period of our church, I ask who supported the men sent to Pennsylvania. And in the fourth period those sent to East Tennessee? They went at God's call and commission and God moved the people to take care of them: true, often the missionary would have to do as Paul did, resort for a period to "tent making", which in my own case, was to teach a school for one to five months.

In the days of my youth, I was often tempted to look at what is called the dark side of the picture. I now regard, that a great change has come to us for the better. In business management, it seemed to me, there were often losses to our church caused by want of a business care for the means used. I am now fully of the persuasion or opinion that all the losses we may have sustained, have been the schooling which enables us to stand in the grand business line which we occupy today. True it is not perfect, it is only good, and the caution learned from our former losses will assist in making further improvement. I rejoice today that we have so many learned and able men, in mid-manhood, who are competent, and are watching the business or financial lines of the church. I also rejoice and praise the name of God that he has given us so many learned and able young men who are learning business, from the last class mentioned, just a little before them in age.

I feel that I cannot close this imperfect and desultory biographical sketch of my life, without giving a tribute of honor to the Lexington Presbytery, in which, the largest part of my membership as a Presbyter has been spent. Some of its present members will remember, that on my retirement from the active and aggressive work of the ministry in the Cherokee Nation, to make my home in Indiana, I informed them of my retirement and location, and asked them if they would receive me into membership upon my Presbyterial letter from Cherokee Presbytery.

I had doubts of the legality, being out of the bounds of that Presbytery, in a different State. I gave them my reasons for wishing to be a member, and whether legal or not, they received me into their membership, and I am thankful to our heavenly Father, I have enjoyed the privilege since, of being with them in several of their precious convocations. It is an intelligent body of servants for the Master. I am led to believe it is the best sample Presbytery in the Cumberland Presbyterian Church. I thank the brethren that they allow me, under the circumstances which I am placed, to hold my membership with them.

It is not necessary for me to say, the Presbytery, since my first knowledge of her, has made great improvements in all points of Presbyterial business. Perhaps most, if not all the Presbyteries of our beloved church are advancing to a business line of doing business - I hope they are. Yet it will take some of them a great while, if ever, to equal the Old Lexington.

The Cherokee Mission

The Cumberland Presbyterian preaching force at this time consisted of Rev. N. J. Crawford, Rev. R. C. Parks, myself and a licentiate [J.H. Kelly, of Arkansas Presbytery]. And from facts I shall hereafter state, perhaps the Cumberland Presbyterian Church would be stronger today in the Cherokee Nation, if there had not come to the territory another Cumberland preacher till now.

The first year of my ministry in the Cherokee Nation came a Rev. Thompson[200] (I have forgotten his initials) of Cherokee blood, and educated at Lebanon University, Tennessee, and was perhaps licensed and ordained by Rich Land Presbytery, and for some time served the Cumberland Presbyterian Church at Franklin, Tennessee, and while in the service there made a character for himself. He, however, became possessed of the idea he could make a vast fortune in the Cherokee Nation, out of wheat farming and Texas cattle; hence, he at once moved his family and located at the Capital of the Nation, Tahlequah. He then set out to select his wheat farm, which he could find on the rich prairies of Cooweescoowee District. He came to N.J. Crawford's the first day of June 1883, and the next day to my temporary home at Chouteau, in the district of above named. I had already learned from Rev. Crawford that he would accompany Mr. Thompson to help him in the selection of his wheat farm, and on the way he would bring Mr. Thompson to see me. I was much pleased at the thought of having learned preacher, of Cherokee blood, added to our number in the Nation.

It was in the forenoon when they got to my house, and of course they would take dinner with my daughter and self. After introduction and a little conversation, my daughter begged excuse, and went to preparing dinner. Conversation was free, and I found him a very polished gentleman.

I said to him that I expected to build a small cottage house somewhere on the Indian lands, that would be a sufficient home for myself and daughter, if the Indians would let me. To which he quickly replied, "Oh! I can fix all of that; I can have the Council grant anything responsible I would recommend."

---

[200]Gideon Thompson, pastor First Presbyterian Church, Tahlequah from 1883-1884.

He appeared to me to regard himself as the greatest human power in the Nation. This caused me to enter a close watch for the delineation of his character. Directly the wheat farm and cattle ranch came up; he talked as if he might have a million dollars to spend for cattle and wheat and appurtenances to carry on his business. Rev. Crawford and I were full of hope as we had expected Mr. Thompson would add much strength to our contemplated new Presbytery, which we wished to shortly organize.

I had decided in my mind Mr. Thompson was a puffer and a blow. I got an opportunity to speak a word to my daughter; I said to her, "This man won't do. He is a bag of wind." After dinner and before he and Crawford left, I got a private word with Crawford. I said to him, and he understood it, ironically, "Mr. Thompson is too great a man to add anything to the mission work in the Cherokee Nation. In word, I am afraid of him." I received the idea for Mr. Crawford's looks and reply, that he thought I was rather hasty in my judgment.

Now at this moment, but neither of us knew it, Mr. Thompson was under agreement to preach in the Old Presbyterian Church at Tahlequah, and their Board of Missions was to pay him $800 per annum. All this had been arranged by a Rev. Chamberland, who had been raised among the Cherokees, and possessed great influence in the Nation. He was interpreter for the Council, and a learned man and he hated Cumberland Presbyterians; hence, he surrendered his place in mission work to Mr. Thompson, in the hope of proselytizing him, and at the same time preventing Cumberland influence and work in the Nation, and especially at the Capital of the Nation.

Our mission board at St. Louis was immediately informed of Mr. Thompson's course, and upon being informed, the President, Rev. Dr.[Claiborne Handly] Bell, came to Tahlequah to change things for the better. Dr. Bell remonstrated with Mr. Thompson, who replied he would rather work for the Cumberland Presbyterian Church than the Old Presbyterian, if he could be supported: whereupon Dr. Bell proposed to give him $800 per annum, and paid $400 in hand, and promised the remaining $400 as soon as he returned to St. Louis. Mr. Thompson now agreed to work for the Cumberland Presbyterian Church. He, however, continued preaching for the old Presbyterian people, and for their salary, while, at the same time he had received $400 from Dr. Bell to work for the Cumberland Presbyterian Church.

Our Board was again immediately informed of his course, and the Cumberland Presbyterian Church Board wrote to the Old Presbyterian Board, and claimed, as Mr. Thompson had worked for them on the money paid him by our Board, they justly owed our Board the $400. I have learned from a reliable source that our Board, by some means, has recovered $200 from the $400.

The conclusion of Mr. Thompson's case in the Nation was that his fortune was a total failure. His brother in the church, and banker at Franklin, Tennessee, had all confidence in him; from said bank he had made large loans to carry his wheat farm and cattle ranch; he broke his brother banker at Franklin, greatly worsted the Conchoe Cattle Company in Texas, and in two years, left the Cherokee Nation disgraced in the eyes of all who knew him. He came to Ash Grove [in] S.W. Missouri, and joined the Congregational Church, and tried to break up the Cumberland Presbyterian Church in that place. From further remarks - excuse.

Some months after the foregoing occurrences, a Methodist preacher, Smallwood, a full-blood Cherokee, and the most eloquent man of the Cherokees, came to us with a letter of dismissal and vouchers from the Indian Conference of the Methodist Episcopal South, and was regularly received a member of the Cherokee Presbytery, of the Cumberland church. The Presbytery gave him work among the full-bloods, and a fixed salary of $200 per year, payable in monthly installments.

Now, this same Rev. Chamberland persuaded him to leave the Cumberland Presbyterian Church and join the Old Presbyterian Church, and they would give him $300 per year. Smallwood said it would be morally wrong. "Oh No," said Chamberland. "You can tell that Uncle Red Bird Sixkiller, who was the interpreter when you joined their Presbytery, led you to believe you were joining the Old Presbyterians." He left us and joined the Old School North, through Chamberland's lie put in his mouth.

Another Case of Obstruction. Immediately after the organization of the Cherokee Presbytery, I came to a meeting of the Lexington Presbytery at Shiloh, Johnson County, Missouri, for the purpose of soliciting help to pay for the two church buildings recently erected. At that meeting, three young men were licensed to preach. One of them was very anxious to go with me on my return to the Nation. I said to him that Brother Crawford had the supervision of the mission work, and that he should remain until he had written to Crawford and had his reply. I had just got back a day or two, when here he was at my place of board at Chouteau.

However, Bro. Crawford gave him work. He went to the place where Bro. Crawford had obtained board and home for him with a half-breed family, familiarly called there: Uncle John Ward's. Uncle John had a very pretty daughter, Victoria, 17. The young preacher at once took the idea he would like to be adopted citizen of the Cherokee Nation. The beauty of Miss Victoria took a deep hold on him.

In two weeks, he came to Chouteau and hunted me up. After a little chat, he revealed to me that he loved Miss Victoria and spoke of what a large farm Uncle Johnny owned, and if he could get Miss Victoria, he would be set up for this world. I said then, "I see, my boy, you are infatuated to such a degree you are in great danger." He quickly asked, "How, Uncle Davie?" I said, "You will show you are crazy in love, and she will kick you sky high" and so she did. This spoiled his boarding place and home. He lingered about one month and went to a Southern Methodist meeting; he said to the preacher that he did not know what to do with himself; he had worked for the Cumberland Presbyterian Church for some time, and they had never given him a cent and his clothes were beginning to get shabby, etc. The Methodist preacher thought it a good opportunity to proselytize, and he did proselytize him with promise of pay.

Another cause of trouble. Rev. N. J. Crawford and I attended the meeting of our General Assembly in Bentonville, Arkansas. A young, ordained preacher came to us, desiring work in the Cherokee Nation. He belonged to the Arkansas Presbytery, and referred us to F.R. Earl, D.D. as to his character and abilities. The Dr. said his natural abilities were good enough, if only other things were equal, saying, he had no raising. This caused Mr. Crawford and I to give him but little encouragement.

After a month or so he came to the Nation and said he had come to stay with us, if we were willing; he held a letter of dismissal from Arkansas Presbytery. Bro. Crawford gave him the outposts to work till the next regular meeting of our Presbytery when he should hand in his letter. His letter was regular, and the Presbytery voted him a member.

It is proper here to state there had already come from the people among whom he had worked some severe criticism on his manners, and Mr. Crawford thought it proper to inform him that he might be more cautious. He desired to have the names of the criticizers, and Mr. Crawford gave them, which only tended to prejudice him against said critics. The Presbytery had many troubles with him, and finally upon a charge of lying, he was suspended from the ministry. He returned to Arkansas and in one year after, upon a petition from thence, and his confession of penitence, the Presbytery restored him.

One other unfavorable case. Later, a gentleman came into the Nation from Kansas; shortly after his arrival, Brother Crawford was holding a meeting on Pryor Creek in which were several conversions and many penitents; the gentleman above spoken of came to said meeting and sought the acquaintance of Brother Crawford, saying, he felt desirous to help him in his meeting, but circumstances would not allow him to do as he felt.

Mr. Crawford inquired of him the circumstances; he said he had, in Kansas, been a Presbyterian preacher, but unfortunately, two years since he and his wife separated, or rather, she had left him and gone to her mother's, refusing to make home with him any longer. Their family consisted of two children; these little children he desired to teach obedience to parents; his wife opposed his exactions, and in the wrangle over the children he had treated her a little roughly, but he thought deservedly. The Presbytery preferred charges against him, and suspended him from the functions of a minister, and finally, for his stubbornness since, had expelled him.

Bro. Crawford thought he saw in the man some signs of good, and said to him, if you wish at any time to make any remarks or talk to the seekers, you are at perfect liberty to do so. Suffice to say, he at once went to work, and profitably, as many souls were saved. He gave us the address of the Moderator and Clerk of the Presbytery which expelled him. From them we learned the majority in his expulsion was only two; his friends in that Presbytery said we should do all we could consistently, to raise him up, upon which advise, we first took him in as a church member, and the Presbytery received him as a candidate, on a written discourse licensed him, and in a regular manner ordained him. He was a good expounder and did much good while he worked with us. He went into the Choctaw Nation, and on his return called for a letter of dismissing and recommendation, which was granted and on his return to the Choctaw Nation, he joined the Old Presbyterians.

I have given these several incidents in substantiating what I have already said, "That it would have been better for our Church in the Cherokee Nation, if no other ministers had come than those in the organization of the Cherokee Presbytery." Notwithstanding these troubles, the Presbytery has made and received a number of good and efficient ministers.

Uncle Davie, a man of staunch personal loyalty, had trouble excusing the weaknesses of fellow ministers in this area.

'Recapitulations'

Ancestors of Rev. David M Hogan

```
                              ┌── William James Hogan (about 1680-1754)
                    ┌── William Griffin Hogan (1705-July 1783)
                    │         └── Elizabeth Griffin (1683-1733)
              ┌── James Shadrack Hogan (1728-11 September 1793)
              │     │         ┌── James Joseph Sullivan (1685-2 October 1750)
              │     └── Sarah Shadrack Sullivan (about 1708-1778)
              │               └── Martha Shadrack (1690-1729)
        ┌── William James Hogan (1 June 1750-2 April 1827)
        │     │               ┌── Dutton Lane (September 1670-8 October 1726)
        │     │     ┌── Richard Tydings Lane (1698-1770)
        │     │     │         └── Pretitia Tydings (about 1674-1770)
        │     └── Silence Lane (1730-circa March 1803)
        │           │         ┌── John Fuller (1686-1735)
        │           └── Sarah Fuller (7 August 1702-25 August 1784)
        │                     └── Sarah Heath (1680-1709)
  ┌── David Hogan (17 June 1781-30 January 1867)
  │     │                     ┌── George Boone (19 March 1666-27 February 1744)
  │     │           ┌── Squire Boone (25 November 1696-2 January 1765)
  │     │           │         └── Mary Milton Maugridge (1668/9-2 February 1740)
  │     │     ┌── Daniel Boone (22 October 1734-26 September 1820)
  │     │     │     │         ┌── Edward Morgan (1670-1736)
  │     │     │     └── Sarah Jarman Morgan (23 September 1700-1 January 1777)
  │     │     │               └── Elizabeth Jarman (1678-1731)
  │     └── Sarah Elizabeth Grant (1 June 1760-16 October 1816)
  │           │     ┌── Joseph Bryan (-)
  │           └── Rebecca Ann Bryan (9 January 1739-18 March 1813)
  │                 └── Hester Hampton (-9 January 1739)
David M Hogan (2 December 1811-20 February 1904)
  │                 ┌── William Dorton (1710-1741)
  │           ┌── William F. Dorton (1730-April 1780)
  │           │     └── Ossie May Maxwell (about 1700-13 January 1790)
  │     ┌── Moses Dorton (1758-12 March 1826)
  │     │     │         ┌── Zachary Lewis (30 November 1669-14 November 1725)
  │     │     │   ┌── John Zachary Lewis (1 January 1702-20 January 1765)
  │     │     │   │     └── Mary Walker (1673-9 January 1724)
  │     │     └── Elizabeth Watts Lewis (1725-13 January 1790)
  │     │               ┌── John Waller (23 February 1673-2 August 1754)
  │     │         └── Mary Waller (30 January 1699-23 March 1781)
  │     │               └── Dorothy Mary King (1675-)
  └── Elizabeth Parmalee Dorton (17 January 1787-3 February 1869)
        │               ┌── John Robertson (1672-5 December 1720)
        │         ┌── Jacob Robertson (1694-4 September 1773)
        │         │     └── Mavell Alsop East (1676-1725)
        │   ┌── William Robertson (about 1735-June 1804)
        │   │     └── Martha Headen (1704-1755)
        └── Laodicea Robinson (1768-after 1840)
              └── Charity Kennedy / Cannedy (1751-1848)
```

INDEX OF ILLUSTRATIONS

24 DMH Family Tree

25 Dorton's Fort
   Daniel Boone
   Wilderness Rd map

26 Bryans Station
   Pineville map
   Hogan's Tavern
   Cumberland Ford
   Dorton's Mansion
   Tri-State marker

52 Ewing-Hogan home
   New Lebanon CPC
   CPC HQ today

53 Maryville College
   Isaac Anderson
   Fielding Pope
   Maryville Seminary
   Circuit Rider

59 Balch painting
   Coffin painting

60 Henry Hoss grave
   Rev. Charles Coffin
   Mordecai Lincoln
   Davy Crockett plinth

61 Andrew Johnson
   Wedding frock
62 Tailor at work
   Tailor shop & home
64 Flatboat on river
71 River trip map
   Flatboat Launch site

72 Trail of Tears map
   Eagle Nest Island

79 Thomas Benton
80 Rev. Finis Ewing

83 Pettis County map
84 Gen. George Smith
   Absalom McVey
   Georgetown marker

101 John C Frémont
102 Agua Fria, CA
106 Frémont Adobe

109 Hogan Ranch map
   Deerfield P.O. desk
116 Jayhawkers in MO

121 Gen. James Lane &
   Gen. Sterling Price
122 Battle Map
123 Dry Wood Battle
125 Cyrus Hogan grave
124 Fort Scott drama
125 Elizabeth & Hiero
126 "Gen. Order No11"
128 Mary Hogan wed
130 Wilson home

156 E. Hogan grave

164 Fred Fraunberg
169 Redbird story map

179 The Central Hotel

188 Redbird Sixkiller
   Sixkiller grave
189 Davie's signature

196 DH Obituary 1904
198 Davie's Grave
199 Hogan Family Plot

201 New Lebanon CPC
218 Davie Hogan's tree
   back 6 generations

MINISTERS

220 Anderson, T
   Beard, R
   Bell, C
   Bird, M
221 Blake, T.C.
   Burrow, R
   Cobb, Belle
   Cossitt, F
222 Farr, WB
   King, RD
   King, SF
   Miller, FM
223 Robert D. Morrow
   William A. Scott
   Jas. 'Scotch' Smith
   John L. Yantis

Illustrations: Ministers & Missionaries

Clockwise from top left:
Thomas Constantine Anderson
Richard Beard
Claiborne Handly Bell
Milton Bird

Illustrations: Ministers & Missionaries

Clockwise from top left:
 Thaddeus Constantine Blake
 Reuben Burrow
 Dr. Isabelle 'Belle' Cobb
 Franceway Cossitt

Illustrations: Ministers & Missionaries

Clockwise from top left:
William Benton Farr
Robert Donnell King
Samuel Finis King
Fleming Mitchell Miller

Clockwise from top left:
    Robert Davis Morrow
    William Anderson Scott
    James 'Scotch' Smith
    John Lapsley Yantis

Illustrations: Ministers & Missionaries

INDEX OF PEOPLE

A

ALLEN, Rev. J. C., 141
ANDERSON
    Pres. Isaac, D. D., 39, 40, **53**
    Thomas C., 205, **220**
ARNOLD
    Finis Sloan, 149, 190
    Katie, 149
AUSTIN Mary Ann, 148

B

BAKER, Norma Jean, 12
BAKER, Rev. E. E., 141
BALCH, Hezikiah, 55, **59**, 65, 219
BASS, A. J., 148, 149, 150
BEARD
    Rev. John, 205
    Rev. Richard, 205, 219, **220**
BELL
    Edward C., 101
    Rev. Dr. Claiborne Handly, 205, 213, 214, **220**
BENTON
    Thomas Hart, 79, 112, 119
BIRD, Milton, 205, 209, **220**
BLACKBURN
    Mary 'Polly', 55, 63, 73, 77, 86, 89, 101, 113, 152, 184
BLAKE, Thaddeus Constantine, 205, 219, **221**
BOONE
    Daniel, 4, 13, 14, 17, 20, 21, 22, 23, **25**, 31, 68, 167, 168, 181, 183, 185
    Daniel Morgan, 68
    Eliza Jane, 11, 16, 23
    Nathan, 21, 68
    Squire, 11

BRYAN
    Rebecca Ann, 23
    William Jennings, 148
BRYANT, D. B., 178, 187
BUCHANAN, President James Jr., 92, 134
BURR, Aaron, 16
BURROW, Rev. Reuben, 205, 209, 219, **221**
BYRD, Col. Joseph, 43, 44, 45

C

CAMPBELL
    Col. David, 169
CAMPBELL, Col. David, 169
CHANEY, Rev. James McDonald, 149
CLAY, Henry, 21, 92
COBB, Dr. Isabelle 'Belle', 160, 162, **221**
COFFIN, Charles D.D., 57, **59**, **60**, 219
COSSITT, Rev. Franceway Ranna, 205, 209, 219, **221**
CRAWFORD, Rev. N. J., 70, 99, 157, 158, 159, 160, 161, 162, 163, 166, 174, 175, 178, 196, 205, 211, 212, 213, 215, 216, 217
CROCKETT, Davy, **60**

D

DEAS, Lt. Edward, 66
DIXON, John, 28, 29
DORTON
    Elizabeth 'Betsy' Parmalee, 11, 14, 20, 28, 29, 30, 85, 113, 131, 136, 137, 139
    Emily (Hibbard), 22, 183
    James B 'US Congress', 15

Moses, 4, 14, 15, 17, 20, 21, 22, **25**, 167, 168, 170, 171, 182
Moses E., 118
William (1792-1880), 15, 20
William F, 11
DUPREE, Hannah Hill, 22

E

EARL, F.R., 216
EWING
Brig. Gen. Thomas, 126, 127
Judge R. C., 206
Rev. Finis, 18, 27, 31, 32, **52**, 70, 79, **80**, 81, 82, 85, 86, 89, 91, 112, 139, 140, 162, 202, 206, 219

F

FARR, William Benton, 104, 105, 219, **222**
FISHER, Maggie A., 147
FOX, Nancy Jane 'Nannie', 139, 145, 151, 153, 178, 190, 194, 197, 198
FRAUNBERG
Frederick William, 164, 165, 166, 172, 178, 179, 190
James Bailey, 178, 181, 185, 190, 191
Roy Humboldt, 172, 181, 185, 190, 191
FRAZIER, Rev. Robert, 58, 62
FRÉMONT, John C., 100, 119, 219
FULLER, 11, 12

G

GRANT
Sarah Elizabeth, 4, 13, 14, 17, 21, 22, 23, 68, 167
William, 11
William Henry 'Gen.', 11, 23

H

HACEY, Rev. J H, 159
HANLEY, Olive 'Ollie' M, 190, 195
HERNDON, Rev. Richardson, 28
HIBBARD, William Wylie, 22
HOGAN
Alice 'Ally', 147
Alice Susan, 147
Col. James E., 102, 129, 147
Cyrus O., 87, 113, 125, 151, 196
Cyrus Titus, 142
David 'General', 11, 13, 14, 15, 16, 17, 18, 19, 20, 21, 22, **26**, 27, 29, 30, 44, 69, 85, 101, 111, 112, 113, 117, 120, 131, 134, 136, 143, 144, 147, 148, 149, 154, 181, 182, 186, 191
David, Jr., 85, 86, 113, 138, 145, 148, 151, 161, 176
Dr. James M., 16, 17, 76, 85, 86, 114, 117, 123, 135, 139, 147, 149, 182, 186, 191
Dr. John D., 14, 30, 33, 75, 76, 85, 90, 94, 102, 114, 118, 134, 135, 146, 149, 179, 182
Dr. Robert Henderson, 21, 85, 114, 133, 135, 148, 182
Dr. Samuel Grant, 22, 76, 85, 103, 114, 131, 182
Edwin Grant, 91, 104, 113, 138, 146, 151, 161, 162, 164, 178, 190, 191, 195, 197, 199
Elijah, 15, 96, 182
Elizabeth 'Betsy' Grant (Beaty), 181

Elizabeth Grant Clay, 21, 85, 95, 113, 123, 124, **125**, 149, 182, 186
Eugene, 102, 129, 147, 185, 187
George Madison 'Col.', 15, 16, 19, 85, 87, 93, 94, 96, 102, 118, 133, 139, 147, 149, 155, 182, 186
Henry Hoss, 70, 85, 101, 113, 118, 126, 127, 139, 145, 151, 152, 153, 178, 190, 191, 194, 197, 198, 219
James, 120, 181
James (b.1752), 15
John (b.1756), 15
John Sr., 12
John Sr. (b.1790), 113, 147, 182
Joseph Warren Turley, 21, 55, 131, 182
Julia P., 91, 96, 113, 137, 138, 145, 148, 149, 151, 153, 155, 156, 161, 162, 164, 165, 172, 178, 179, 181, 185, 187, 188, 190, 191, 197, 199
Lucy Ann (Carroll), 182
Mary 'infant', 23, 29
Mary Elizabeth, 89, 91, 113, 128, 131, 137, 138, 139, 140, 145, 146, 151, 153, 178, 191, 197, 199
Medora, 94, 102, 129, 147, 185
Moses Dorton Jr., 191
Moses Dorton Sr., 21, 85, 97, 113, 117, 119, 133, 135, 139, 140, 148, 149, 176, 182, 186, 191, 197
Nancy, 14, 15, 28
Nancy (Herndon), 181
Patrick, 13

Rev. David Madison 'Davie'
1811—Dec. 2nd birth, 14
1817—to Cumberland Gap, 17
1818—log schoolhouse, 20
1829—Tanner's apprentice, 27
1832—move to Missouri, 31
1833—Conversion, 35
1834—Maryville Seminary, 39
1835—CPC Circuit Rider, 40
1836—Greenville College—Weds Elizabeth Hoss, 55, 61
1837 MO boat move, 65, 66, 69
1837 Oct 21—CPC License—son Henry Hoss born, 70
1840—son David, Jr. born, 85
1841—Finis Ewing dies, 86
1843—son Cyrus O. born—bankruptcy, 87
1844—Rock Spring CPC, 89
1845—daughter Mary born, 89
1848—daughter Julia born, 95
1853—son Edwin G born, 104
Family Tree, **24**
signature, **189**
Samuel, 182
Samuel Benton, 106
Samuel Grant, 22
Samuel Lane, 33, 103, 148
Sarah 'Sallie' (Grider), 182

Sarah Ann, 14, 22, 35, 85, 95, 132, 133, 134, 136, 139, 140, 146, 149, 182, 184
unnamed 'stillborn', 29
Wilkinson, 14, 16, 22, 23, 27, 29, 30, 33, 76, 85, 89, 94, 96, 105, 106, 113, 120, 132, 135, 137, 139, 142, 143, 144, 146, 147, 148, 149, 182, 183
William, 181
William 'Cousin', 147
William Griffin, 13
William James 'Capt.' II, 13, 14, 15, 17, 19, 20, 22
William James 'Col.' III, 44
William Jr., 129, 147
William M. 'Col.', 15, 16, 29, 55, 69, 75, 85, 92, 93, 94, 96, 102, 105, 113, 118, 128, 129, 130, 133, 134, 135, 136, 138, 143, 144, 145, 147, 149, 155, 182, 185, 186
HOGAN (FREE)
Amanda, 132, 138
Esther, 112, 128, 132, 138, 151, 153, 154, 155
George Washington, 138, 154
John, 133, 138, 143, 144, 145
HOLMEAD
Anthony, 92
Cornelia Virginia, 92, 93, 94, 102, 113, 129, 133, 134, 135, 138, 144, 147, 155
James Beaury, 129, 138, 155
HOPKINS, Samuel, D. D., 39
HOSS, 69, 73, 76, 99, 149, 181
Alfred, 56, 63
Archibald Blackburn, 63, 73, 100, 101, 103, 149
Edwin, 63, 73, 101, 102, 103

Elizabeth Blackburn, 55, 57, 63, 66, 85, 86, 103, 104, 145, 149, 151, 152, 195
Emily 'Emma', 63, 149, 190
Henry, 55, 56, 58, **60**, 61, 63, 70, 152, 195
Julia (Parke), 63, 73, 149
Samuel Blackburn, 63, 73, 101, 149
HOUSTON, Sam, 92
HOUX
George, 78
William, 78
HOYT, Prof. Darius, D. D., 39

J

JEFFERSON, President Thomas, 170
JOHNSON, President Andrew, 58, 60, 61, **62**, 130
JONES
Evan, 39, 40
John B., 39, 158, 166
John Buttrick, 39, 40, 158

K

KELLY, Rev. J. H., 161, 211
KING
Rev. Finis Ewing, 90
Rev. Robert Donnell, 91, 202, **222**
Rev. Samuel, 90, 91, 92, 202
Rev. Samuel Finis, 159, **222**
KLONTZ, **109**, 194
Calvin, 184
John, 153
Miss, 194

L

LANE, 11
James H., 121, 123, 124
Mary M 'Polly', 23, 30, 33, 113
Silence, 12

LEWIS, 11
  Mary Ellen, 114
LINCOLN
  Mordecai, **60**, 62
  President Abraham, 62, 117, 118, 119, 128, 137, 155, 204

M
macAITHEIR, Ógán, 12
macCENNÉTIG, High-King 'Brian Boru', 12
macCOSGRACH, Aitheir, 12
MADISON, President James, 16
MARTIAU
  Nicholas, 12
McCORKLE
  Rev. Archibald, 38
McVEY
  Absalom, 74, 76, **84**
  Mary Edmondson, 74, 75, 76
MILLER
  Everett, 147
  John, 70
  Rev. Barnett, D.D., 69
  Rev. Fleming Mitchell, 69, **222**
MOAD
  Rev. Granville Linfield, 159
MONROE
  Marilyn (actress), 12
  President James, 17
MONTGOMERY, James 'Col.', 121
MORGAN, Sarah Jarman, 11
MORROW, 202
  Rev. Columbus, 104
  Rev. John B., 104
  Rev. John D., 89
  Rev. Robert D., 32, 78, 89, **223**

N
NIADH NAR, Crimthann of Ireland, 12

O
OGDEN, Rev. John W., 204

P
PARKE, Mary, 149
PARKS, Rev. R. C., 157, 161, 162, 163, 211
POPE, Prof. Fielding, D. D., 39, **53**, 219
PRICE, Sterling 'Gen.', 121

R
RAMSEY
  Colonel, 42, 43, 44
  James W, 42
RANKIN, Elizabeth Robb, 87, 147
READ, Rev. Robert Alexander, 69
RED BIRD
  Dotsuwa, 169, 170, 171
  Sixkiller 'son of Dotsuwa', 171
ROBINSON, Mr.'bookkeeper', 75, 76
ROBINSON/ROBERTSON, 11
  Laodicea 'Dicy', 21, 22, 167, 182, 183
  William, 167, 168
ROOSEVELT, President Theodore, 16, 170
ROSS, Chief William Potter, 158
ROUCH, Amanda E. 'Jennie', 147

S
SCOTT, Rev. William A., 204, **223**
SEWARD, William H., 118, 128
SIXKILLER
  Lt. Redbird, 166, 171, 188, 214, 219
  Rufus, 171

SMALLWOOD, Joseph, 162, 163, 214
SMITH
  Elizabeth E. P. (Hogan), 161, 190, 191, 195, 197
  Gen. George R., 75, 76, 77, **84**
  James 'Scotch', 204, **223**
STAHR, William P., 179
STETTINIUS, Samuel Endredi, 92

T

TATE, Rev. Robert, 49
THOMAS
  Earnest Augustus, 145, 178
  Harry, 131, 137, 138, 140, 145, 178
  Julia Ethel, 139, 145, 178
  Orlando, 137, 138, 140, 145, 178
  Phillip Yelton, 128, 131, 137, 145, 146, 178, 191
THOMPSON
  Rev. Gideon T., 212, 213, 214
  Rev. Samuel, 90
TURNER, Nat, 29

V

VAN BUREN, President Martin, 79
VANNICE, Rev. R. L., 141

VENNER, Margery, 11
VORIS, Hortensia Gertrude, 85, 114, 134, 135, 146

W

WALLER, 11
WARD, Rev. Robert Baker, 149, 152
WASHINGTON, President George, 13
WEAR
  Robert B., 90
  Samuel, 136
  William Duke, 90
  William G., 101, 136
WILSON
  Elizabeth 'Mrs. Goodlander', 147, 186
  Hiero Tennent 'Col.', 95, 113, 124, **125**, 126, 139, 147, 149, 186
WRIGHT
  Bros. Orville & Wilbur, 195
  Mary M., 97, 113

Y

YANTIS, Rev John Lapsley D.D., 205, **223**
YOUNG
  Arthur Galbraith 'Maj.', 95, 136, 140, 141, 146, 149

INDEX OF PLACES

A

ALABAMA, 4, 14, 17, 19, 22, 67
  Madison, Huntsville, 14, 17, 19, 22, 43, 64, 65
  Talladega, Talladega, 44
ARKANSAS, 124, 176, 211, 216
  Benton
    Bentonville, 216
    Pea Ridge, 127
  Franklin, Ozark, 126
  Ouachita, Camden, 127, 139
  Sebastian, Fort Smith, 126
  Washington
    Fayetteville, 161
    Prairie Grove, 161

Index of Places

C

CALIFORNIA, 99, 100, 101, 102, 103, 112, 137, 145, 148, 149, 151, 176, 195
  Coloma, Sutter's Mill, 99
  Mariposa County, 99, 103
    Agua Fria, 100, 103, 119
    Magoon Creek, 148
  Merced River, 103
  Sacramento, 151, 161
  San Joaquin, Stockton, 103
California Trail, 99, 100
COLORADO, 151
  Kokomo, 146, 149, 151, 178

D

DISTRICT OF COLUMBIA
  Washington, 92, 93, 94, 102, 113, 128, 136, 144, 155

I

ILLINOIS, 68, 141, 145
  Alexander, Cairo, 64, 68
  Marion, 148
    Salem, 139, 148
  McDonough, 141
    Colchester, 139, 195, 205
  Randolph, Kaskaskia, 68
INDIANA
  Marion, Indianapolis, 199
  Wayne County, 165
    Cambridge City, 7, 149, 179, 181, 185, 188, 193
IOWA, 28

K

KANSAS, 111, 116, 122, 164, 179, 216
  Bourbon, Fort Scott, 186
  Cherokee County, 172
    Baxter Springs, 166, 172, 191
  Douglas, Lawrence, 127

KANSAS
  Bourbon, Fort Scott, 113, 117, 118, 121, 123, **124**, 139, 146, 147, 191
  Labette
    Chetopa, 178
    Oswego, 164
    Parsons, 140, 146, 165, 179
  Shawnee, Topeka, 199
KENTUCKY, 13, 14, 16, 17, 18, 21, 22, 23, 28, 29, 81, 148, 167, 168, 181
  Bell County, 168
    'The Narrows', 13, 25, 26, 168, 170
    Log Mountain, 168
    Pineville, 20, 22, 168
    Strait Creek, 168, 169
    Wallsend, 22
  Clay, Hibbard Branch, 22
  Fayette, Bryans Station, 13, 16, 181
  Fayette, Bryans Station, **26**
  Garrard, Lancaster, 205
  Harlan County, 15, 21, 195
    Cumberland Ford, 13, 14, 15, 17, 20, 21, 22, **26**, 168, 182, 183
    Dorton's Mansion, 14, 15, 22, **26**
    Hogan's Tavern, 14
    Robertson's Station (fort), 168
    Cumberland Gap, 13, 15, 17, 18, 21, 27, 30, 111, 168
      Three State Cornerstone, 17, **26**
    Cumberland Gap National Park, 17
  Knox County, 14, 15, 17
    Barbourville, 28

Index of Places

Dorton's Tavern, 15
Herndon's Tavern, 15
McCracken, Paducah, 64, 67, 68
Wilderness Road, 17

M

MARYLAND
  Baltimore, 74
  Colony, 12
MEXICO, 68, 93, 94
MINNESOTA, 28
MISSISSIPPI
  Oktibbeha, Starkville, 14, 96
Mississippi River, 68
MISSOURI, 23, 27, 28, 30, 31, 44, 55, 62, 111, 141, 205
  Cooper County, 31, 131
    Boonville (Boone's Lick – historic), 68, 69, 73, 133
    Elkton (later Otterville), 70, 73, 195
    Ewingsville (renamed New Lebanon), 28, 30
    New Lebanon, 30, 31, 32, 33, 35, 38, 41, **52**, 69, 70, 73, 195, 206
    New Lebanon (Ewing-Hogan House, 32, 51, **52**, **201**, **219**
    Otterville, 73, 101, 113, 120, 131, 140, 197
  Henry County, 30
    Leesville (was Tebo Grove), 30, 33, 35, 114, 148, 172
  Howard County, 31, 32, 185
    Boone's Lick State Hist. Site, 31
    Boonslick Road, 31, 68
    New Franklin, 31, 32, 93
  Jackson, Kansas City, 87, 100, 147, 165
  Johnson County, 107
    Chilhowee, 90, 94, 104, 105, 113, 139, 146, 149
    Holden, 89, 101, 144
    Knob Noster, 129, 130, 133, 138, 144, 145, 147, 149, 185, 191, 197
    Leeton, Shiloh CPC, 94, 215
    Rock Spring (Holden), 88, 89, 91, 94, 96, 99, 104, 106, 142, 143, 195
    Warrensburg, 94, 130, 137, 138
  Lafayette, Lexington, 32, 121, 124, 139, 140, 146, 149, 152, 176, 204, 205, 206
  Missouri Territory, 21
  Morgan, Haw Creek, 69, 70
  Pettis County, 186
    Arator, 55, 69, 70, 73, 77, 78, 85, 87, 96, 101, 113, 118, 119, 120, 131, 137, 139, 148, 149, 191
    Elk Fork, 113
    Georgetown, 15, 55, 69, 75, 77, 78, **84**, 85, 89, 90, 152
    Sedalia, 75, 76, 133, 138, 143, 144, 145, 155, 165, 166, 171, 175, 176, 197
    Smithton, 55, 103, 120, 131, 148, 191
      Providence Baptist Church, 103
      Providence Cemetery, 55, 103, 131, 137
  Saint Louis, St. Louis City, 68, 90, 213, 214
  Saline County, 205
  St.Charles

Index of Places

Femme Osage Creek, 21
St.Charles, 31
Vernon County, 76, 107, 110, 112, 116, 127, 129, 141, 146, 194
    Badger Township, 108
    Big Dry Wood Creek, 107
    Big Dry Wood Ranch, 107, 108, **109**, 113, 122, 126, 128, 129, 145, 147, 153, 184, 194
    Big Dry Wood, Battle of, **121**, 123
    Coal Township, 145
    Deerfield, 107, 108, 110, 112, 121, 127, 129, 142, 149, 151, 153, 178, 190, 191, 194, 195, 196, 197, 198
    Deerfield Cemetery, 125
    Deerfield Township
        Ellis CPC, 108
    Hogan's Ford, 107, 121
    Montevallo, 108
    Moundville, 138, 141, 146, 161
    Nevada, 108, 110, 121, 130, 153, 161
Missouri River, 68
Mormon Trail, 100

N

NEVADA, Virginia City, 148
NEW FRANCE, Upper Louisiana, 68
NORTH CAROLINA
    Colony, 13, 167, 168, 181
        Yadkin Valley, 13
Northwest Territory, 68

O

OKLAHOMA (INDIAN TERRITORY), 28, 40, 188, 191
    Cherokee Nation, 164
    Mayes
        Chouteau, 70, 160, 174, 176, 177, 187, 212, 215
        Hogan (town), 177
        Locust Grove, 163, 166, 177, **188**
        Pryor Creek, 177, 216
    Muscogee Nation, 67
    Wagoner, Gibson Station, 159, 160, 176, 178
Oregon Trail, 100

P

PENNSYLVANIA, 29
    Allegheny, Allegany City (Pittsburgh), 27

S

Santa Fe Trail, 31, 68
SOUTH CAROLINA, Battle of Kings Mountain, 20, 170

T

TENNESSEE
    Bledsoe, Pikeville, 47
    Blount, Maryville, 39, 43, 44, 45, 50, **53**, 195
    Campbell's Station, 169, 170
    Clinch River, 42
    Decatur
        Eagle Nest Island, 66
        Havana (historic), 65, 66
    French Broad River, 65
    Greene
        Greeneville, 55, 61, **62**, 130
        Greeneville College, 55, 56, 57, 61, 62, 63, 64, 65, 152, 158, 195

Tusculum, (was
    Greeneville College),
    56
Hamilton
    Chattanooga, 66
Knox
    Knoxville, 65
McMinn
    Athens, 44, 45
Monroe
    Madisonville, 40
Nolichucky River, 56, 64, 65,
    71
Putnam
    Pinhook, 46
Rhea
    Rhea County, 50
Roane
    Kingston, 42, 43, 45
    Roane County, 42
Sequachee Valley, 41, 43, 44,
    45, 46, 50
Shelby County, Cordova
    CPC Headquarters, **52**
Tennessee River, 63, 64, 65,
    66, **71**
TEXAS
    Austin, 158, 195
    Bastrop County
        Bastrop, 75, 90, 102, 114,
            139, 146, 149
    Ellis County, 186

Ennis, 142, 148, 149, 154,
    155, 156
Ovilla, 90
Nacogdoches County
    Nacogdoches, 94
Navarro County, 94, 96, 100,
    102, 142
    Chatfield, 93, 94, 96
    Muskete (Chatfield), 96,
        155

U

UNITED KINGDOM
    ENGLAND, 11, 16
        Devon, 11
    IRELAND, 11, 12
        County Tipperary, 12, 13
            Cranagh Castle, 13
        Thomond, 12
    SCOTLAND, 11
    WALES, 11

V

VIRGINIA, 29
VIRGINIA COLONY, 169
    Brunswick, 13
        New Brunswick, 13
    Russell, Dorton's Fort, 11, **25**

W

Wilderness Road, 13, **25**
WISCONSIN
    Crawford
        Prairie du Chien, 28

ABOUT THE AUTHOR

BRIAN HOGAN, third great grandnephew of Rev. David Hogan, and, like Uncle Davie, a Church Planter and Missionary, earned his Master's in Ministry from Hope International University specializing in World Christian Foundations. He is a sought-after speaker, trainer, and coach. Brian serves full time with Church Planting Coaches, a global ministry of Youth With A Mission (YWAM) and is the President of Disciple Making Mentors (4DMM.org). He enjoys being a catalyst, historical sleuthing, board games, reading, traveling, and trying anything new, novel, and different.

He is also the author of "There's a Sheep in my Bathtub", "An A to Z of Near-Death Adventures" and "Boy Centurions". Brian's training course *Keys to Church Planting Movements* and books, video and audio are available at: 4dmm.org/shop/.

www.ingramcontent.com/pod-product-compliance
Lightning Source LLC
Chambersburg PA
CBHW020420010526
44118CB00010B/337